Barcode in Back

It All Begins with the Music: Developing Successful Artists and Careers for the New Music Business

Don Grierson and Dan Kimpel

D1232713

Course Technology PTR

A part of Cengage Learning

HUMBER LIBRARIES LAKESHORE CAMPUS

3199 Lakeshore Blvd West

TORONTO, ON.   M8V 1K8

COURSE TECHNOLOGY
CENGAGE Learning·

Australia • Brazil • Japan • Korea • Mexico • Singapore • Spain • United Kingdom • United States

COURSE TECHNOLOGY
CENGAGE Learning

It All Begins with the Music: Developing Successful Artists and Careers for the New Music Business
Don Grierson and Dan Kimpel

Publisher and General Manager, Course Technology PTR: Stacy L. Hiquet

Associate Director of Marketing: Sarah Panella

Manager of Editorial Services: Heather Talbot

Marketing Manager: Mark Hughes

Executive Editor: Mark Garvey

Project Editor: Kim Benbow

Editorial Services Coordinator: Jen Blaney

Copy Editor: Andy Saff

Interior Layout Tech: Macmillan Publishing Solutions

Cover Designer: Luke Fletcher

Indexer: Sharon Shock

Proofreader: Sandi Wilson

© 2009 Don Grierson and Dan Kimpel

ALL RIGHTS RESERVED. No part of this work covered by the copyright herein may be reproduced, transmitted, stored, or used in any form or by any means graphic, electronic, or mechanical, including but not limited to photocopying, recording, scanning, digitizing, taping, Web distribution, information networks, or information storage and retrieval systems, except as permitted under Section 107 or 108 of the 1976 United States Copyright Act, without the prior written permission of the publisher.

For product information and technology assistance, contact us at
Cengage Learning Customer & Sales Support, 1-800-354-9706

For permission to use material from this text or product, submit all requests online at **cengage.com/permissions**
Further permissions questions can be emailed to
permissionrequest@cengage.com

All trademarks are the property of their respective owners.

Library of Congress Control Number: 2008940612

ISBN-13: 978-1-59863-863-9

ISBN-10: 1-59863-863-7

Course Technology, a part of Cengage Learning
20 Channel Center Street
Boston, MA 02210
USA

Cengage Learning is a leading provider of customized learning solutions with office locations around the globe, including Singapore, the United Kingdom, Australia, Mexico, Brazil, and Japan. Locate your local office at:
international.cengage.com/region

Cengage Learning products are represented in Canada by Nelson Education, Ltd.

For your lifelong learning solutions, visit **courseptr.com**

Visit our corporate website at **cengage.com**

Printed in the United States of America
1 2 3 4 5 6 7 11 10 09

Acknowledgments

Our sincere gratitude and thank yous to all of those who gave so freely of their expertise, knowledge, opinions, and experiences that we hope enrich these pages.

The authors also wish to thank Kenny Kerner, and our students past, present, and future at Musicians Institute in Hollywood, not only for accepting our input, but for keeping us inspired in these new days.

We appreciate the expertise and dedication of Cat Veit in transcribing and copy editing many of the interviews, Brian Lam for his author photos, and Michael Kurniawan and Raymond Ho for their support.

Thank you to Mark Garvey and Kim Benbow, who shared our enthusiasm for this project.

About the Authors

Don Grierson, a legendary A&R executive, has worked with many of the most notable artists in modern music history. He was involved promotionally with the launch of Apple Records and The Beatles. Don worked in record promotion internationally and marketing, principally for Capitol Records. He was then a founding member and VP, A&R, for Capitol's sister label EMI America Records, signing and working with acts such as Sheena Easton, Kim Carnes, Kate Bush, Sir Cliff Richard, J. Geils Band, and Kenny Rogers. This was followed by a very successful stint as VP, A&R, back at Capitol, where he signed and helped guide a number of hit-making acts, including Heart, Joe Cocker, Steve Vai, Megadeth, George Clinton, Tina Turner, Bob Seger, Duran Duran, Thomas Dolby, Billy Squier, and others. He later became Senior VP, Head of A&R, at Sony/Epic Records, working with such acts as Cheap Trick, Celine Dion, Bad English, Gloria Estefan, The Jacksons, Living Colour, and Cyndi Lauper. Don currently operates his own independent consultant company and is a faculty member at Musicians Institute, Hollywood, California. Visit Don online at www.dongrierson.com.

Dan Kimpel, acknowledged as one of the American media's foremost authorities on popular music and songwriters, contributes to numerous interactive CDs, magazines, web sites, podcasts, documentary films, videos, in-flight audio programs, and new media. His notable interviews include conversations with Leonard Cohen, Holland-Dozier-Holland, Green Day, Metallica, Fergie, Elvis Costello, Jackson Browne, and Dr. Maya Angelou. Dan is the author of *Electrify My Soul: Songwriters and the Spiritual Source, How They Made It: True Stories of How Music's Biggest Stars Went from Start to Stardom, Networking in the Music Business,* and *Networking Strategies for the New Music Business*. A noted music business educator, Dan lectures at colleges, universities, and conferences across the U.S. and Canada, and for five years conducted a master class in networking for graduating seniors at the Liverpool Institute for Performing Arts (LIPA) in the UK. He is a current faculty member at Musicians Institute in Hollywood, California, where he was recently named MBP Teacher of the Year. Visit Dan online at www.dankimpel.com.

Contents

Chapter 2
The Artist   23

Chapter 3
The A&R Exec/The Label   53

Chapter 4
The Producer   79

Chapter 5
The Mixer   99

Chapter 6
The Manager   109

Chapter 7
Film/TV   **129**

Chapter 8
The Lawyer   151

Chapter 9
New Days, New Directions, New Ideas   165

Chapter 10
The Publisher   199

Chapter 11
The Performing Rights Organization   211

Chapter 12
The *American Idol*   223

Chapter 13
Music as the International Language 237

Index 251

Preface: Dan Kimpel

It all began with a suggestion made to Don Grierson by Kenny Kerner, a vice president at the Musicians Institute in Hollywood, California, and the head of the Music Business Program (MBP), where both Don and I are on faculty. Kenny, noting that there was not a book in existence on artist development, told Don he should write one. Don quite reasonably responded by exclaiming, "I'm not a writer!" Kenny then suggested that Don contact me with the idea of teaming up.

Working for two non-profit songwriter organizations, first the Los Angeles Songwriters Showcase (LASS) and later the National Academy of Songwriters (NAS), I had long been aware of Don Grierson. While it was often a struggle to persuade even the lowliest A&R (artist and repertoire) representatives to screen songs at our weekly events and our annual Songwriters Expo, Grierson, one of the most high-powered A&R executives in the business, with a sterling string of massive hits, would gladly give of his time and expertise to listen, advise, and educate hopeful songwriters.

I am proud to say this about Don: In all of my years in this business, I have never heard a single negative word said about him. His reputation as a man of honor is airtight.

From the Van to the Dan

My perspective on the music business is vastly different than Don's. I began my career performing in local rock bands in and around my hometown of Lima, Ohio; I lived and worked in Nashville, toured the country, relocated to New York City, and eventually made my way to Los Angeles as a songwriter and performer. It was in Los Angeles that I reinvented myself, so to speak, on the other side of the desk.

Working with songwriters came very naturally to me. I held positions with two non-profit songwriter organizations, the LASS and the NAS. Over time, I began writing articles for the Los Angeles Songwriters Showcase newsletter—*The Songwriters Musepaper*—and this led to my first book, *Networking in the Music Business*. Since then, additional titles have marked my path as an author. I am pleased to contribute articles about songwriters, film composers, and music industry professionals to a wide range of publications, including a regular column, "Song Biz," for *Music Connection* magazine. I have also programmed, interviewed, voiced, and produced in-flight entertainment for Delta and United Airlines.

As I read the stories of the people in this book, it is apparent that there is a similarity in philosophies between our interview subjects, Don's, and my careers. There is a Zen saying: "Leap and the net will appear." Intention is a powerful force, and having the faith and determination to follow an unknown path can create a powerful alchemy.

Music Biz 101

As I mentioned, both Don and I are currently on faculty at Musicians Institute in Hollywood. Our department, under the formidable authority of Mr. Kerner, pointedly does not hire traditional teachers to conduct the courses. Only credible music industry professionals are invited to be a part of the program.

Over time, music business education has become an increasingly vital element of my life. In 1998, I received a fax from Arthur Bernstein—then head of the Music Department at Liverpool Institute for Performing Arts (LIPA), a school co-founded by Sir Paul McCartney—inviting me to conduct a one-week master class in the UK. This commitment turned into five years of classes, hundreds of students, and the rich worldwide roster of friends and professional contacts that exists for me today.

What I have discovered in teaching students from England, Norway, Japan, the Philippines, the Dominican Republic, Denmark, Sweden, Germany, Switzerland, Serbia, Brazil, and beyond is that, although the business of music might be different in various regions, musicians and those who work on their behalf are essentially the same. Now, teaching at the epicenter of the entertainment industry at Hollywood and Highland, I witness this truth confirmed, as hopeful players and music industry professionals converge on this phenomenal vortex of the entertainment world to make their mark with determination and commitment.

The music business is built on trust and enduring relationships. I am proud to extend my working relationship with Don Grierson through the creation of this book. He possesses the highest respect for artists and executives alike. With these words, it is our intention to honor that creed, not only to demystify and disseminate information about the music business, but, through conversations with often unsung behind-the-scenes motivators, to illuminate the essence of its soul.

Dan Kimpel
Los Angeles, California

Preface: Don Grierson

I begin by explaining my life in music with these words: "None of this makes sense." I was born in England, my family immigrated to Australia, and we landed in a village in the Outback, the bush country: 9,000 people, legions of kangaroos, very few streets, one movie theater, and a single radio station. After leaving high school, I worked at a menial job for two years, not knowing what I really wanted to do with my life. I played sports, especially tennis, but I wasn't a drinker (that really puts you on the "outer" in that environment), and believe me, there was little else to do.

Although I had no plans for the future, I was totally fascinated with listening to records and the radio. For every pop song I heard, I would write the title down in a book with the name of the artist and label—especially the American labels. When I could get reception, I would listen to the big Sydney Top 40 stations (AM only played in those days, of course), which would introduce and back-announce the songs they played with exhortations like, "This is breaking real big in America: number 22 on *Billboard*. This is an import on Capitol Records from the U.S." I would write all of this down. My buddies looked at me like I was a freak of nature. I couldn't then, and still can't, explain how I came to that. Listen, yes, but take notes? My only real interests were listening to music and in my mind "picking the hits."

By chance I met a disc jockey from our one local station, and he invited me to come by. Instead of sitting with the jock in the studio, I would go to the library and play records. I just loved that. When the DJ asked, "Did you ever think about being a DJ?" I thought, "No, I never had, but...?" So at home, I took the newspaper, hid in the bathroom, and read it like I was reading the news. I wondered, "Could I really do this?"

I was due a two-week vacation from my going-nowhere job. I found a little radio school in Sydney, so then I told my boss I wasn't coming back. I went to the big city, stayed in a bed and breakfast, got a job in an appliance store trying to sell refrigerators, went to this radio school at night, and learned the basics of radio. I wasn't making much money, and I realized I couldn't afford to stay, but I did finish my course. Then I came home to see my family and decide what to do next. Coincidentally, I ran into the program director from the radio station, who said, "We might have a startup post at the radio station for a 'cadet' announcer— maybe you'll get on the air." He gave me the job!

I learned how to write copy, log and file records, and be around the vibe of a funky little radio station, 2DU, DUBBO. We programmed everything: news, soap operas, farm and stock reports, horse racing, and pop music in the afternoons and on weekend nights. And when someone passed away, we had funeral announcements three times a day with Tchaikovsky's "Swan Lake" playing underneath. We catered to the community.

Then one day, a jock got sick, and it was, "You're on, kid."

I was there for four years. I soon became a full-time on-air personality, had the evening shift, 6:30 to 11:30 p.m., five nights a week, and "Party Time" on Saturday nights. That was a request show, but I'd sneak in my own favorites, my own "requests" as well. During the week shift, I had to play mostly "middle-of-the-road" music, along with British Broadcasting Corporation (BBC) specialty programming. I did have a pop show for an hour and a half that started the shift. I could program my own music. The station was getting *Cashbox* magazine (then an important music publication in the U.S.), but it arrived six weeks late because it came by sea. I didn't care; I read every word on every page. I was fascinated! I would close the station down at 11:30 and go home to—what? We didn't even have TV in our town. So I'd stay at the station and devour *Cashbox,* and for every advertisement run by a label that had an address—Capitol Records, 1750 North Vine Street, Hollywood, California—I would write those labels and ask them to send me promos. You couldn't find my town/station on the map, but I didn't care. I wanted American imports! Of course, very few labels did send anything, and most of it was junk. Imperial Records put me on their LP list—they had mostly blues material, Brownie McGee and Sonny Terry, etc. They didn't send me any hits, and as I remember, most of the albums arrived warped anyway. There was no black music at all in Australia in those days, but I created a late-night blues show for one night, jazz on another, Latin on another, and so on. I can't imagine there were too many listeners, but I was playing great music that inspired me and living it up! I certainly didn't have to worry about ratings!

There was one small label that did send me hits, Cadence Records in New York (www.bsnpubs.com/cadence/cadencestory.html). They had the Everly Brothers, the Chordettes, Johnny Tillotson, and a young Andy Williams. They put me on their mailing list. I was ecstatic! They released maybe one single every two or three months, but each one was a smash. After every 45 single I received, I wrote their National Sales/Promotion Manager, Bud Dollinger; I told him that I loved his records and that I was playing them on my show. I couldn't break an egg, let alone a hit single, and the listeners couldn't buy these records anywhere even if they wanted to, as they weren't released. And you know what? No one cared either. But I was playing American imports. How cool was that? I was a happy kid!

At the beginning of my fourth year at the station, I took a vacation to Surfers Paradise, Queensland, the Miami of Australia: sun, surf, and girls. Driving home after a wild two weeks, I just decided, "I have to go to America." That's where most of the great music comes from. I liked being a disc jockey, but I knew I would never be great, an original—it wasn't my future. I found out I could immigrate to the U.S. I made a reservation on a ship but then canceled the trip. I wasn't ready physically or mentally, but I'd resigned from the station. The program director gave me my job back, but said that it wouldn't happen again. I did rebook on another ship. I just knew I had to make the move. I had no clue what I was doing; all I knew was that I had to go to America to do something with music—this weird thing that drove me. My buddies thought I was nuts. The ship sailed from Sydney to New Zealand, New Zealand to Fiji, Fiji to Hawaii, Hawaii to Vancouver, Canada, down to San Francisco, and finally to Long Beach, California. Two and a half weeks of wonder and fear. I bought a transistor radio on the trip. As we were getting close to Hawaii, I could actually hear American radio. I was listening to Top 40 in Honolulu—this was a new, exciting world for me.

The ship arrived. I fell off of it in Long Beach—literally, because I was drunk for the first time in my life. Let me explain: In Vancouver, a bunch of Australians who were heading back to Australia on the round-trip boarded, and I was getting close to arriving in the U.S. We decided to celebrate. There was a girl in the group I had my eye on and so did another guy. There was a dance floor and a band—a not-very-good quartet. We were dancing, and I was drinking vodka with lemonade. I didn't like the taste of alcohol, but I did want to get a little crazy. I thought nothing was happening, so I kept drinking—then it kicked in. I must have drunk an entire bottle of vodka. I was sick. I couldn't walk. I lost the battle for the young lady, as did the other guy, because he couldn't function either. There was a closed swimming pool on the top deck with a big, heavy rope net across it so no one could fall in. I remember, in my drunkenness, swimming that net. I crawled into my bunk, sh*t-faced, at 4:00 a.m.

We berthed a few hours later. People were getting off the ship, and I was whacked out of my brain with a hangover, trying to get my things together. I'm sure I had alcohol poisoning; it stayed with me for a week. Somehow I staggered through customs and immigration, and there I was, standing in Long Beach, California. It was hot and smoggy and I was wondering, "What am I going to do now?" The logic in my brain told me to get on a bus and go to downtown Los Angeles. In Sydney, that is where all of the action would be, downtown, so that's where I went. After paying for a week in a funky hotel, I had $16 left in my pocket. Back then, when you immigrated you had only to prove that you had enough money to support yourself for three months. I had sent over $275 to a bank in the U.S. Where I grew up, we didn't even have locks on the door, so I didn't lock the door at my hotel. During that first night, someone came in and stole my $16. Fortunately, I still had the $275 in the bank.

I had three letters of introduction from a label promotion person in Sydney who dealt with international companies in the U.S.—Liberty Records, Dot Records, and Verve Records, which was in New York. I called Dot, and the guy was overseas! I called Liberty and that guy was also overseas, but his assistant was English and he took pity on me. He said, "You're downtown, no way. You've got to come to Hollywood. All the music companies are here." I moved into the Hastings Hotel on Hollywood and Argyle for $80 a month; it had clean sheets, but no TV. Then I was on the phone. "I'm from Australia, I was a disc jockey, and I'm looking for a job." This was my introduction to the U.S. music industry.

I found no job, but someone did recommend that I check with California Music One Stop. I had to take a bus to a "rough" area at Vermont and Pico Boulevards. I didn't even know what a "one stop" was. (I soon discovered that they, especially in those days, sold 45s and LPs to mostly the small record store accounts that now no longer exist.) The owner was a rotund ex-New Yorker, Sam Ricklin. California Music One Stop's building was essentially a giant room with tables and racks of singles and albums—every record by every artist I'd ever heard of or read about was in this room, and I thought, "I've got to work here; this is paradise—this is me."

I was told that there were no jobs, but somehow I got to rambling in my Aussie accent about how I knew all of these labels. I was running out of money and scared of what might happen if I didn't get a job soon. And I couldn't go home, as I only had a one-way ticket! Fortunately, Sam asked me how I knew all about the labels and artists, saw my enthusiasm (and maybe had a little pity, too), and said, "You know what? We have a guy who has been drafted, and he won't be back until January. I'll give you a job until Christmas [this was early October] at $1.60 an hour, and you can work overtime." He kept me on after Christmas, and I got a big raise, to $1.75.

I was now selling records, listening to all the new release single samples that were sent by the labels, and in my mind I was still "picking the hits." This interesting character, Bob Kane, used to come in often. He was an art director type, and he'd check out all of the new releases to see the artwork. (His wife was go-go dancer, in a cage with hanging beads—that was new to me, too.) I found out he was also a Jerry Lee Lewis fanatic. I think he would have left his wife for Jerry if he had called! After getting to know each other over time, Bob asked, "What do you want to do?" I was now thinking about what a next step would be, as a $1.75-per-hour job had little future. I thought by now that I could do promotion. I'd met a few of these guys when they came by from time to time. Music was obviously my passion, and I was telling everyone which new release could be a "hit." Bob said, "I've got a good friend; let me talk to him." This friend happened to be the number-one DJ at KMPC, Gary Owens. Being from radio, I was now a big-time listener to the L.A. stations, and I certainly knew who Gary was. (Later he was also a featured personality on the TV show *Laugh In*.)

Somehow, Bob set up a dinner for me with Gary. We met on Vine Street in Hollywood at Clifton's Cafeteria (it's gone now). He was, and is, an amazing man—gracious and kind, a great human being! He said he knew a lot of record people, and if he heard of anything, he'd let me know. I never expected to hear from him again, but a couple of months later he called: "I have a friend who has a label through a local distributor. I mentioned you to him. He told me he had been trying to get his distributor to hire a junior-level promotion person to promote the lesser-known artists and 'oddball' stuff he and the other labels released that wasn't really being handled." That friend was A&M Records' Jerry Moss who had co-founded the label with Herb Alpert. I first knew that label from Australia. I'd played "The Lonely Bull" by Herb Alpert and the Tijuana Brass on my show many times. Jerry wanted to meet me at lunch at the Brown Derby in Hollywood (also gone now). Nervous time!

Don Grierson, Herb Alpert, and Gary Owens (seated)

I had to take a bus, of course. I went in, saw the caricatures on the wall, and the room full of schmoozers—it was a real Hollywood hang. I had walked past this famous gathering place many times, but I never expected that I would actually get to go inside. I sat with Jerry, another amazing human being. Somehow he liked me; my accent must have been a plus. He said, "Let me talk to my distributor, Record Merchandising." He set up an appointment with the owner, Sid Talmadge. Off I went to that meeting. You can imagine how nervous I was, just being one year off of the boat and still very naïve to the real world of the record business.

There was a desk and a partition, and while I was waiting to meet Sid, I heard a name being called to the phone: Bud Dollinger. That certainly caught my attention. I asked if he would come out. Here in Los Angeles was the guy from Cadence Records in New York who had put me on the label's mailing list when I was a jock. He said, "What the hell are you doing here?" So before I actually met Sid, Bud must have told him I had some kind of big balls, coming all the way from the Aussie bush to the States; plus I somehow must have given a good interview. Sid gave me a job for $135 a week. I was now a promotion man!

I worked there for two years, and during that time I got drafted. I had three alternatives: go to Vietnam and probably get my ass shot off, go home to Australia and maybe not be allowed back into the States, or try and join the Reserves. Johnny Grant, the late honorary mayor of Hollywood, was also then at radio station KMPC, where he often dealt with the armed forces doing public service shows. I knew him because I was often at the station doing promotion. I called him to see if there were any Reserve units he knew. He made some calls and found an opening in the Marine Corps unit at Chavez Ravine. I did six months of active duty and five years Reserve duty after that. And, they made me cut my hair—I hated that!

Record Merchandising had kept my job for me during those active duty months, and I rejoined them after I came back. Then, six months later, Capitol Records called. They were looking for a promotion manager. I went to the famous tower for the first time and was hired as West Coast singles promotion manager, and then became the Southern California promotion person for all releases. I wasn't only promoting singles, but also albums—acts such as the Band, Pink Floyd, and the Beatles. Life was good!

When I was at Capitol (the EMI-owned label in the U.S.), the Beatles formed their own label, Apple Records, but it was still owned by EMI. Everyone in the world was waiting for the new Beatles record. In their creative wisdom, the Beatles decided to release four singles simultaneously to introduce their new label. Fearful that everyone would only focus on the Beatles single, the Apple office created a "Golden Apple Award" for the promo person who could achieve the most airplay on all four singles: "Hey Jude" by the Beatles, "Those Were the Days" by Mary Hopkins, "Sour Milk Sea" by Jackie Lomax, and an instrumental brass band single "Thingummybob" by John Foster & Sons Ltd. Black Dyke Mills Band, which Paul McCartney produced. I worked my butt off, won, and George Harrison flew in from the UK to present the award to me at a party at the Playboy Club in Century City. That was an incredible evening!

I spent four years at Capitol until an executive change restructured the promo department. I subsequently worked West Coast promotion for Chess Checker/Cadet. Cool people, but not a lot of product. I was then asked to take the same position at MGM Records. I stayed for six months before they made major changes—typical promotional politics. I was next offered a job as A&R coordinator at RCA Records, West Coast, coordinating all the independent labels distributed through RCA. It was there that I learned how the inner operations of a label worked—such valuable lessons. I was with RCA for four years; during that time, the label had four presidents, and I had three bosses on the West Coast. A new president came in and

George Harrison and Don Grierson

tried to tell Elvis Presley what kind of records he should be recording—that didn't work, of course—and then he decided basically to close the West Coast creative office at a time when the West Coast music scene was exploding with the Eagles and such—a brilliant move.

I was then very fortunate to get to return to Capitol Records as manager of international A&R and promotion, a unique position. Half of this job was A&R'ing incoming EMI-owned music from around the world. EMI had companies in all the major markets, and they all had local artists they hoped would be released in America. Interestingly, from my early days of being a listener, then in radio, and through my promotion years, I was always mentally "picking the hits." Now I was actually being paid to do so. My first signing was the Little River Band from Australia. They had a long career and sold many millions of albums.

The other half of this new position was promoting Capitol artists/releases internationally: Anne Murray, Bob Seger, Steve Miller, Helen Reddy, Natalie Cole—all of the company's priorities. They sent me overseas to London, Paris, Stockholm, Cologne, Amsterdam, Tokyo, New Zealand, and Australia—back home! This was unbelievable! I was working my ass off, but I loved it. How could it be better?

All that changed two years later when Capitol "promoted" me to the head of merchandising and advertising. As you can imagine, after traveling the world for two years, this was very different territory. I did have a choice, but in those days we didn't have attorneys to negotiate for us, and back then there was a loyalty factor involved when you worked for a company. The department needed a creative kick in the butt. I was now going to New York, Detroit, Boston, and other U.S. locales rather than London and Paris. My department was responsible for the creation and implementation of all national advertising campaigns and merchandising elements: trade ads, TV and radio spots, and store displays. I worked with the art department, saw how they functioned, and I always looked outside the box creatively. For example, typically every poster was square or rectangular. I said, "Let's do a circular one," or, "Let's do die-cuts." We created stickers that could actually be pulled off of the trade ads. The key was to get attention and make an impact. Although this was not the sexiest position, I learned a great deal and had the opportunity to be a part of the very important area for the marketing of music—my passion! The company wanted flair and creativity, and my department gave it that. All good!

Two years later, Capitol created EMI America Records, a small sister label to the major. The executives said, "You're the head of A&R." Wow! I had no experience at A&R in terms of starting from scratch, so this was a new challenge, dealing with talent and the related people involved: managers, attorneys, producers, and songwriters. And I was still "picking the hits." Our first single was "Bluer Than Blue" by Michael Johnson, which went to number 12, followed by Kim Carnes' "Bette Davis Eyes," a monster number-one hit around the world. We had major hits with Sheena Easton, the J. Geils Band, the Michael Stanley Band, Marty Balin, Sir Cliff Richard, Robert John, and Gary U.S. Bonds (produced by Bruce Springsteen), and huge hits with Kenny Rogers, especially "Lady," which was written and produced by Lionel Richie. I was there four years. It was an amazing run.

Don Grierson with Heart and record company personnel

Time to move again. I was asked to return to the Capitol label and become head of A&R. Another four years with great success: I signed Heart, who had been on Epic and included Ann Wilson, one of the great voices of all time, and sister Nancy, an amazing guitarist. I found hit singles for them, and we had a series of multiplatinum albums. I signed Joe Cocker and helped to resurrect his career, especially internationally. Other artists I worked with included Freddie Jackson (six number-one R&B singles), Melba Moore (six top-10 R&B singles), and George Clinton (the number-one R&B single "Atomic Dog"); among other great artists were Tina Turner, Queen, Anne Murray, Duran Duran, the Motels, Megadeth, and many other unique distinctive career artists who were a joy to work with and for.

Don Grierson with Frankie Beverly and Maze, Joe Cocker, and Martha Davis (The Motels)

I grew up in the Capitol system to a great degree. It wasn't a cold or cutthroat company—it had a British heritage, and those were my roots. But the business was changing and Capitol wasn't. A new challenge presented itself.

Tina Turner and Don Grierson

I resigned from Capitol to join CBS Records (which became Sony Music) as senior vice president, A&R. At Sony/Epic Records, I had the privilege to work with such unique talent as Celine Dion, Cheap Trick, Bad English, Cyndi Lauper, Gloria Estefan, REO Speedwagon, Living Colour, the Indigo Girls, and The Jacksons. I was used to success at Capitol, but CBS Records was a monster. It was an amazing five years. Companies change, staff changes—you move on.

Don Grierson with Cheap Trick and producer Ron Nevison

Since that time, I've been in the exciting and fast-changing independent community. I was a partner in a small company, Drive Entertainment, but now focus as an independent consultant, working with artists, managers, small companies, and so on, in the U.S. and overseas, as well as doing music supervision and being a faculty member at Musicians Institute in Hollywood, California. Teaching at MI, and being able to give something back from the experiences and challenges I've had, is inspiring and a great joy.

I believe my A&R and career successes have always been because I'm a passionate listener, basically playing the role of the public, the audience, evaluating on their behalf how and why a song, track, or singer might connect with them. I can't sing or play an instrument, but I guess I have what they call "great ears." On the professional side, someone has to "listen," to be the objective voice while always respecting the artist and the art. This is not something you can go to college to learn, and I didn't. I've taken nothing for granted, worked very hard, never ever lost my passion, and always believed in the music!

Don Grierson with Kenny Aronoff

Trends are always there potentially to affect the thinking, but the true responsibility of a music industry A&R person is to seek talent, yes, but also to help create and deliver music that sells. You need to be a leader in creative thinking, not to follow like sheep. One does have to comprehend the sphere of the market, but never live by its trends. Sure, I do understand the need by some to create music to fit the slot for what is selling today, but these things change—often very quickly. Unique talent and great songs will straddle time.

What my co-conspirator Dan Kimpel and I intend to do in this book is to introduce you to the vast perspectives of the major music business players in this age—to offer insights from successful entities in all areas of the amazing, wonderful world of music and its mechanism, to reveal interesting histories of talented people as well as journey into the stories of those who are very much involved today. To survive in our business, it is necessary to be fluid and to understand trends and timing while never losing sight of the big picture. And, as you will read—it all begins with the music.

Don Grierson
Hollywood, California

Introduction

Popular music is an ever-evolving phenomenon—a way of life, a soundtrack for successive generations, a barometer of social changes, and a global business of massive proportions generating in excess of $40 billion per year. Despite every cataclysmic shift in the modern music business, the raw ingredients of every musical genre—pop, rock, hip-hop, R&B, country, and Latin—remain essentially unchanged. It is a precious formula of talent + songs + timing. Now more than ever, the fortunes of multinational conglomerates are dependent on the ears and instincts of an exclusive coterie of highly prized professionals who discover, nurture, and promote talent. It is a delicate dance of enthusiasm, resolve, and imagination.

In the not-so-distant past, record companies were fully engaged in artist development. A typical scenario might involve an A&R (short for "artist and repertoire") person discovering new talent, signing them to the record label, nurturing their songwriting and recording ability, and arranging for the label to fund them until they are prepared to meet the marketplace. Historically, artists were extended multiple opportunities to build their credibility, discover a market for their music, and ultimately emerge into the general consciousness.

Those days are no longer. Now, it is more often independent artists and independent labels that create their own buzz, using much smaller budgets, recording, marketing, and publicizing music, and who consequently then generate a demand for the artist's work. And it is this initiative that they've shown, coupled with a solid track record that comes with it, that can then make these artists appear to be more signable for a major record label, such as an Interscope, Warner Bros., or Island/Def Jam.

Understanding when the market is ready for a certain style of music or the introduction of a particular artist is not a science. If this were truly measurable, then the most powerful companies would totally dominate sales. True, while pop music is often cyclic, the majority of consumers of popular music are not imbued with advanced musical faculties; they do, however, respond on deep levels to songs and artists to whom they can relate, and those who can emanate that ever-elusive "vibe."

Why This Book?
The impetus for this book evolved from the absence of information that can help artists, managers, and others who would like to be involved in the real-world process of finding and shaping future recording artists to understand this process through the stories told by this

book's interviews. These stories reveal the struggles and successes from the past through to the present. The entertainment industry, and especially the music business, is invested with long-standing rags-to-riches mythologies—invented media fodder that makes for engrossing reading, but has little or nothing to do with the ways that artists can be propelled from obscurity into the mainstream. As long-standing professionals in the music business, we, the authors, have access to the real information, and more important, to the behind-the-scenes players who make it all work. Our relationships and credibility permit us to conduct intimate, one-on-one conversations rich with insider information and to reveal the real-life secrets that can make an artist or aspiring industry professional's career.

If artist development back in the proverbial day was the business of the record company, in the modern music business, artist development is everyone's business. There is no single route in. The rise of technology has ushered in an era of self-empowerment for artists. Using the latest digital gear, it is possible to create market-ready masters at home. More-over, it is now possible to license these recordings directly to television shows and films for lucrative publishing and synchronization fees. In earlier eras, someone—a label, a manager, a music publisher—had to believe in an artist's viability before he or she recorded a note. Today, this is no longer true. Consequently, the market is glutted with music.

So where do recording artists come from? What are the ingredients imperative for their success? How can a rising artist cut through the clutter to make a formidable impact and sustain this power in today's volatile music business climate? What can artists and aspiring industry entrepreneurs gain from lessons already learned? Audiences learn about artists through videos, radio, tours, promotional tie-ins, the Internet, viral marketing campaigns, commercials, festivals, soundtracks, television shows, and, most significantly of all, word of mouth. But before any of these mechanisms can be engaged, there has to be something to promote. And as you will read in these pages, it all begins with the music.

1 The Songwriter

If it all begins with the music, it certainly must be said that contemporary music definitely radiates from the song. The greatest singer, band, or rapper in the world can't convey a message without words and music. And all the technology in existence will not give anyone the ability to create great songs. For songwriters who are students of the craft, there is no better way to learn how it is done than by studying other writers and successful songs.

Jeffrey Steele (www.jeffreysteele.net), a songwriter who penned 500 songs recorded in an eight-year period with 95 singles off of 75 gold and platinum records, says, "The most important thing any songwriter needs to have is that drive, an 'against all odds' instinct to keep writing through all the rejection and all the hardships. These are your stories, the stuff that turns into your songs. I think a lot of people run from these things, but they need to realize that that's what you're gonna be writing about for the next 20 years." Early on in Nashville, Steele was told that his songs were nowhere near the marketplace. "Off by a mile. But I knew that I loved to write. It gets to a point where you either slough it off or think maybe they're right. But look at the criticism and see if it has any weight. These guys are critics, and they'll say things to discourage you. Over the years it's become fire for me."

Around 1998, things changed. LeAnn Rimes cut his song "Big Deal," Kevin Sharp had a hit with "If You Love Somebody," and Diamond Rio struck gold with "Unbelievable." Says Steele, "All hell broke loose. I can't explain it and I don't want to. I just kept doing the same thing and working harder at it. It's not unusual for me have three writing appointments a day like I'm in a doctor's office. People say, 'How can you do anything artistic when you're writing that much?' First of all, I'm a freak; that answers that question," laughs Steele. If his first appointment of the day is productive, it inspires him for the next two sessions, and keeps his adrenaline running until the late hours. "I know there's something wrong with me, when I can't shut my brain down, when I'm getting up and writing at three in the morning. I want to keep practicing my lyric craft, get as good as I can. I want to use fewer words to say more things. Instead of having two lines, I try to get it down to two words."

Writing songs to reveal emotions, putting real words out there, Steele acknowledges, is key to why songwriters do what they do, and he includes himself among this assembly. "But it's definitely not in the actual finished process. It's in the process of writing it, and you're feeling like you really touch on something. And it comes out the right way, and there's this sigh of relief, and you realize something in your own life as you're writing it down—it's really healing."

There are songwriter/producers, working musicians who write, and some writers who exist in their little creative environments, and this wonderful thing called music comes out of them. Some songwriters—especially songwriter/artists—literally inhabit their songs, and their melodies and words define who and what they are. Some are most effective as co-writers, and some write by themselves. It's a craft and a business; the most successful songwriters often possess a facility for both art and business. For the great Diane Warren, who you will meet in this chapter, songwriting is her entire life. Writing songs is often a magical process. The greatest songs touch the world.

Kara DioGuardi: Integrity Time

"I don't necessarily believe the people who are in the music business are the most talented people; the most talented people are in a bed somewhere, curled up. And that's because the GM of some business who is at a label and doesn't know anything about music said, 'I'm not sure I hear the hit,' and the kid went home and hasn't spoken for a year."

If she were simply a songwriter, Kara DioGuardi would be a formidable industry force, but she's much more: a stunning vocalist; an accomplished producer; and the founder of Arthouse Entertainment, a music publishing firm that also provides corporate branding, management for artists, writers, and producers, and an interface with film and television productions and record labels. DioGuardi is also currently a vice president of A&R at Warner Bros. Records. "Business can overshadow many things," she states. "Even though you're running a business—and business is business—you have to be very careful because your main commodity is your creativity," she says. "It always has to come from the song, it has to come from a point of truth, it has to be the best you can make it, and it has to have integrity. Once you start selling those things out, your business is going to go down. I have to protect my gift at all costs, whether it costs me money or not."

In 2009, DioGuardi became the fourth judge on the pop culture juggernaut *American Idol*—joining Simon Cowell, Paul Abdul, and Randy Jackson behind the desk. "I work with so many great artists that have been really successful, so I kind of know the common denominator, and I'll be sure to relay that to the audience and to the contestants," says DioGuardi.

When the decision was made to include her in the cast, DioGuardi says it caught her off guard. "It didn't make sense; like I'll be on the biggest show on TV right when I was really about to settle down, are you sh*tting me? It was like, 'Well, all bets are off now.' It's just one of those things. It just happened. This is just part of a journey. I have to do it, but along the way I want to help these people. There will be a few contestants—forget the audience, forget the cameras—I hope I can impart something for a few of them that they take with them and that will change their lives. That's the whole thing: You have to give back. I hope I can give it to them."

And as the new kid on the team, so to speak, DioGuardi is well apprised of the weight of her inclusion. "You've got to be a team player, respect the brand, when it's uber successful and be really honest, too. In the beginning, it is difficult because of the elephant in the room. You know there's the camera, and it's hard to be you under those circumstances. But as it goes on, I hope I get to the core of who I am, and as we go on I will make sure that this comes through."

Song Goddess

With her colossal list of cuts, DioGuardi is undeniably the current queen of the pop songwriting cosmos. Named BMI Songwriter of the Year at the Broadcast Music Incorporated (BMI) 2007 award ceremonies, DioGuardi contributed to multiple songs for Christina Aguilera's *Back to Basics* album, including the smash single "Ain't No Other Man." The list of artists who have recorded her songs includes Celine Dion, Anastacia, Britney Spears, Enrique Iglesias, Ricky Martin, Ashlee Simpson ("Pieces of Me"), Kelly Clarkson, Kylie Minogue, Hilary Duff, Marc Anthony, Pussycat Dolls, Jewel, Gwen Stefani ("Rich Girl"), Bo Bice, Clay Aiken, Santana, Jessica Simpson, Lindsay Lohan, and Paris Hilton. Recent tracks with Avril Lavigne, the Jonas Brothers, Kelly Clarkson, and Faith Hill continue to enrich this eye-popping discography.

Among DioGuardi's recent projects was writing "Sober" with Pink. "I love her; I had so much fun," she says. "It was one of the best sessions of my life. We just synced up, and it was like playing a great game of tennis. She had an idea, a tag line, we built it around that. And beyond that, she's the most incredible singer—I think she sang it in three takes. Incredible. I had chills; my hair was standing on my arm, and the producer and I were looking at each other dumbfounded." Pink, DioGuardi says, writes from the heart. "Whatever's she's feeling, she's totally in the moment of what she's feeling and she wants to express it. She is a true artist. She has her own style and she knows what fits her. It's so refreshing to work with somebody who is that invested in her art and knows themselves that well."

"There is a spiritual component in what we do in that I have to be true to myself and to the people out there," DioGuardi says. "I made those mistakes in my career sometimes—'I wish I hadn't put that lyric in that song'—because it's bigger than me. And you don't realize that when you're coming up, you think it's small, just what's happening in the room, but when it starts going out into the universe, you can't control it. If there's a lyric that's kind of racy for kids, for example, now I feel like I have more responsibility. What do I want to express, but how can it be positive for the world, too? What I'm writing personally is my responsibility. When I'm co-writing with an artist or a co-writer, I have them to consider. So I'm not infusing the room only with what I want. So that's why I've been able to do this for so long. I don't feel like it's my record—I'm helping the artist."

Background Check

DioGuardi was supposed to go to law school. That's what her family—including her father, Joseph, a former congressman—expected when she graduated from Duke University. Instead, she began waitressing and singing with a garage band in New York. When a college friend landed a job with *Billboard* magazine, but was offered another position for more money, DioGuardi slid into her gig. The magazine's Larry Flick was an early believer. "He used to call me 'Runway' because I'd walk up and down the hallway, delegating all of my work so that I could write," she recalls. "About three or four months into our relationship, I thought, 'I've got to get his opinion on my stuff, but I can't tell him it's me. He'll feel forced to listen to it and if he doesn't like it, he'll say he likes it anyway.' I gave him a tape and said, 'This is my friend, and she's been bugging me.' He rushed over after listening and said, "Oh my God, who is this girl?' I said, 'It's me.' He introduced me to Clyde Lieberman [BMG Music Publishing], and that started my career."

Working with *Billboard*'s legendary editor Timothy White gave DioGuardi deeper insight into her own creative past and future. "As a kid I felt very lonely. I don't think my family understood I was creative. I was a circle in a square. Timothy had this thing where he felt that great art came from pain. And a lot of his favorites were artists who'd had rocky childhoods and misfortunes. I never understood that until I began doing my own writing. I think he helped me. He was a kind, great man who loved music."

Casting Lots at Warners

As a vice president of A&R for Warner Bros., DioGuardi has been responsible for a number of new signings, among them a brother act, Laze & Royal. "I heard a song that I believed in. I thought it was a really good pop song, and I thought they were good producers. I liked their style, their story. They've been through a lot of in their lives. Their mother is very ill, and they never knew their father and basically supported themselves through music their whole lives, since they were 14–15 until now. They have an incredible work ethic, and I thought, 'These guys are going to stumble onto something, and I want to be in business with them.'"

But DioGuardi isn't writing songs with them. "I can't 'homie in this club.' I can't—I'm f**king wiped. It's not my thing. I want them to be aligned with the street, what's going on right now and what is really current. I'm not trying to make these artists a vehicle for my songwriting and me. I want them to stand alone and shine for what they do and not for what I do."

Laze & Royal

"Our whole camp is ecstatic," says Royal. "Kara is a real creative person. At labels, there aren't people like that anymore. They're sitting in a room with a laptop hitting 'refresh' on media bases like BDS [Broadcast Data Systems]. People are treating it like a nine-to-five—like a regular job. That's why we chose Warner Bros.—Kara was a songwriter first, she understood our vision. We've got our own style and an image thing. She didn't care; she respected that we write, we produce our own stuff, and that's what she wanted to utilize. She was one of the only ones to recognize that. She's like my sister or my mother; she's got her super ADD mode going on. She calls us at three or four in the morning with ideas. People don't do that these days. We like people around us who work as hard as us."

Laze concurs. "What attracted us to Kara is that our sound has a lot of pop elements. When she called us in, she only knew the one record. When we told her we produce everything from pop to rock, she was blown away. She signed us as writers and producers. It's a blessing to have A&R in your corner who understand the creative side."

"Our whole project is breaking down barriers, killing stereotypes," says Royal. "We've been influenced by so much. There's no such thing as genres; there's good music and bad music."

Jason Reeves: Heart on Sleeve

DioGuardi also signed singer/songwriter Jason Reeves. Although he is newly affiliated with a major label, he has solid credibility from his series of indie CDs, the most recent of which, *The Magnificent Adventures of Heartache (And Other Frightening Tales)*, has been picked up by Warner Bros. and is available for the first time at retail with new mixes of four songs plus a rerecorded version of a key song, "Gasoline."

The 24-year-old Iowa City native relocated to Los Angles in March 2005. When he met producer Mikal Blue and Blue's partner Ken Callat—father of emerging artist Colbie Callat—Reeves became a major co-writer for Colbie's platinum debut, *Coco*, including the smash singles "Bubbly" and "Realize." These songs, he says, evolved from an unaffected approach. "We were writing between going to the beach or climbing a waterfall in the mountains. It was so relaxed; we did it because we loved it. I think that it would be different if we went for it from the beginning, to take over the world. There is an element of surprise that this happened."

"I love Jason," says DioGuardi. "I'm obsessed with him. I don't know how you don't get Jason Reeves. I fell in love with his record: the songs, the lyrics, and way he intertwines things without being obvious. His sense of melody I thought was incredible and his sensitivity to love and hurt and joy I thought was unparalleled. I love the journey of it. I fell in love while listening to his record in Maine—that's where I met my boyfriend. And I felt a very strong connection to it. I listened to it every minute of the day while we were up there."

Signing Story

DioGuardi finds artists through a variety of methods. "They come to my world. People call me up, 'Can you hear this?' If someone gets it to me, I have an obligation to listen to it."

DioGuardi credits her academic background with instilling a strong sense of discipline. "When you're trying to be a writer or an artist, you'd better know how to structure a life or you'll fall into a deep depression. It's about staying in the game. I don't necessarily believe the people who are in the music business are the most talented people; the most talented people are in a bed somewhere, curled up. And that's because the GM of some business who is at a label and doesn't know anything about music said, 'I'm not sure I hear the hit,' and the kid went home and hasn't spoken for a year. True creationists can't always take that kind of rejection. To be a great artist or writer, you've got to be that sensitive. And you've got to have pain, or joy, and to feel really deeply."

www.karadioguardi.com

Billy Steinberg: A Hit Songwriter's True Colors

"As a songwriter, you can't worry about every nickel and dime that you're owed. You're lucky to get even a tiny percentage of what you're due."

Words, anthems, hits: Songwriter Billy Steinberg is one of pop music's most eminent songsmiths and the co-writer, with longtime collaborator Tom Kelly, of huge songs, such as "True Colors" (Cyndi Lauper), "Eternal Flame" (the Bangles), and "Like a Virgin" (Madonna). Steinberg teamed up with writer/producer Rick Nowels for "Falling into You" (Celine Dion) and now works with a new collaborator, Josh Alexander.

"Cyndi Lauper did an amazing production of 'True Colors,' and sang it better than anyone ever would," says Steinberg. "But it's a universal message, and it has had more incarnations. Kodak used it for an ad campaign; Phil Collins had a version and used it in a movie called *Save the Last Dance*. In a similar kind of way, "I'll Stand by You" [the Pretenders] has the same universal quality. Another gratifying thing has been that, since *American Idol* has started, there isn't a time when the contestants don't sing our songs."

Steinberg's collaboration with Josh Alexander is decidedly cross-generational. "I'm in my late fifties and Josh is in his twenties, so there is a big age difference. You know that those of us that are involved in music business are always getting phone calls saying, 'Listen to this.' I got a call from my uncle, and he had a friend who was a professor at University of Califorina, Berkeley, and a friend of his son was songwriter and would I meet him? I was struck immediately with his musicianship and songwriting talent. 'Too Little Too Late" by JoJo is so far our biggest single."

Steinberg traces his interest in pop music to the influence of two neighbor boys in Fresno in the late 1950s who were pop music fans. Soon, he was amassing his own collection of 45 rpm singles. "I would play them over and over until my parents were alarmed," he laughs. "My family moved to Palm Springs in 1958, and then the Beatles came out in 1964, and it absolutely blew me away. The age that I was, 13–14, you're really open to that kind of experience. And I put together a rock band, and we'd play at dances. I still wasn't playing an instrument. I'd sing lead and we would do covers."

Writing poetry, Steinberg says, was the next step in his evolution toward becoming a songwriter. "My grandma got me a Gibson acoustic guitar. I never got really good, but good enough to write some songs. Then I went to Bard College in New York, where I was a literature major there. I wrote one song a day and played my songs for my friends, and it was cool 'cause I realized there was a more receptive female audience. I could take the poetry, put it to music, and all of a sudden I had a song. I really feel like in some way, as a child, I was studying the structures of those early records. When I started writing songs, I had the ability to intuitively understand song structure. I knew it from all the records I had listened to."

Returning to California, Billy formed a band, Billy Thermal, and was signed to producer Richard Perry's imprint, Planet Records. He also obtained his first covers from an outside artist: Pat Benatar. "I got the idea that people were more interested in my songs than me as an artist, but I was hooked on the idea of having a record in the marketplace. Billy Thermal broke up, and it occurred that it might benefit me to co-write. By that time, I was 30 years old, and I had been writing for 12 years. I didn't know who to work with. In August 1981, I rented a house in Pacific Palisades and called Keith Olson on the phone who had produced my two Pat Benatar cuts. He was really warm and said I was one of his favorite songwriters. He invited me to his house. One of the first people I met at the party was songwriter Tom Kelly. Keith had produced a song for Pat with Tom titled "Fire and Ice." And that's how we met. One of the first songs we wrote together was 'Alone' in 1981—a power ballad that became a number-one hit for Heart. I didn't like it at first, it sounded slow and stiff. But when we rewrote it and added a new line and sped it up, it made all the difference in the world."

Riding with Roy

Given his history as a fan of pop music, certain historic reference points have influenced Steinberg's craft. He relates that he and Tom Kelly, both enamored of the orchestral style of Rock 'n' Roll Hall of Fame legend Roy Orbison, wrote a song, "I Drove All Night," that reflected the majestic splendor of the great singer. "At one point in the eighties, Tom and I saw little ad in the 'Calendar' section of the *Los Angeles Times* showing that Roy was performing at a supper club in Orange County. We waited in line at the club where most of the people were our age or older. I was kind of bracing myself, saying, 'I can't expect too much.' His vocals on the recordings were other-worldly good. Out comes the band and background singers, who start singing 'Only the Lonely.' And out walks Roy and he steps up to the mic and sang every hit from his catalog probably better than the record—it was mindblowing: 'In Dreams,' 'Pretty Woman,' 'Crying,' 'It's Over.' All my favorites. We eventually met him, and Roy agreed to put his vocal on our demo of 'I Drove All Night.' I was at Tom's house, and Roy was scheduled to come over that day. And we walked out to get the mail and saw a red convertible Ferrari driving really slow. And I felt like I had died and gone to heaven. As a kid, I owned every one of his records. And he was driving up the street to work with us. He was such a gentleman. He was so modest and so genuine. He put down two tracks of vocals. Sang it through twice. Then Roy got together with Jeff Lynne and had a comeback."

Cover Me

Since he is such a well-established songwriter, it might be imagined that Steinberg has intermediaries in place to pitch his songs and garner subsequent covers. He contradicts this assumption with the reality that he gets his own cuts. "I never really take for granted that someone else is going to get me a cover. Whether it's calling A&R people or producers or managers, I've been pretty aggressive about it. My experience with publishing companies is that they for the most part have so many songs, they spend more time making contracts and collecting the monies and making statements that I think they're more effective in those matters than in song-plugging."

"Some people assume erroneously that it must be easy to get my songs covered. The only advantage is that I can get people to listen, but I don't see people predisposed to recording my songs. Any new song is judged by its own merits. It takes a lot of money to launch a single, especially today, and nobody is going to give you that spot because you have had success in the past. It's hard to get my songs listened to and to get them covered."

Strengths in Song

"I learned a valuable lesson in 1981 when I met Tom. I had written songs on my own up until that point, and I didn't really know what my strengths and weaknesses were as a writer. I was a songwriter: I wrote chords and melodies and lyrics, and then when I worked with Tom, he was such a better musician than I was. I realized my strong point is in writing lyrics. Make an honest assessment of your capabilities. Find somebody who fills in the blanks and who brings to the collaboration strength in something that you lack."

Diane Warren

"You can't just be good—you have to be great."

With an astounding roster of top-10 hits in a dizzying range of diverse musical genres, Diane Warren has penned a legacy of incomparable smashes: "How Do I Live," "If You Asked Me To," "Unbreak My Heart," "I Don't Want to Miss a Thing," "Music of the Heart," and "Nothing's Gonna Stop Us Now." Warren has written for such notable artists as Aerosmith, Elton John, Tina Turner, Barbra Streisand, Aretha Franklin, Patti LaBelle, Roberta Flack, Celine Dion, Whitney Houston, and Roy Orbison. Recently, a diverse group of artists—including Lenny Kravitz, RBD, the Pussycat Dolls, Carrie Underwood, Pet Shop Boys, Mario, Joss Stone, Daniel Bedingfield, Christina Aguilera, Sugababes, Kid Rock, Enrique Iglesias, JoJo, Jessica Simpson, and Mary J. Blige—has recorded her songs. She was the first songwriter in the history of *Billboard* to have seven hits, all by different artists, on the singles chart at the same time.

Her songs have been featured in nearly 100 motion pictures to date, and she has been nominated for four Golden Globes and six Academy Awards, in addition to her nine Grammy nods. Her accolades also include a star on the Hollywood Walk of Fame. "Isn't that funny? People can walk all over me and sh*t all over me," she says.

View from the Valley

"Songs spoke to me since I was little," says Warren. "I was a shy kid, and they saved my life. I grew up in a house with a lot of music in it. My parents had lots of soundtracks and show tunes. And my sisters were a lot older than me, and I was hearing all kinds of records, Elvis and stuff, and it all had an impact. And at seven, I started looking to see who wrote the songs. I remember the first was 'Up on the Roof' [Gerry Goffin and

Carole King]. When I was around 10 or 11, my neighbors wanted to start a band, and I wanted to be the songwriter. We didn't really have a band—I just knew I wanted to be a songwriter. At 14, I got obsessive, and I'm still that way."

Few who know her would disagree. "These songs are like my kids. I protect my kids. It's like I don't think people can believe like me. I'm just passionate. It's fun to play songs for people and see things happen. You know me: I'll call radio stations, and I'm a good promotion person. It's all about believing and having passion. It gets me to work every day. Why do I have to stop at just writing the songs? Why can't I do all the other stuff? No one's going to do it like me."

Sometimes these "song children" travel to unexpected destinations. Warren recalls this one: "I remember when I wrote 'I Don't Want to Miss a Thing.' It was like a Celine Dion song, and then [Universal Music executive] Kathy Nelson got Aerosmith to do it. I remember getting the CD, and my mind was blown; it was a genius record. It wasn't anything I thought it would sound like. It was beautiful. Fast forward to. . .today, I'll meet rappers and they love that song. That's part of the journey—songs definitely have a life of their own."

Office Time

For 24 years, Warren has occupied the same suite of offices in Hollywood. "I just show up and go to work. I just do this everyday. I get up early in the morning; I kind of know what I do, but I don't like to describe it. I'll have a title. I show up and see what happens."

Very significantly, Warren owns her own publishing company, RealSongs, a rarity in the business of music. She recalls when RealSongs was named ASCAP Music Publisher of the Year. "That's a career achievement. That was amazing; underneath me is EMI and Warner/Chappell Music—and I'm just one writer." Her concept for owning a firm came early in her career when she was embroiled in a lawsuit. "I was signed to Laura Branigan's producer, and we had disagreements with the contract. It turned into a law-suit, and I couldn't sign with anybody else. I was bummed out that I couldn't do any-thing. So I came up with the name 'real songs.' Everything I aspire to is in that name. I was lucky to keep the name of that company. And I wrote a bunch of songs on my own, and I never looked back. I own them—how cool. The amounts of money that I have been offered are staggering. I don't intend to sell."

A State of Great

A huge career highlight happened recently for Warren, she explains. "I was a guest of the president of Israel, and I wrote a song that he wants to be the theme song for Middle East peace. It was unveiled at the Shalom Prayers Peace Center with Palestinian and Israeli children singing. And Elliot Yamin performed it." In addition to her never-ending cycle of work, Warren contributes generously to the well-being of animals through PETA and Best Friends, an animal society. "I love animals. They don't have a voice, so whatever I can do to save them and help them, I will do," she confirms.

But Warren does have a voice, and she uses it to continue creating an unbroken string of songs. "Hunger and fear drive me. Clive Davis has the same kind of thing. It's not about money. It never inspired me to go to work. I just love writing songs."

And for aspirants she offers this credo: "Be great and work hard, whether you are a songwriter or an athlete. You can't just be good—you have to be great."

www.realsongs.com

Keith Stegall: Rebel on the Row

"When you hear someone sing live, it's more heart than hit."

Although the average fan of country music might not recognize Keith Stegall's name, his words, music, and productions would certainly resonate with fans of Alan Jackson, Randy Travis, and George Strait. Stegall is a revered Nashville-based producer, songwriter, and musician whose golden touch has guided a jukebox full of hits.

"I grew up with music, since my father was a musician." Says Stegall, "I went to college in Shreveport, Louisiana, and got my degree in religion. When I went off to grad school, I was miserable. My advisor asked me what I enjoyed doing, and I said, 'writing songs,' so he advised me to go and do that."

Stegall began his career at Blackwood Music in Nashville, CBS's music publishing division under Mitch Miller. "My first cut was 'Sexy Eyes' with Dr. Hook," says Stegall. He was no stranger to Music Row. "While I was still in college, I was making trips to Nashville once a month. It took four years to get that first break. But thank God for my advisor."

Helen Reddy, the Commodores, Johnny Mathis, and others tracked Stegall's songs in L.A. Most notable among the subsequent recordings was Al Jarreau's huge hit "We're In This Love Together." Stegall, who was pursuing his own artist career, didn't consider himself a country writer per se, but country artists began recording his songs. Charley Pride, Jerry Reed, Eddy Arnold, Moe Bandy, Conway Twitty, George Strait, and Steve Wariner all had hits with his compositions.

By 1985, Mickey Gilley and Glen Campbell had taken Stegall's tunes to the top of the country charts with "Lonely Nights" and "A Lady Like You." "That starting kicking things up," says Stegall. "Shortly after, I met Randy Travis. That was the beginning of me being a record producer. I was still working at being an artist at the time and had several record deals before I produced Randy's breakthrough album. I got a royalty check from Warner Bros. and thought, 'What am I doing out here on the road?' So I made a decision to come back and be a record producer. Alan Jackson was the next one I ran into. He and I started writing together and those demos secured his deal with Arista. And I have been doing it ever since." Among the many Stegall productions for Jackson are signature songs "Where Were You When the World Stopped Turning" and "It's Five O'Clock Somewhere," recorded by Jackson with guest Jimmy Buffett.

Stegall estimates that he has written and/or produced over 40 number-one and top-10 records. His accolades include CMA Awards, Grammy nominations (including Soundtrack Compilation of the Year for a Motion Picture for *Bridget Jones' Diary*), and a Producer of the Year Award from *Music City Magazine*. "Once I got successful, I got calls from labels to do things. I wanted to work with George Jones and Merle Haggard for the experience of working with those guys. Basically, I look for people that are unique. Alan and Randy—when that sort of music was not considered 'in' in Nashville. It's a gut thing. When you hear someone sing live, it's more heart than hit."

Hot Man on the Bandstand

The Zac Brown Band has the requisite heart of which Stegall speaks. "We saw them perform over two years ago. I went to the bar and I saw him and the band and knew there was something magical going on—something extremely authentic and Southern and real, and it just knocked me out. I didn't know if it would work on radio. I just said I'd love to sit down and talk with you and get involved with what you're doing. We had a meeting in Atlanta, and I asked him about working together. He wanted to make a record, but the people in Nashville wanted him to hire session players and fire his band and make him the singer."

"But I wanted to use his band. I said, 'I don't care how long it takes, but let's use your band, so it's really you.' It took about a year to make the record, and I used only a few outside players for color things. I played a little accordion and organ on it." Brown's career received a major boost when he signed with Live Nation (home to Madonna and Jay-Z). "A great team of people came along with that—veterans from the music industry. I was asked to put a promotion staff together, and the single, 'Chicken Fried' went to number one and the album is well on its way to gold status."

Stegall hears similar alchemy in the music of the Harters, a family trio originally from Arizona, now living in Nashville. "When they take the stage, there's magic that takes place. It's not forced; it's a very natural display of talent. Artists with the ability to captivate people on stage are the ones that become iconic. Just because someone is a songwriter doesn't mean they're an artist. The Harters should be playing on their records so that it doesn't sound like a machine that's being cranked out."

Into the Mix

From 1992 to 2002, Stegall was the head of A&R at Mercury Records Nashville, where he championed a gold and platinum roster of artists he worked with, including Mark Wills, Jamie O'Neal, and Terri Clark, all who had number one hits. Since Stegall doesn't work for a label now, he says he has even more leeway to develop artists. "I don't know if the industry is set up to nurture the artist anymore. I set up a creative world, where artists who I think are talented can come and grow and develop and realize their potential. I don't think there's much time for that at a label. Labels have brains that are dictated from the top down. If I had a label, I'd do it my way."

Having a studio in which to operate also gives him control of the developing and the established artists' sounds. "I've owned a mix room for the last 20 years. And I have favorite studios in town with big open tracking rooms, especially for an Alan Jackson record. I track with a large section, seven to eight people. Once we get the tracks, if we capture something, I bring them back to my place and spend the next three to four months getting Alan's vocals on there and overdubbing guitars."

Synthesizers, Stegall says, are used only if the budget is running out. "The last seven years have seen the rebirth of the Hammond B-3 organ. When I came to town, they were stuck in the back of studio, but now they've been showing up on records again."

Spotlights and Cat Fights

The creative pressure cooker environment of the studio can exert tremendous stress under the audio microscope of a high-level recording session. "I had one experience in the studio when a creative fight broke out between a couple of artists," says Stegall. "I thought, 'I can't believe I'm witnessing this.' When you walk into a studio with high-level, high-profile people, it's an interesting experience. But I try to be diplomatic. These people are under a tremendous amount of pressure because they live in a fish bowl."

www.keithstegall.com

Lauren Christy: Baby, Remember Her Name

"It was so liberating to finally make that decision—to drop trying to be a star."

As the female component in the hit-making writing and production trio The Matrix—writers and producers of hits for a roster of artists that includes Avril Lavigne, Britney Spears, and Jason Mraz—Lauren Christie is often behind the scenes. But it wasn't always this way. Originally, she had her own aspirations to be an artist.

A just-announced project for The Matrix is creating music for the remake of the beloved musical film *Fame*. "I was such a fan of the original movie, and I went to a performing arts school just like it, so it's very close to my heart," Christy told *Entertainment Weekly*. "When I heard that they were doing a new version and needed people to work on the soundtrack, I said, "We have to do it." [Matrix partners] Graham [Edwards] and Scott [Spock] were like, 'Don't stop Lauren. She's really crazy to do this.' But once they saw the original movie, they realized how significant it was. And nowadays, with the whole of America watching *American Idol*, everyone wants to be an entertainer. I think the new version is going to be really relevant."

Crawling with Susie Reptile

Christy is the child of parents who had ties to the entertainment industry. Performing poorly in school, she switched to the Bush Davies Ballet School when she was 11 years old. She remained there until she was 17, when she chose to focus on music rather than dance. She pulled together a band, Pink Ash, and remade herself into Susie Reptile, the leader of the band of seven in which she was the only female. Over the course of a year, she holed up in her room to write and record, using a four-track and some keyboards. She emerged with 15 new compositions and dreams of a publishing contract. Christy signed a contract with publisher EMI and was set to begin recording for Polygram Records. She moved from London to Los Angeles, and in 1993 put out her eponymous debut, an effort that is largely autobiographical. She garnered some success as a songwriter, with credits including feature films *Batman*, *Great Expectations*, *Raising Helen*, and *13 Going on 30*.

Christy's career as an artist followed this timeline of small accolades. She earned a Golden Globe nomination for Best Original Song for "The Color of Night," co-written with Jud Friedman and Dominic Frontiere. Still, as mainstream success eluded her, she was convinced that she was destined to be a "starving musician." She was admittedly frustrated by what she characterizes as the "whole artist thing," as she recalls. "I like my records, which is a good thing looking back on it, but at a certain point I realized I wasn't going to be the superstar I was hoping to be. I never thought I was the sh*t when it came to singing, and I never thought I had this huge star quality. It was more like, 'I need my songs to be heard, so I guess I'll sing them.'"

Christy credits manager Sandy Roberton (Worlds End Management) with changing her life and career for the better. Roberton offered to help her get a new record deal after the release of her second album, but it was a meeting with an A&R rep in England that provided the epiphany she had been waiting for. "He said, 'I really like your music, but do you think I could give some of it to Natalie Imbruglia?' That was a big turning point for me. 'I don't have to sing it anymore, and I can let go of that dream I once had.' I vowed I would never be an artist again, and I wasn't going to cry about it."

Meet The Matrix

The foundation of the hit songwriting and production trio The Matrix was beginning to take shape through conversation Christy was having with her husband Graham Edwards, as they toyed with the idea of starting a network where artists could develop their talents. They joined forces with Scott Spock, born in St. Louis, an accomplished trumpeter turned programmer and remixer who had worked with Diana Ross, Nick Carter (Backstreet Boys), and Chaka Khan. Spock had first met Edwards when he remixed tracks from Edwards' group, Dollshead, and Spock and Christy had also recorded together. When manager Sandy Roberton suggested that the three co-write and produce one song, it was a radical circle.

"We can't believe we've gotten to where we are," marvels Christy. "It seems like only yesterday Sandy said, 'I'm going to make you the biggest producers in the world,' and we were like, 'Yeah,' and kept our heads down and worked." The Matrix actually came out of a project that didn't succeed, a girl group for whom they wrote songs. "Nothing came of the group," explains Christy, "then people were saying 'but the production sounds great,' which was the real lynchpin. We went, 'let's try something.'"

"Sandy suggested we come up with a name because it was hard to constantly describe the three of us," explained Christy. "So we came up with the name 'The Matrix.' The matrix is a name for the womb, or the rock, which everything comes from. Our name wasn't inspired by the movie *The Matrix* [which came out later]."

The Matrix began procuring cuts and projects. One of their first projects was writing and producing a song for Christina Aguilera's Christmas album, and they wrote and produced songs for Irish artist Ronan Keating. But their big break was when Roberton hooked them up to collaborate with a new, then-unknown Canadian artist named Avril Lavigne, who had been signed to Arista Records. With Lavigne, the trio created mega-hits "Complicated," "Sk8er Boi," and "I'm with You."

Says Christy, "Avril really wanted to rock out, but the record company had a different approach, yet it was too middle of the road for her. We said, 'You can't do System of a Down; you're beautiful and you're 16. We really have to find the key for the door for you.' We were carving out a nice living for ourselves. But we never had a big hit. We were getting a little bit nervous. Our publishers dropped us right before the Avril record came out. The people were nice, but they knew that we hadn't had a hit yet. It was the most beautiful gift to sign a new publishing deal."

Sandy Says

All three members of The Matrix are in awe of the commitment and vision of their manager, Sandy Roberton. "You can send Sandy an e-mail at three in the morning," says Edwards, "wake up at six, and have a reply." Christy disagrees about the time. "It will be earlier," she avows, "because he goes to the gym at 5:30 a.m. And you'll see him at the Viper Room at 1:00 a.m., checking out acts. From day one, he's had the same enthusiasm he has today, and you can't help but catch it. Whether it's a brand new artist or Ricky Martin, he calls later in the day, 'How did it go? When can I hear it?' It's hard to find someone who will put their name on the line, go in when no one has ever heard of you, and say, 'These guys are the sh*t—you've got to use them.' When we had nothing, he made us feel totally special and successful. I'll always be grateful. Coming from being an artist, doing a record deal, I was going, 'What am I going to do?' He said, 'This is what you're going to do with your career, and you'll be brilliant at it. The three of you are going to conquer the world."

Cutting Korn

One of The Matrix's most unexpected turns came when they collaborated with the hard rock band Korn. "We heard [lead singer] Jonathan Davis wanted to collaborate with people, and he called Sandy. He took a chance and spent two days in the studio with us, and it wasn't really working and the band thought it wouldn't work. Then something happened the last day, and we all just clicked. From there, we spent three weeks with them every day and wrote 23 songs. We pretty much wrote that whole album (*See You on the Other Side*) with them. They had a lot to prove, and we did too; that's when you get the best stuff happening when you're kind of nervous about it." When collaborating with co-writers, Christy rationalizes, "There's always something that you can get from somebody. I could write with my mother even—she might instill frustration in me and I could write a song off that energy. Just having someone in the room could change the way things are going."

Music in the Mill

Christy confirms that The Matrix, having been through the artist mill themselves, understands "the record company thing. We know if they're having a bad day. Sometimes we'll spend an hour bitching with the artist about how tough it is. I remember the problems in the system, when people at the label you're attached to are fired."

And choosing artists to work with, Christy says, comes down to communication with the music. "It's rare that it's a lot of money, but if we don't love the music, we don't do that. It may have happened in the beginning because we had to pay bills. The other thing is, the music might be fabulous but the people are just such a**holes! And life is too short. I've had that happen too. Other factors are who the people are, will it be successful, the A&R person, is the record company going to restructure? I hate to look at that stuff, but you have to."

"Sometimes the stars don't align, and people don't quite get who that person is. They might have the most amazing songs but just don't look right. Or it's not the right time—so many different factors. A lot of people in the business will do well even if they're not that talented because they have energy. But if you find someone with talent and energy, they're unstoppable."

Tom Shapiro: Turn Right on Music Row

"You write a bad song to get to the good songs. You have to write the crap out of you."

Meet Tom Shapiro, whose credits include *Music Row* magazine's Top Country Songwriter, two CMA awards, four BMI Country Songwriter of the Year awards, and the Nashville Songwriter Association International's first-ever Songwriter of the Decade award, with 23 number-one songs and 52 top-10 charted singles. Among the wealth of hits are "Ain't Nothing About You" by Brooks and Dunn, "Thinking About You" by Trisha Yearwood, "Your Heart's Not in It" Janie Fricke, "Highway Robbery" by Tanya Tucker, and "Watch Me" by Lorrie Morgan.

He co-produced and co-wrote Billy Dean's string of smashes, including "Only the Wind," "You Don't Count the Cost," and the number one "If There Hadn't Been You." He continues to top the charts with songs like "If You Ever Stop Loving Me" by Montgomery Gentry.

Born and raised in Kansas City, Shapiro was fascinated by movie music and was already playing the piano by the time he was 10 years old. After his senior year in high school, he spent the summer at a French university where he met an Oklahoman who played guitar when he wasn't learning French. When his new friend explained that he was writing songs, Tom began to write with him. "Later he would write themes for *Roseanne* and *Home Improvement*," Shapiro remembers.

After a year at Whittier College in California, Shapiro moved to Boston University, where he majored in music and minored in English. He also spent a brief time teaching at the Berklee School of Music, and in 1973 he helped found a school of contemporary music. But he wanted to write, not teach, so a year later he sold his share of the school and moved to L.A., where he made do with a variety of jobs, including one at a dental lab in the San Fernando Valley, where he worked as a courier, driving the freeways of Los Angeles to deliver false teeth and bridges to dental offices. His first major publishing deal was with Heath-Levy Music. "I got a cut here and there, but nothing much. Finally, I had to quit the business. I was working at a music store in Santa Monica, hating it and hating my life, going through a divorce. I had written this song after I left Heath-Levy with Michael Garvin. George Benson was doing a greatest-hits album, needed one more song, knew my publisher, and asked if I had any songs to pitch. So I get a call on Monday morning, saying, 'We got it!' I was trying to get a song into a 'Grade Z' porno movie for $200, and I thought that's what he meant, but the publisher said, 'George Benson cut your song this weekend.'"

Nashville Bound

The Benson cut, "Never Give Up on a Good Thing," provided Shapiro the credibility he needed as a songwriter and instigated a major move. "Monday I got word that the song had been cut over the weekend," he says. "Tuesday I quit my job. Wednesday I packed my clothes, and Thursday I headed for Nashville because I was tired of L.A. and I knew I could get an advance on the Benson cut to keep me going in Nashville for a while. I write for acts. Being a country writer, you have to be in Nashville. You can't do it from afar," Shapiro notes.

"I'm a nine-to-five writer, five days a week in the room. It's a great job. You can walk away from the room. There's no rush. The magic that takes place—you find something that entertains or interests you. If it doesn't interest you, it won't interest anyone else. Get a reason to write a song. Every time you write a song, it's not a failure, 'cause it will lead eventually to the good one."

Magic notwithstanding, Nashville is much more collaboration-driven in this modern age. "In the seventies, I wrote by myself. It is sort of a numbers game, and you're writing with a lot of artists, so a lot of co-writing is happening. Unless you're a genius like Paul Simon or Jimmy Webb, you will be writing with artists who have certain things that they want to say. To this day, I'm still learning things as the business changes. I do work with writers that are younger than me 'cause at this point, most of the writers *are* younger than me."

Shapiro shares that while major artists are open to cutting outside songs, newer artists are not. "And it's a weird phenomenon. Fewer artists are cutting now. There used to be a time when the new artist would want to write their own because they were getting grade C material. Now, when people would be willing take a chance on a new act and they could get top material, they insist on writing the songs themselves. Unless I totally believe in them, I don't like dealing with new acts."

Hooked on Hooks

Shapiro recalls a valuable lesson he learned from hit songwriter Mac Davis, who was then experiencing massive successes as a songwriter with hits for Elvis Presley and B. J. Thomas. "He said, 'Never forget what brought you to the dance. It really comes down to the fact that you're a songwriter. Politics mean nothing—it's the fact that you create something special that people want.' That has stuck with me, with all the side things that have happened in the business. In the end, it's how good you are as a writer."

www.eminashville.com/bios/tshapiro.html

Pam Sheyne: Collaborative Confluence

"I love the process and I hate the process—when it comes easily, it is the most amazing feeling."

"A girlfriend said to me, 'The next time you go to L.A., you've got to write with David Frank,' Pam Sheyne recalls. "I called him, and we had one day to put in. I said, 'If we've only got one day, we really should get another writer so we can nail a song.'" Frank invited hit songwriter and collaborator Steve Kipner, his neighbor down the road in L.A.'s rustic Topanga Canyon, to join in the writing session. The song the trio wrote that day, "Genie in a Bottle," became the breakthrough hit for Christina Aguilera. For Pam Sheyne, it was—after almost 17 years in the music business—a catapult to the highest echelons of pop songwriting.

Now based in Los Angeles, Sheyne occupies an increasingly rare position, that of a "pure" songwriter. In recent years, the success of Disney's team pop machine have been a boon for Sheyne, as she has landed cuts on the *Camp Rock* CD (featuring the Jonas Brothers in the starring roles) and *The Princess Diaries*, penning the film's end title. Additionally, Sheyne works frequently in Nashville and writes for a roster of international artists from the UK to Italy.

Born in New Zealand, Sheyne moved to England, where her brother and sister were already living. "I was always into music in school. I played guitar from age seven and sang. My parents were big fans of country music and music in general." In the UK, her sister helped find her an office job that Sheyne hated. She began perusing the classified ads in the trade magazine *Melody Maker* and found a gig singing covers with a band at the Sheraton Skyliner at Heathrow Airport.

Over time, she began singing backup for recording sessions with artists including Lulu, Sisters of Mercy, and William Orbit, and even toured the world, performing onstage with the Pet Shop Boys. But Sheyne wanted to move into more creative endeavors. "I didn't see myself doing this forever. I wanted to do more, to try my hand at more things. I wanted to write. That is definitely my home. I came into it effortlessly."

A Nudge from Nigel

When Sheyne met Nigel Rush, her first publisher—now her husband and manager—the business side of her career began to evolve. "I traveled to Stockholm and Sydney for co-writes. Nigel took me to every possible event, reception, and party—even the opening of a French door—it was exhausting! He introduced me to everybody. The industry is not as big as you think. We went to every function and built up a great network of people, but we realized we would have to keep traveling. The world is bigger than the British market. We started coming to America. It seemed that Los Angeles was the center of the pop writing community—it has spread to Nashville and New York, but a lot of writers had come to L.A."

"Nigel has been with me since the beginning as a writer, and he's been a huge part of the process. I've always been a little shy and not as tenacious as he is. He has gone for every opportunity possible, and this has furthered my career."

Sheyne and Rush were on holiday in Greece when "Genie in a Bottle" hit number one in the United States. "Nigel kept me waiting. He called Steve [Kipner] in America and found out." Rush kept Sheyne guessing while he requested that the restaurant put champagne on ice. When the restaurant didn't have any on hand, a friend was called on to deliver the requisite celebratory bubbly. "We partied," Sheyne laughs, "my poor liver!" A few weeks later, she landed at the airport in Los Angeles and was picked up by music publisher Suzan Koc. "She said, 'It will be on in a few minutes, it's all over the radio.' When it came on, I stood up in the car and put my head through the sunroof: 'It's my song!'"

Prose with a Purpose

Over the past decade, Sheyne says, songwriting has become much more project-oriented. "You have to find who is looking for songs. I used to get together with writers and just ask: 'What do you feel like writing today?' Now it's much more of a business. You get together, and you have to be damn focused on what you're doing. I may go to write with a producer or the artist, but very seldom do I get together and just write a song for the fun of it. Even if it is fun, it's for a specific purpose. You have to focus in on the creative direction you've been given and hope that it's correct."

Sheyne refers to the information about what type of song an artist might require as "a brief." She explains how she comes by this knowledge: "You call around and talk to as many people involved in the process as you can. Still, you're shooting in the dark a lot of the time. It always helps when you're writing with the artist or with the producer."

Naked in the Writing Room

Sheyne is what is referred to in the UK as a "top line writer"—that is, she creates both melodies and lyrics. "I don't like writing by myself. I have this alter ego on my shoulder saying, 'That's terrible.' I prefer energy in the room and bouncing ideas off of other people."

"It's difficult; writing with someone is like taking your clothes off on a first date," Sheyne says. "You have to get a bit thick-skinned, to throw all your good ideas and your bad ideas into the mix. It still amazes me. I love the process and I hate the process—when it comes easily, it is the most amazing feeling. It can start with the tiniest nugget of an idea, a title, or a chord sequence, and it just takes the people involved in the writing to go, 'I love that,' and you're off. It's all about positive energy, and it goes to prove that a human being can do anything if they believe in something."

But once the song is completed, it will then face rigorous scrutiny. "It's tough out there these days. Everyone has an opinion. It doesn't mean that they are right. It can crush and destroy you if you believe what people say. If you think you're good at what you do, keep doing it. This doesn't mean you'll succeed, but give it a good go. Listen to the radio. Listen to what people are buying. Melody is king, even more than lyrics sometimes, and I love lyrics."

"Be as positive as you can. Don't get too personal; be more general, and think about the listener. We're all human beings; we all go through the same emotions. Think on a world level. People want to be uplifted. Music is an amazing thing that can bring people up and change their lives. And there are many more hits that are positive than negative."

www.pamsheyne.com

2 The Artist

Successful artists embody something truly special: an essence, a vibe, and magnetism. Their attributes might include a vibrant stage personality like Gwen Stefani or incomparable voices like those of two of our next interviewees: Ann Wilson of Heart and Joe Cocker. Often, even the most seasoned professionals in the business cannot explain exactly what it is, but the ability to identify it is an essential element for music industry professionals. Timing can be crucial, but in truth, it is all about the talent.

The best artists have personality, image, identity, and the ability to communicate with millions of listeners who can instantly identify their sound. No, artists are not generally "normal" people. The artist is the delivery system, but so much more: In the truest sense, artists are at the center of the storm.

Gene Simmons: The KISS of Money

"Black and gay is always hipper and cooler than straight and white."

Larger than life: With his horrific bat-like make up and protracted tongue, Gene Simmons is one of the music business's most recognizable icons. His business savvy is equally prodigious: With the band KISS, Simmons created an immense trademark and a 30-plus-year legacy of music and merchandise.

KISS continues to be the juggernaut of licensing and merchandising, with over 2,500 licenses. Along with relationships with Holiday Inn, Nike, Pepsi-Cola, Coca-Cola, and Universal Hotels, KISS has licensed KISS Visa cards, Canon KISS cameras (Japan), KISS comic books, and, among other projects, the upcoming KISS cartoon show from Warner Bros. Outside of KISS, Simmons discovered Van Halen, managed Liza Minnelli's recording career, produced New Line Pictures' *Detroit Rock City*, created the hit Nickelodeon cartoon *My Dad the Rock Star* (seen in 24 countries), created the Oxygen series smash *Mr. Romance*, and has two TV series, VH1's *Gene Simmons' Rock School* and A&E's *Gene Simmons' Family Jewels*, among a dozen other TV projects such as *Trophy Wife* (New Line TV). Author of two *New York Times* best-sellers, *KISS and*

Makeup (Crown Books) and *Sex Money KISS* (Simmons/Phoenix Books), he has published his own magazine, *Gene Simmons Tongue* (Sterling MacFadden) and is debuting a new magazine, *Gene Simmons Game*. He heads his own publishing imprint, Simmons Books (with Phoenix Books); has a DVD label, Simmons Audio Visual; and has a record label, Simmons Records. Simmons has co-starred in such movies as *Runaway* and *Wanted Dead or Alive*, acted in television programs such as *Third Watch* and *Miami Vice*, co-hosted NBC's *Extra*, served as a guest judge on Fox's *American Idol*, and been on NBC's *The Apprentice*.

"KISS is bigger than ever," boasts Simmons. "This last summer we did 30 stadiums. When we go out again, we'll do a year and a half. We sold out in 20 minutes. This sounds like bragging, but you can never take it for granted. You can't be yesterday's heroes, and you have to prove it every time you get in the ring. Next we pitch *KISS: The Next Generation* reality show with Mark Burnett. I have five other shows coming out. Just a ton of stuff."

Given this preponderance of projects, it would seem that Simmons has little time for rest, for good reason. "There's an RIP waiting for all of us," he muses.

Back in the Day

"Thirty-five years ago we had a bizarre notion," Simmons begins. "This sounds like a catch phrase, but it was important for a marketing position. We said, 'Let's put together the band we never saw onstage.' The epiphany was that when people go to a concert, they're actually listening with their eyes. If you want just the music, then stay home. Band after band was disappointing live. They would look at their shoes or turn their backs. We got tired of seeing bands that looked like pizza delivery boys with tie-died t-shirts. Stage was a holy place, and we believed we should dress for the occasion. What that meant, we didn't know."

"So four guys completely unqualified to do any of it got together at the right time and the right place. If we tried to do the same thing in the fifties, then we'd be looked at as Martians. You had to have the British Invasion come and go, and you had to have the Bleecker Street glitter glam scene and other pieces of fertilizer in the soil to make this life form spring forth. KISS never had hit radio stuff. We did it the old-fashioned way: We went out and toured. Within a year and half, our record sales were in the dumper. Three records in, we were selling 300,000 pieces yet playing stadiums; we were selling out stadiums before people were playing stadiums. We had bands opening up for us that had been on tour way before us. It was clear that the live experience was what people wanted to see."

Wicked Lester Left to Fester

Prior to KISS, Simmons and guitarist Paul Stanley performed together with a band, Wicked Lester. "I had $20,000 and bought Marshall amps, knowing that bands need equipment so I could rent it out. The band I had in college disbanded, and I came to New York with my gear. I saw Paul Stanley in a band called Uncle Joe at a club. He had a great voice and presence, and somehow we wound up being in the band Wicked Lester together. He was a guy who wrote his own songs. I thought I was the only one in history who ever wrote his own songs; and somehow the Beatles weren't human beings, weren't real people, so they didn't count. I remember I met him and asked to hear his songs, and he thought I was an arrogant prick and didn't like me at all. I thought I was king of the earth and should have it all. He played the song 'Sunday Driver' that he wrote. Eventually we recorded that as 'Let Me Know,' and it knocked me out. It sounded like a Stones song or something. We looked at each other hesitantly—we were complete opposites. You're better off not being in a band with your friends; I look at it as a business. It's not called 'music,' it's called 'music business.' I recognized that and thought I should be in a band with a guy who thought I was an a**hole."

Wicked Lester was signed to Epic Records, but the band failed to make much of an impression. "It was a five-member Doobie Brothers kind of band—no style, everyone looking sloppy and hippy-ish. It wasn't the band we wanted to be in. We were insane. Paul and I literally decided to fire the rest of the guys, but they wouldn't go, so we quit and we took our songs with us. The record stayed at Epic. Once we started KISS, we understood rights and trademarks, and so we bought back our record. It had cost $44,000 to record, and we paid $120,000 to buy it back. We own it to this day, and it will come out soon enough. I was all of 23 years old then. Paul was 20."

"The name KISS came right away—Paul came up with it. I said, 'Let's call ourselves F**k'! But reality stuck its hard nose into it. Ace Frehley [guitar], who delivered liquor for a living at the time, he actually drew the first version of the logo and then Paul redrew it. We use that logo to this day."

The KISS makeup, possibly their most recognizable visual element, came about this way, according to Simmons: "It was a bizarre notion because we thought we were geniuses. We were going to play big halls, and we wanted to reach to the last seat. We went to see the Who in Philly, and you couldn't see them onstage. We decided, 'Put on white face like a mime and outline the lips so you can see us.' Once we had mirrors in front of us, we came up with our own things. Scarlet Rivera, who was the guitar player with Bob Dylan, was so fascinated by the KISS thing she went back and talked to Bob, and he started wearing white face onstage."

Merchandise and the Media

With an extensive merchandise line that even includes a KISS coffin, the band commands a vast profit-driven empire. "Marketing and merchandising weren't words that existed back then," says Simmons. "I saw a $3,000 check for the rights to do Rolling Stones t-shirts. Why not do $3 million? It's the Stones! They just didn't know it. We didn't hesitate doing toys and stuff like the boy bands, such as New Kids on the Block. I wanted to make this as close to the Disney model as possible."

Simmons was born in Israel and immigrated to New York City at age eight with his mother, a Holocaust survivor. When Simmons was young, it has been speculated that his mother's long absences while working two jobs in order to make ends meet left emotional scars that gave him a strong desire for wealth. "I'm Jewish," he confirms. "It's people of the book who read. All the same information that rich guys have, the poor guys have, too. A library is a House of God and continues to be. Ignorance is no excuse. That's what the cops tell you: If you break the law, you still get the same punishment as the guy who didn't know any better. I started reading *Billboard* and *Cashbox* magazines before I was in a band. They told me the secrets. 'Here's what's working and what the marketplace responds to.'"

"It's not really about how good you sing or how good looking you are—it is some quality you can't put your finger on. Madonna is not the beauty of all time. She or I or Mick Jagger wouldn't make it on *American Idol*. We don't sing all that well. I look like something that crawled out from under a rock! When I first saw Sly and the Family Stone, I wondered, 'What is it?' I couldn't put my finger on it. They were black, but they weren't doing Temptations' steps. Most rockers don't learn it. They fall victim to the clichés of drugs and alcohol. Remember: They're morons, they're not rocket scientists that chose to play guitar. They're not qualified to do anything else. For those few that do make it, they go broke really fast because they're not qualified to understand any of it. People that win the lottery blow it and commit suicide in a year or two. If squirrels know what to do with their nuts, how come people don't?"

Improbably, Simmons at one point managed Liza Minnelli. "She came to me as a friend. I said to her, 'You're singing like Ethel Merman and that doesn't work anymore. Do cabaret and put a beat to it, and you could be in gay clubs around the world and then straight folks will come cause it's popular in the gay clubs.' Because gays will always lead the charge—they know what's hip faster than the straight people do because they are all about style and music and celebrating life. Black and gay is always hipper and cooler than straight and white. That's where rock 'n' roll came from and dance and disco."

Although the Minnelli project was a success, Simmons has refrained from other management opportunities. "I like making money too much. By owning my own content, I don't even use assistants. I use others' infrastructures. I'm like a Navy Seal: I swim underwater and sink big battleships by connecting big decision makers with other decision makers and doing big deals."

Rules and Tools

Simmons has one hard-and-fast directive for his business endeavors. "I get paid first. With capitalism and supply and demand, the guy who owns the company and funds everything himself gets paid last. If it fails, he's on the hook. Whatever venture I have, I'm the first to get paid. And it works. I'm really work-friendly—I'll do anything within my power, but not if I get paid last."

And the changes in the music business, Simmons conveys, are the result of greed and lack of forethought. "The record labels allowed foxes to come into the hen house. Downloading put hundreds of thousands out of work, and whose fault is that? The labels! I don't care about the tech. Apparently, commerce decided it wasn't wrong; it was only wrong if there were repercussions. Go ahead and steal people's livelihoods. But then don't think commerce can come after you. Try and steal something from me and see what happens."

"This is the time of the entrepreneur. Be creative and stop giving away your stuff for free. You are training people to not pay for what you have. And now every band has to be smarter because labels weren't smart enough; our economy and everyone got greedy and stupid, and there *are* repercussions for that. Bands are going to have to be more like Gene Simmons. Get rid of drunks and drug addicts in your band because they will suck the life out of you. Look at every opportunity and educate yourself. Fire your mother if she's a drug addict. Don't get married before your career starts. Every girl has 'Yoko Ono disease.' Nothing and no one should stop you. Everyone you think is important will try to stop you and demand your time. Give yourself all the time and attention because no one else will pay your salary or your rent."

www.kissonline.com

Heart: The Musical Pulse of the Wilson Sisters

Author's Note   Some artists have a true gift. In the case of Heart, that is without doubt the case. The band is led by two sisters: Ann, who has one of the most inimitable voices in rock/pop music history, and Nancy, who is an amazing guitarist and vocalist and, as has been shown in recent years, is a truly talented composer of music scores for film. They are the nucleus of Heart, a prolific, worldwide-acclaimed act for well over 30 years.

I had the great fortune to meet them and sign them to Capitol Records in the mid-eighties. They had had a long run of success at Epic Records, but their sales had slipped and their contract was up. They wanted a new home. Here was an act with a great history, amazing talent, and a defined image. I believed they could again be back on top of the charts, with the right songs and production. We focused on these critical areas, took no prisoners, and accomplished this. The Capitol team did a brilliant job marketing and promoting their first album for the label. It was certified multiplatinum, and featured a number-one hit and three other top-10 singles. That album was followed by their second and third for Capitol, both having number-one hit singles. Major sales, tours, big-time MTV exposure, and well-deserved success! They continue to tour and shine these many years later.

I am the number-one Heart fan. They are always professional, dedicated to their craft, and an act whose talent and uniqueness will always be respected.

—Don Grierson

"There was something strong about the two of us doing it, not just being the cute girls in front, but tearing up the stage and taking command of the music. I think that was fresh and in many ways, it still is."

Thirty million records, 21 top-40 hits, sold-out arenas worldwide, and a profound influence on rock music, the band Heart are, by any measure, genuine superstars. "Alone," "Barracuda," "Crazy on You," "Magic Man," "Straight On," and "These Dreams" are among the Heart songs that have become classics.

The band has spent over three decades together, but since the band's two principal members, Nancy and Ann Wilson, are sisters, they share a lifetime together. After taking a break in the late 1990s to start families and pursue individual projects (Nancy scored five films for her husband, Cameron Crowe, including the Academy Award–winning *Jerry Maguire* and Grammy winner *Almost Famous*, while Ann toured and also appeared in several theatrical productions), the Wilson sisters came back together as Heart and released a highly acclaimed album, titled *Jupiter's Darling*, featuring 15 new original recordings. They have been touring ever since and are beginning plans for a new record.

"We were in bands together, from the minute we picked up acoustic guitars in our teens," says Ann. "We put together folk groups that did vocal harmonies like Simon and Garfunkel, or whatever songs we liked in the top 40. We had the Viewpoints,

Rapunzel, and one with our sister Lynn, called the Prunes—this was before the Electric Prunes. It was a natural progression to electrify."

Nancy says that a mix of acoustic and electric was one of Heart's early trademarks. "When I finally joined the band, even though I had an open invitation, it was discussed that this is what I would bring to the band, a marriage of two genres. It's like Led Zeppelin, which had both of those areas covered. We thought there would be more opportunities with the two of us in the band to stretch out and have more variety and stylistic freedom."

Nancy says at the point she joined the band, they were already a major draw in Vancouver, B.C. "I walked into a lucrative situation on a club level. Not long after that, we tried to get picked up by every major label, and everybody turned us down about twice. They tried to come after Ann as a solo performer, and she said 'No.' We found a producer, Mike Flicker, who saw us playing at Oil Can Harry's in Vancouver and thought there was something to it. He started developing us through a small label in Vancouver called Mushroom Records."

Ann says Mushroom's owners were a family whose primary business was a paint company. "The Vogel family—they were the entrepreneurs of our success. It took us several years after we'd arrived in Canada to where we were shopping a demo. We'd been driving out to Alberta, and Saskatchewan, into the interior of Canada to play these dances, grad parties, so we put in a lot of time in the people to get there."

Nancy adds, "When the heater in the van broke down, it was life and death. There are a lot of dues in becoming live performers, getting our sea legs on every type of stage and every type of situation. There is a real good reason why those types of hard beginnings are vented on the young," says Ann. "You have to have so much stamina and to be so rubbery and to come back."

Nancy continues, "That's the difference these days as opposed to the days where we came from, when performers would go out and learn their craft the hard way, by playing live. It wasn't the construct of some producer trying to create a 'star' in the studio and putting them in front of the mirror with a belly bar and teaching them to move."

A Flicker of the Future

Working with Flicker, a musician, the duo polished their songcraft. "He helped us arrange the songs, and we'd hammer them out in the studio. We would come in with lyrics, melodies, and chord progressions. Those were the days when being a producer was being even more of a producer than it is now. He helped scratch 'Magic Man' out of stone," says Ann.

"As a musician, he came through a musician door rather than a star-maker door," notes Nancy. "And it wasn't technical; it was about the groove, the sound, and the vibe. The most important thing about the way that music imprints is that it is on a soul level, not on a technical level. It's instinctive: I think that's what a producer or a musician can bring, or someone with music in his soul whose ears are not painted on."

Feminine Wiles

The Wilson sisters say that when they began their careers, women in popular music were either earnest folkie types or disco queens. Nancy clarifies: "Before [the album] *Dreamboat Annie* was a success, we were going around to radio stations in a rented car, and it was more like a novelty that we were these two unusual rock women fronting and leading a band. We would go to the radio station and the promoter would say, 'Put on your lipstick, put on something sexy.' And we'd be trotted out there, trying to impress these programming guys. And then the promoter would payola them, illicit contraband was probably exchanged, and that put us on the map as women. Usually in Canada, they didn't play more than one woman act an hour."

"Once the album caught fire, the fans, the true barometers, were knocked out. There was something strong about the two of us doing it, not just being the cute girl in front, but tearing up the stage and taking command of the music. I think that was fresh and in many ways, it still is."

Eighties Ladies

The band made a big impact with the advent of videos—as they recall, "Big hair, big budgets." Nancy has a theory about the decade of excess. "Even though some good songs did come from it, it turned from the mind-expanding seventies into the cocaine eighties, and it became a different style of what the music was about. It became more of the image and the ego. Just like the cocaine experience: A little over the top, too much to say, too many notes, and too many layers of production."

When that decade evolved into the grunge-infused nineties, Heart was intrigued that the Seattle bands held them in high esteem. Ann recalls the shift: "A lot of the guys would come and play with us. Soundgarden, Pearl Jam, Nirvana, we were really accepted with wide-open arms by those bands, which we thought would reject us because we'd been in those over-the-top eighties videos. But they were cool and sweet, and we found out they had been influenced greatly by us, which was wonderful to find."

"They made an exception to their rules. We were doing everything they were rebelling against, but because we came from Seattle and knew them, they were like, 'You guys are all right, just not everyone else.'"

New Beats from Heart

Spent by the decades of touring, the sisters took a break from the Heart machine. They formed a local band, Lovemongers, with hometown friends and performed mainly at benefits. Nancy recorded a live album at McCabes guitar shop in Santa Monica, California, and Ann enlisted a stellar list of partners like Shawn Colvin, Gretchen Wilson, Elton John, k.d. lang, Wynonna, and Rufus Wainwright for an album of duets. "You know this," says Ann. "I'm a team player, and I get off on working with Nancy. I didn't have that deep inner thing of wanting to be solo. I think that's why it took me so long. It took Nancy to do the scoring on Cameron's movies, where I couldn't get to her."

Now, inspired by a cross-country tour with Journey and Cheap Trick, they are ready to reenter the studio. "It's a good time for us; the world is in an uproar, and people need to be uplifted," says Nancy. "As artists, that is our essential job—to uplift humanity and give hope, to bring love and goodness to anyone who is willing to listen or who finds out that it's there. The reason we've been able to stay with the creative process for this long is we know how meaningful it is for people and us. When you can go on a stage in front of thousands of people and get off and have a communal experience that's transcendent, you're doing something right."

And for aspiring artists, she adds this coda: "Stay with your art, as long as you're passionate and doing it for the love. If you are doing it for any other reason than the right reason, then forget about it. The other advice I would give is to know your music history, steep yourself in it, and take the good things that came before. And don't let anyone tell you who to be or how to look or what to sound like."

www.heart-music.com

Joe Cocker: Soul Master

Author's Note   I'd always been a fan of Joe Cocker, but I never expected to meet or even work with him. What a unique artist, one of a kind, with a voice that resonates in your soul! I knew his manager at that time, Michael Lang of Woodstock fame, and one day he called me at Capitol to ask if I'd be interested in possibly signing Joe. He was actually signed to Island at the time and recording a "country-pop" album, but all was not well with the relationship. It was possible to buy him out of his deal.

Knowing that Joe had had his "problems" over the years, I hesitated, but decided to check with our EMI offices overseas, as I knew he'd had much more success there, especially in Europe, than in the U.S. Their reaction was immediate: "Yes, sign him." They believed they could sell serious numbers if he delivered a great album. Knowing that it would be at least possible to recoup Capitol's investment, to include the cost of buying him out of Island and recording an album, and most importantly, believing in his artistry, I believed this was a good deal to do.

Interestingly, the president of Capitol at that time, my boss, wasn't into signing a "has-been drunk" who he believed wouldn't sell in the U.S. He didn't agree with me artistically, but he did agree that if this was important for our affiliates overseas, then we should support them wherever possible.

It was now time to meet Joe, to be sure he and I could relate, could work together—also for me to get a sense of his "state of mind." We met at my office in the Capitol Tower, and it was immediate: I had to work with this man. Yes, in those days, Joe still had moments when he "lost it," but he was dead serious about wanting to make great music and do the promotional things that would be asked of him. We bonded! I was excited! I was going to have the opportunity to work with a "legend" who actually wanted A&R help and was a believer.

Seeing that Joe wasn't a songwriter but an interpreter of other's songs, the challenge would be to find great material. Importantly, we both agreed that he needed to go back much more to his "Cocker the rocker" roots than being purely a pop ballad singer à la his big hit singles "Up Where We Belong" and "You Are So Beautiful."

We did accomplish all of this, especially in Europe (Capitol's promotion/ marketing support in the U.S. was minimal). Major album sales, big-time touring successes, and a revitalized career! Joe, a truly soulful artist, a survivor of so many tough moments in his life, a man I'm so proud to have met and been touched by, was back on top!

—Don Grierson

"I studied Ray Charles when I was young, and he had the beautiful way of making a song his own. You can't just hand it over. I never wrote songs and that is why I put so much more into that side of it—putting my own feeling into the songs."

Joe Cocker doubts that his style would go down well on *American Idol*. "Flinging my arms around—maybe I was the first air guitarist. It was all my frustration of not playing, or playing drums rather than piano or guitar, that I was physically mimicking. But this evolved into my singing style. If I were to stand like a tenor would in an opera to use lungs and diaphragm, it would turn off quite a few people. Whenever I do a new song, I don't choreograph it; it just falls into place."

Pub Rub

Cocker began his career in his hometown of Sheffield, UK, as a drummer. "I always had a decent sense of time. It was difficult back then. Back in my day, I strapped a mic onto a stand so I was singing behind the drums. And it was a weird thing to do; it wasn't like playing guitar and singing. But I really enjoyed playing like that. It was so clumsy to have all that gear around. In my band, we had a good-looking guy singing who was also singing for us, but he couldn't really sing. They said, 'Joe, we need you to do the singing.' I was thrust into the spotlight and took it from there."

Cocker's rise was fast. "Coming from drinking six pints a night to living in London. Only a year later we were at Woodstock—it was a remarkably fast journey. And then Leon Russell, I keep getting these calls he wanted to put the Mad Dogs & Englishman band together. That was a different thing. There were 40 of us on the road with all the backup singers. I don't think it's the type of thing that we could ever put back together today."

It was an era of mythic excess, of powders and potions, as drugs and alcohol infused the rock lifestyle, substances that affected Cocker's professional day-to-day life. "In many ways, I almost lost it completely in the mid-seventies," admits Cocker. "I could have been another statistic."

Predictably, after Cocker's stratospheric career rise came a fallow period. "There was a lapse, one of those strange things…the scene changed, and we were out of touch with this world, and the music went back into the hands of the businessmen. And for a while, it got too insane. I did an album with the Crusaders. Germany and France were great audiences for me. Then I did the Grammys and sang 'I'm So Glad I'm Standing Here Today' with my peers all sitting in the audience. It was nice that I could take a step towards a new beginning."

Songs Sustain

Audiences worldwide once again became aware of Cocker with the Grammy-winning performance of "Up Where We Belong," sung with Jennifer Warnes for the film *An Officer and a Gentleman*. Cocker recalls his first impression of the song. "I hated the demo they sent me. It sounded like an old country song. [Producer] Stewart Levine said, 'I have faith in this. Just come down to studio,' and he had already put the track down and guessed the key I would sing in. I sang it on my own as solo record. When we finally got Jennifer's voice on it, I knew it would be a big record."

"You Are So Beautiful" is another of Cocker's signature performances. "That was a time period when I was feeling very insecure and I was a bit lost. Jim Price, the sax player, came to see me in London and said he had this song and he wanted to produce an album. When he played it on the piano for me, he didn't even say that it was Billy Preston's tune, but I said, 'I have to record that.' We recorded it in L.A. I was a little screwed up at the time, drinking heavily. It was a top-five record in U.S. I wasn't on the road or anything back then. I was a bit arrogant and wasn't aware of its success."

A major success for Joe during his early Capitol years was his incredible version of "You Can Leave Your Hat On," produced by Richie Zito for the film *9 1/2 Weeks*.

Long Time

"It's about 40 years," Cocker muses of his enduring career. "We still go to Poland and Russia, and I still like to go to Ukraine. They went nuts in Georgia—amazing audiences. I'm an ambassador for rock 'n' roll and can still keep doing it, and it's a buzz and an ongoing thing, still. I'm thinking maybe I should call it a day in five years because I'll be 70, but you look at B. B. King, and he's still making music. It makes you wonder if it's better to keep that music train moving. It amazes me that the audience has stuck with me all these years."

Amazing shows keep Cocker energized. He recalls this one: "I did a show in Austria where Mozart grew up. It was on a Saturday night in the town square, and everybody in town came to see it; there were people hanging out of windows. It was a beautiful night and the sound was perfect. A lot of those shows stay in my memory. That's why I do it—because of those nights."

"It's a lot different world now, but there's something to be said for live performances. If I were 17 or 18, I'd hone my craft by doing as much stage work as I could. I find when I tour, promoters say, 'We can't get young artists to perform five shows in a week.' But at the same time, when we worked an hour on and 10 minutes off in the sixties, it was great for the voice because we learned so much. Look at Pink—she's come through from being a teen artist and developed her own style. Just give it your best and build a repertoire. It will take a few years."

"Every decade there are gaps, but every five or 10 years, I'd have a hit that would sustain me. As a young artist, you have to be aware of that and build on things."

www.cocker.com

Death Cab for Cutie: Indie Band Speeds to New Destinations

"Things started shaping up really strangely, not only for us, but obviously in relation to Postal Service and all these weird cultural things—the Garden States and the O.C.s, and just this weird kind of rebirth of indie-rock culture on a much larger level."

Rain-shrouded, introspective, coffee-infused, Seattle is a city with a hard-rocking musical legacy and a vibrant scene. Physically isolated from the cultural mainstream, it is an historic locale for bands that flourish with originality and independence. Death Cab for Cutie qualifies on both counts: A gleaming link in the city's sonic chain, the band's music is atmospheric and orchestral, with sweeps of guitars painting expansive soundscapes, shadowing emotional, eloquent lyrics wrapped in an undeniable pop sensibility and rendered through Ben Gibbard's distinctively honest voice.

Deathcab for Cutie had its origins in Bellingham, Washington, a college town where Gibbard and guitarist Chris Walla bonded as students at Western Washington University. It started out as a solo project when Gibbard turned a freshly broken heart into nine songs that he wasn't embarrassed to share. To record, he recruited fledgling four-track producer (and fellow Teenage Fanclub fan) Chris Walla and bassist Nick Harmer, the most amiable (and comic-book–obsessed) musician on campus. After a cassette-only release, *You Can Play These Songs with Chords*, became a local hit, Death Cab for Cutie became a full-on band. Their name was purloined from a song title by a sixties cult band, the Bonzo Dog Band. Gibbard explains. "I saw the Bonzo Dog Band in the Beatles' *Magical Mystery Tour* film. I was a huge Beatle fan. I'd never been a fan of the Bonzo Dog Band; they were pretty grating, but after seeing that movie in college, I thought. 'You know, if I ever start another band, I'll call it Death Cab for Cutie.' And I've cursed myself ever since because journalists always ask questions about the name."

Refining the Straight Job

Prior to Death Cab for Cutie's ascent, Gibbard worked a straight job. He'd graduated from college with a degree in environmental chemistry and, during his school days, had had an internship at an oil refinery. When he graduated, he was employed to do environmental testing. "It was a dangerous job, and I knew I wasn't planning on doing that for the rest of my life. In the early years of the band, by the time we started going on tours, I was making $14 an hour, when I was paying $250 a month for rent. I'd go to my bosses and say, 'I'm leaving on tour for a month. You can fire me if you like, but you know it'll take a year and a half to train someone to be where I am now.' So I had 'em by the balls. Everyone has those jobs. I thought, 'I could do this the rest of my life or the foreseeable future, and live and exist, but it doesn't make me happy.'" And, of course, there was the pungent smell of the refinery itself. "You could smell that sh*t for miles."

The straight job was soon history. Relocating to Seattle, Death Cab for Cutie recorded their full-length debut, *Something About Airplanes*. Generating a Seattle-area buzz, they became a proper band, releasing their official debut in 1998 on the burgeoning area indie Barsuk.

Independence Days

Barsuk Records began as a venture by Josh Rosenfeld and his partner, Christopher Possanza, to release the album by their band, This Busy Monster. Taking its name from the Russian word for "badger," the label, based in Seattle, became home to Jesse Sykes and the Sweet Hereafter, Rilo Kiley, Nada Surf, and many others. "We used to accept unsolicited demos," says Rosenfeld. "We got too much stuff. It's harder now than it was 10 or 15 years ago. It's so easy now for someone to make music with a home computer. There's so much, it became overwhelming. We started the label because we were in a band, and we couldn't find a label who wanted to put out our music. I remember thinking at that time, as I looked at the rosters of labels I admired, that it seemed cliquish: 'Oh, of course they signed you because you know the guys in that band.' I've come to realize exactly how that functions over time. The one huge place where we find music we like is when bands on the roster are on the road, play shows, bring us a CD back, and say, 'This band is really good.' I share a taste in music with bands on the roster, so there is a lot of overlap. It's not a clique; that's how I hear music I like."

After the band's debut, they began touring. And more albums were tracked, including 2000's *We Have the Facts and We're Voting Yes* and 2001's *The Photo Album*, each more successful, in content and sales, than the last. The band is distinctive for a cast of rotating drummers. Just prior to the release of *We Have the Facts*, Good left the band, replaced by drummer Michael Schorr. Schorr would first appear on *The Forbidden Love* EP, released in fall of 2000. The following year, another LP was released, entitled *The Photo Album*. Limited editions of this album contained three bonus tracks, which were later released separately as *The Stability* EP.

Seattle Sonics

Gibbard says that Seattle has a number of geographic factors that make its popular culture distinctive. "Back in the day, bands wouldn't even come here to play because it's so far off the beaten path. You come from San Francisco to Portland and Seattle, and then you've got to drive two days to get to anywhere else worth playing."

Having created a substantial body of work as a band, Death Cab for Cutie took an extended hiatus. Chris returned to his first love, producing, working on widely hailed releases by the Decemberists, the Thermals, Nada Surf, and Travis Morrison. Ben spent some time in the L.A. neighborhood of Silverlake recording electropop songs with his friend, producer Jimmy Tamborello, singer Jen Wood, and Jenny Lewis from the band Rilo Kiley. This little side project, called the Postal Service, yielded an album, *Give Up*, that has to date sold over 600,000 copies with no tours and no promotion. "We made the record because it sounded like a fun project, and it turned into a far larger entity," he says. "We don't play shows, promote the record, or do interviews. The record quietly continues to sell, and people are into it. Jimmy will send me songs, and I'll work on them in my own time. He's down there and I'm up here. He'll send me a fragment of a song he's working on and we'll put the pieces together, make a song out of the parts, just a kind of playing a video game." Gibbard stayed with Tamborello for a spell, in his residence down the street from the club Spaceland. "It's the epicenter," notes Gibbard. "It seems that for every band who's trying to make it big, so to speak, there is another band who is purposely trying not to do that."

In 2003, refreshed and renewed by their time apart—and inspired by the recruitment of ace drummer Jason McGerr—Death Cab recorded and released the rave-spawning *Transatlanticism*. Milestones began to fall like dominos: sales that doubled those of any previous release, successful tours of Japan and Australia, magazine features, TV appearances (including a memorable spring 2005 performance on *The O.C.*), and a personal invitation to join Pearl Jam on the Vote for Change Tour. Death Cab's 2004 Transatlanticism Tour is documented on the DVD *Drive Well, Sleep Carefully*, directed by noted filmmaker Justin Mitchell. *Transatlanticism* received critical praise and also became the band's top-selling album, with 225,000 copies sold during its first year out. In addition, tracks from the album appeared in the soundtrack of television show *The O.C.* Other television shows, movie trailers, and feature films brought Death Cab for Cutie and Postal Service to international audiences by utilizing both bands' songs.

In the fall of 2004, Death Cab for Cutie inked a worldwide deal with Atlantic Records. Leaving their long-time label Barsuk Records and the ranks of indie record labels, Gibbard stated on the official website that nothing would change except that, "Next to the picture of Barsuk holding a '7,' there will be the letter 'A' on both the spine and back of our upcoming albums."

The band's major label debut, *Plans*, was released in August 2005. The notably indie band had arrived at a crossroads. "Things started shaping up really strangely, not only for us, but obviously in relation to Postal Service and all these weird cultural things—the *Garden State*s and the O.C.s, and just this weird kind of rebirth of indie-rock culture on a much larger level the last couple years. But also, and I certainly don't say this to toot our own horn, I feel like we're an exception to the rule in so many cases. When people have come to me talking about, 'Hey, somebody just came to our band, a major label wants to sign us,' or even some band that we're friends with that Atlantic's been talking to, I feel like I need to always qualify that we're a very special situation in this whole major-label world."

In 2008, the band's *Narrow Stairs* became their first number-one album on the *Billboard* charts, garnering a Grammy nomination for Best Alternative Music Album.

www.deathcabforcutie.com

Sara Bareilles: Between the Lines

"It sounds like a cliché, but it has made all the difference in my life. Listen to your intuition and trust yourself completely."

Song by song, gig by gig, year after year: While studying communications at UCLA, singer/songwriter Sara Bareilles took incremental steps, recording a series of low-budget indie releases, performing in local Los Angeles venues like Genghis Cohen, Temple Bar, the Mint, Molly Malone's, the Troubadour, and Hotel Café; penning an impressive body of songs; building a loyal online audience; and impressing fellow musicians and industry insiders alike with her sheer musicality. It sometimes seemed a slow uphill climb, she says. "There were multiple years when it was, 'Are we doing anything?' And I'd step back and think, more people are coming to the shows, we're selling more CDs online, people are telling me they found me through this and that. It was apparent to me. And maybe that's what helped moved things forward intrinsically— just knowing that we were actually making progress."

These small steps became a giant jump when Bareilles was signed to Epic Records, and her performance of "Love Song," from her full-length major label debut *Little Voice*, was used in a Rhapsody commercial. Viewed over 8 million times on YouTube and named iTunes single of week, this feisty piano-driven track pumped *Little Voice* to the top of the iTunes chart and the full-length release debuted at number 45 on the *Billboard* charts. Bareilles has since toured across the U.S. with Maroon 5 and Counting Crows.

My Fair Lady

Eureka, California, a bucolic, redwood-shaded town near the Oregon border, is Sara Bareilles' hometown. She credits this rural upbringing with inspiring her active imagination. Radio hits and show tunes were parallel musical influences as she taught herself to play piano, sang with local choirs, and graced the stages of community theater productions. When she enrolled in UCLA in Los Angeles it was as a communications major, but music was close to her soul. Among other endeavors she joined a vocal group, Awaken a Cappella.

Her career advanced considerably when she signed with artist manager Jordan Feldstein of Career Artist Management, whom she met through mutual friends. It was Feldstein who introduced her to Epic Records' Pete Giberga, the A&R executive who brought her to the label in 2005. Bareilles lauds Goldstein's assured management style. "When we were out trying to—I guess shop around, sort of taking the demo around and doing showcases for labels—he never made me feel like we were in a desperate position. I remember when we took a flight to New York to meet with everybody at Epic, and I was nervous and I said, 'I don't know what to say in this meeting. I've never done this before.' He said, 'Don't worry about it. Be honest and say anything you want to say, and if it doesn't work out with them, it's not a big deal.' This is a really nice thing to hear when you're going into a meeting that makes you freak out."

Big Choices and *Little Voice*

Producer Eric Ivan Rosse (Tori Amos, Lisa Marie Presley) was selected to work with Bareilles on her debut, and it took almost two years to record. "We listened to my whole catalog," notes Bareilles, "and made choice selections that were important to me but also felt like they made a cohesive whole. There were songs I wanted to record that stuck out like a sore thumb. And I know my writing style is kind of diverse anyhow. I didn't want to make an album that felt disjointed, that was so sporadic that it was hard for a listener to understand my sound. Eric felt the exact same way." Among the selected songs was "Gravity," a longtime audience favorite she'd penned back in 2000. "From playing it, I see that people have a connection to it. It's one of the songs that for some reason I never get tired of singing."

As the story goes, when Epic requested an additional song—a love song—Bareilles responded with her breakthrough hit "Love Song," and it's declarative lines, "I'm not going to write you a love song/'cause you asked for it/'cause you need one." Many listeners identify Bareilles because of their continued exposure to the track. "It's a great problem to have," Bareilles laughs. "I have my moments—especially after the Rhapsody commercial came out. I don't know that I wanted to be that 'Love Song' girl. To see it going in that direction was a little unnerving. What I hope 'Love Song' is for me is a window into the rest of the work that I've poured my heart and soul into. 'Love Song' is an important song for me. It was when I wrote it, and I'm proud of it; but I'm also proud of these other pieces of work that we did, and I hope people are interested enough to check them out."

The Soul of the Song

Bareilles believes that songwriting is a sacred act. "The most intense emotional moments I have come through songwriting. Whether I feel like I'm connected to something bigger than myself, or placing hands on keys and hoping something comes out, it's all an act of faith. I hope that always stays at the core of what I do. I think sometimes people dissect the craft too much. For me, it takes the magic out of it. I think songwriting is a craft, something you can get better at, but I don't know that it's something you can dissect to the point of knowing how to write a hit song. That's always felt strange to me—the idea of 'we figured out the formula.' There are always exceptions to the rule, and I love the exceptions."

While reworking and rewriting are not processes over which Bareilles obsesses, her lyrical standards are high. "I don't keep going back over lyrics and want to change one word to another. If it comes out that way naturally, or if it feels pretty organic, I'll let it be. But I am detail-oriented with lyrics. I want to make sure I'm saying something interesting and saying it in somewhat of a unique way. I'm not big on the cliché—I like getting to say things in an interesting way."

Only one song on *Little Voice*, "Love on the Rocks," is a co-write. Otherwise, Bareilles pens solo. "It isn't that I don't want to co-write; I'm just not very good at it. I think maybe someday, but I've tried to write and I come away feeling disconnected to the material. And I can't put my energies into songs that I don't feel are honest representations of myself. I'm hoping I will get better at it—there are amazing collaborators out there. Maybe it would be with an artist or with somebody that it felt really organic. I've tried the whole, 'Throw 'em in the room together and see what happens,' and it's miserable for me. I won't be doing that."

Given her relentless touring schedule, Bareilles now finds little time to devote to new songs. "I try to write when I go home. I'm a little nervous of being in the position of not having songs ready for going back in the studio. It's tough for me on the road. I'll have to write when we have some time off. For a keyboard player, it's hard to find time with your instrument. I wish I played better guitar."

Sonic Sense

Bareilles possesses a persuasive, communicative vocal tone perfect for conveying both the sassy attitude in her more driving songs as well as the depth of her most perceptive sentiments. She explains that she needs to maintain a strong center for the vocals and not be overwhelmed by production and arrangement techniques. "I'm looking for things that are going to serve the song. I love the idea of moving more into a funky jazz place someday. I'm not looking for players with super chops who are showing off. I want the song to be at the center of everything and make choices that are going to serve the song. And I wanted to create a soundscape, and I tried to pick instruments and voicings and tones that were going to be interesting to the ear. My litmus test for each song was if I played it in the car and I loved the way it sounded. And I totally did. I closed the chapter on each song, loving what we had done. Of course, I would have changed a million things now, but what moves you forward is you want to make another record to experience another part of your brain."

Essential Trust

This is not an era of piano-driven female singer/songwriters, but the success of Sara Bareilles proves that solid songwriting and musicianship can override prevailing trends.

For anyone hoping to accomplish what she has done, she offers this thoughtful advice: "Listen to yourself. It sounds like a cliché, but it has made all the difference in my life. Listen to your intuition and trust yourself completely. I think if you're doing something that's not good for you, or not natural, or doesn't resonate with who you are, then it won't work. The more in tune you are to what you're telling yourself, the better off you'll be."

www.sarabmusic.com

Karmina: The Kiss of Persistence
"It's so hard and cutthroat that all you can do is give 100 percent—100 percent of the time."

—Kelly Rudisill, Karmina

Two sisters who communicate with one voice in intricate, intertwined harmony; gorgeous girls who play their own instruments (Kelly keyboards and Kamille guitar) and write deeply affecting songs; and add a devoted mother and manager, Robin, with the foresight and means to relocate the family to Los Angeles and introduce them to the music industry—it would seem like formula for certain success. Why then did it take Kelly and Kamille Rudisill (known collectively as Karmina) nine long years to get signed to a record label?

Not that it hasn't been worth the wait: Their CBS Records debut, *Backwards into Beauty*, is a sparkling gem of insightful songs. Their single "The Kiss," an undeniably hooky single coupled with a powerful video, is the perfect introduction to the duo's exuberant musicality. *Backwards into Beauty* is also a CD that the pair completed on their own without the involvement of the label. Along with producer Guy Erez, Kelly and Kamille are credited as co-producers.

"That's rare," says Kamille. "A lot of times they sign you and say, 'We'll hook you up with this producer. Put these strings in, take this electric guitar out.' It can drive people mad, but we didn't have to deal with that because they signed us with our sound already made." Kelly adds that the beauty of their deal with CBS is mutual as exemplified through their video for "The Kiss," which depicts couples overcoming love that might be deemed forbidden, including gay and lesbian, multiracial, and multigenerational couples. "We sat down with the director, the head of the label, the marketing executive, and us, all brainstorming. We wanted to do something deep, impactful, and meaningful."

Teen Dreams
Kelly was born in Germany, Kamille in Hawaii, and their family moved to Northern California. When the girls were eight and 10 years old, their mother enrolled them in

the San Francisco Conservatory of Music, where they studied music theory, composition, and classical voice training. Kelly, the eldest sister, began writing pop songs when she was 11. "We started going to the West Coast Songwriters Association Conference, hearing information and trying to stay as open-minded as possible without getting crushed."

Kelly recalls their initial industry encounters. "We had some of our first record company meetings when we were 14 years old—we used to dance when we sang. And we'd mix it up: Kamille would get on guitar and I'd play piano. Then someone from Interscope said to us, 'I'm confused. What do you want to do? It's too much.'" Subsequently, the sisters defined themselves as singer/songwriters.

With the manufactured assembly line that turns pretty girls into stars with mass-marketed merchandise, the two have been shaped into teen-friendly product. "When you're that age, you want to resist anything any adult wants you to do," laughs Kamille. "As soon as we got into songwriting, we couldn't imagine ourselves as Disney artists. What Disney artist other than the Jonas Brothers writes their own songs? We didn't see ourselves going in that direction."

Kelly clarifies this position. "If Disney approached us and said, 'Do you want to be on a show as Karmina?' would we turn it down? Of course not. But someone isn't telling us to fit into a mold; we've developed our own mold."

The sisters believe that having their mother as a dedicated manager and a support system was key. Robin Rudisill has a formidable corporate background as an executive at Bank of America—a position she left to build her daughters' careers. "If we went to a meeting and a label turned us down with 'Keep writing, keep going,' Kelly and I would be so bummed," says Kamille. "Our mother would say, 'What a great meeting that was. Now we can work on this and this.' If it was a rejection, we'd try to get better."

School of Thought

In Los Angeles, both Kelly and Kamille graduated from the Music Business program at University of Southern California, USC. Kamille says it was an important choice. "We wanted to learn the business side of this business. It was really important for us to understand. I think we learned more after college. But having an education helped us put it together." After undergraduate studies, Kelly earned a master's degree in music education. "About halfway through the master's program, we were approached by CBS. I wanted my education so badly." The way it worked out, by the time the group was done negotiating their contract—six months—Kelly was finished with classes.

During their learning process, Kelly and Kamille competed in the John Lennon Songwriting Competition, ASCAP's Lester Sill Songwriters Workshop, and the San Francisco

Concerto Orchestra Competition and were multiple winners at the California State vocal competition. They were a constant presence at virtually every music business seminar and conference held in California. Recalls Kelly, "Sometimes the same classes would be offered every year. We'd say, 'Mom, I've been to this class—we don't need to go.' She'd say, 'You'll learn something new every time that you go. It might make sense now because you have more experience, or you missed something they said, or there is something new to say.'"

Kelly avows that making the move to Los Angeles was a key decision. "Throughout our early process, everyone kept saying, 'You have to move to L.A.' I hate telling people that because there are so many beautiful places in the world to live. L.A. is cool, there are special parts, but someday we'll live elsewhere. But it's so important to be in that scene because when you're in it, and an opportunity comes up, you're right there to take advantage of it. Rather than someone saying, 'Can you do this today?' and you have to drive seven hours or take a flight."

Live Time

Although the CBS name is one of the media's most recognized media trademarks, the company's history as a record company is a bit more complex. The label is affiliated with the television network and the business strategy is planned to save on music licensing by building a viable stable of acts whose recordings are owned by the parent group and will subsequently generate revenue for CBS when the acts attain hits. For music supervisors, the label offers a one stop for music; for the artists, this deal comes with a five- or 10-second promo at the end of the show their music appears in, directing viewers to the artist's website, iTunes, or Amazon. For Karmina, a song on *Beverly Hills 90210* introduced them to millions of new fans.

Performing on the CBS *Early Show* also revealed them to television audiences, albeit at an hour more befitting a rooster than a vocalist, as Kamille recalls. "The call time was 3:00 in the morning in New York. Our eyes were so bloodshot that the makeup lady had to put in drops and make up our faces so we were not so pasty." And Kelly continues, "Everyone thinks it's a dream and it is, it's so amazing, but it's work. It's what you've signed up for, to go into a radio station at the drop of a hat, hardly warmed up, and sing like we did on the album."

Beholding the Beauty

In the two years since Karmina signed to CBS, they've essentially been performing the same songs that got them signed, only for new audiences. "It gets frustrating," Kamille confesses. "All you want to do is play your next stuff and make the next album, but you have to work that first album and that first single a long time." Kelly says that John Mayer taught her lot about loving a signature song. "I went to a show and he did a version of 'Your Body is a Wonderland.' He said, 'This is my baby. I've played it more times than I care to admit, but I will forever love this song because of what it has done for me.' I thought, 'What a great attitude.' No matter how many times we play 'The Kiss,' I'll love it forever. Part of being an artist is re-creating it every time you play it for people who have never heard it before."

They both believe that songwriting and performance cannot be underestimated. "What it comes down to is music," concludes Kamille. "To us, the most important things are the songs. We learn more and more to have amazing songs, and build everything else around them."

www.karmina.com

Kyler England: An Artist of Independent Means

"There's no set path—it's wide open now with all these creative options. You just have to be willing to work hard."

Meet Kyler England, a vibrant independent artist whose career is proof that if the songs and performances are stellar, and are matched by equal focus and fortitude, it is possible to maintain a vital career outside of the confines of the conventional record business. She currently has three full-length CDs, two EPs, and two live recordings. Her latest release is titled *Simple Machine*. She is also a member of the ad hoc acoustic "super-group" called the Rescues.

"As far as a career, I put out my first indie record in 2000. I moved to New York City. I'm doing it full time now because of September 11th—it was a totally practical reason. I had been doing some touring but making my living through temping. After 9/11, there was no temp work available. I had no work and no money. I had to get a full-time job, or had to start touring a lot and make money that way. So I just started touring and never looked back."

"It's not like I went from 0 to 60 in a few days. I had been gigging for a while. I had a couple gigs where I could make enough money. That was the key to the early touring: I was sure I had an anchor base. I knew that I could do it again full time and build a fan base and stay on the road enough to make a living. I still do all the booking; I want to be at the helm. If you're organized and driven, it can be done, although sometimes I would love to have someone do it all for me."

Currently, England plays approximately 100 dates annually. "I've done as many as 150 to 200, but I'm scaling back a little bit so that I have more time to be a songwriter. When I first started, I just looked at artists that were similar and one step ahead and playing the venues I wanted to play. For example, I would notice that when they went to Philadelphia, they would play here and there. The Internet is such a great resource, and you can always contact artists and ask their opinion about venues. That's how I started booking, seeing where other singer/songwriters were playing. These days, I have so many friends at various stages in their career with a wealth of knowledge. By creating these relationships, you have all these resources. Making friends and having touring buddies and sharing information is key."

Fan Land in Cyberspace

For an independent artist, connecting with fans online is an immense resource. "There's not another way. I'm so thankful that those old days are over. When I started, I kept a snail mail list in addition to my e-mail list. I'm so thrilled I don't have to do that anymore. It's expensive and time-consuming. You will need a mailing list and a Myspace page and a street team of uber fans that love the music and also want to help you by putting up posters or collecting e-mails. There are so many resources for indie artists on the Internet. You definitely need help from fans to make the best use of your time.

Concerts in the House

For acoustic artists, house concerts have become a viable method of performing for dedicated fans and selling music. There is a national community of committed fan/promoters with room to stage concerts. "I do a lot of them," England notes. "A show in someone's living room or a recreation room. The idea is to create a listening environment in a home. Fans of acoustic music don't necessarily want to go down to a smoky, loud bar, and not every city has a venue like the Hotel Café in Los Angeles. The idea is to create that environment. I'll play a house concert in a city I haven't played before, or if I don't have the fan base to fill and play the club I want to play in that town. Or it's a town I would never go to on that tour because there's no venue. The host takes on personal responsibilities and gets a lot of their friends and people they know that love music and they form an audience for you. They get maybe 50 people in their house for you, whereas at a club you'd get 10. Fans always ask, 'Why don't you come to my small town?' So it's totally a win-win. A house concert is all about the music."

And somewhat about the money: "They're often financially more profitable than club sales because the host will collect a cover or suggest donation for the artist," England clarifies. "Maybe they ask for $50 to pay for some of the food. Also, the audiences are more inclined to be devoted to music and they tend to buy more CDs than at a club or venue. It's a special experience hearing someone in that environment, and they tell their friends about that."

Studio Matrimony

It helps that England's husband, Richard Furch, is a world-class recording engineer. "My husband produced all my stuff, and he's my partner in crime; we met in music school. Right now he's working with Prince and doing really well as an engineer. When he has time to work with me, we write songs together. He co-produces and arranges the music on my records and engineers them, so I've been really lucky in that respect. I save money by not having to hire someone. He also happens to have a studio where we record most of my stuff. I recommend marrying your producer! By law, you share everything anyway, but if you find someone you want to have a partnership with, if you can't afford to pay them up front, there are creative ways to share some of the masters."

Networking Notions

Visual uses of her songs in films and on television have provided additional revenue and exposure for England and include the film *The Lucky Ones* starring Rachel McAdams and Tim Robbins and small-screen dramas including *Ghost Whisperer*, *Army Wives*, *Guiding Light*, *Zoey 101*, *Rollergirls*, and *Paradise City*.

"Every one of these has come about because of someone I know—it's all about relationships. I placed songs on *Army Wives* on Lifetime because I know someone who works at a music supervision company. I've had a lot of music on *Guiding Light*; that has been bread and butter for me. Another supervisor I met at (Hollywood-based monthly get-together) Hunnypot. You need to be able to meet these people and develop relationships."

Last Chorus

While Kyler England's gossamer songcraft draws favorable comparisons to revered songwriters such as Sarah McLachlan and Patty Griffin, there is a steely core of pragmatism that drives the course of her career. "The key to a successful indie career is diversifying your income. I write country songs; I do session singing, licensing, and I help others on their gigs. That's the key—diversifying."

www.kylerengland.com

James Lee Stanley: Trail of the Troubadour

"I have never considered the money. If you make a great record, it's always going to be a great record."

He's been doing it a long time, and he's damn good at it. He's James Lee Stanley, a singer/songwriter with 25 albums to his credit. "When I first came to Hollywood, I wanted to be a songwriter; and people thought I sang well so I should be an artist. I always wanted to do it, but I didn't have the courage. But based on this encouragement, I went for it. I got a deal with a small label, Wooden Nickel."

"It was two albums a year, and I had to write all of the songs for it. So I was writing 20 good songs that deserved to be recorded every year. The president of the label then tried to get me to record songs that he thought were hits. I wasn't experienced, but I was savvy enough to know that if I sang some song I didn't like, and it became a hit, I would have to sing that song for the rest of my life. The label wouldn't have to; they'd be getting their money anyway, but I would be saddled with that song. So I was very careful about the songs I recorded by other people. They had to be consistent with who I was as an artist."

"I think the downfall of so many artists is that they get a hit song that isn't who they are. Then they make an album with stuff they love and the hit song. People will buy it, listen to the hit, and say, 'What's this other stuff?' Because it isn't all part of the same tapestry."

That said, Stanley believes that unknown artists can benefit by putting one recognizable song in a collection if they can create their own interpretation of it. "I went to a DJ seminar and one of the DJs said that the first thing he does when he sees a new CD from an artist he's never heard of is look at the songs. If there is one he recognizes, he puts that on to see what they did to it."

Market Shares

After recording the two albums with Wooden Nickel, Stanley launched his career as an independent artist. "We're all independent artists now," he laughs. Marketing as an indie, Stanley says, has become much more difficult over time. "There was an interesting service provided by the major labels. It was a filtering system, so not that many CDs showed up in the marketplace, considering how many people wanted to do them. There was a level of expertise. Now, anyone with a computer and some time on their hands can make an album. They can burn CDs and they can 'put them out,' and it looks just like everybody else's album except that it's nothing but ca-ca. Who has time to go through every CD that comes out to find the good ones? For independents, it's hard to go international or even national."

So he markets himself to specific regions where he has a fan base and he can make an impact. "I examine where I have a constituency. I'll concentrate on playing there, having my music distributed, and being on those radio stations and in those clubs and newspapers. If I have a thousand dollars to promote a record nationwide, it won't make an impact. But if I spend a thousand dollars where I play, say in San Diego, it will have more impact. I suggest that artists create retail situations for themselves in an area. Because once that happens, then they can begin to branch out."

"I have a music guide with all of the labels, radio stations, and promoters. I don't send the CD to any station that I don't think will play it. I do my diligence; I find out if there a station and a guy from 2:00 to 5:00 p.m. on Saturday who plays my type of music, I send it to him. I don't send it to the station manager and expect him to know where it goes. That's asking a lot of people to go out of their way. There are more of us now than there ever were and these guys can't wade through everything."

Stones Roll

One of Stanley's recent projects is *All Wood and Stones*, acoustic versions of Rolling Stones songs performed with John Batdorf and, on two tracks, Eagles bassist Timothy B. Schmit. The concept came serendipitously, when Stanley was at a wedding reception and the band took a break. When the groom asked him to sing something, he enlisted two other singer/songwriters in attendance and they sang an acoustic version of the Rolling Stones' "Ruby Tuesday." The effect was immediate. "We did a three-part harmony and it was so magical that the wedding party stopped what they were doing. The whole crowd came to the stage and listened and sang along." In addition to Batdorf and Schmit, stellar musicians such as Lawrence Juber from Wings, Paul Barrere from Little Feat, and Peter Tork from the Monkees played guitars.

Since Stanley owns his own fully equipped recording studio, his recording costs are minimal. But he says he doesn't consider the budgets for a project. "I lay out the songs and what kind of vision I have for them, and then I call friends of mine who are willing to play with me and we settle on something I can pay then and I go from there. I'm not a good business model for that. I have never considered the money. If you make a great record, it's always going to be a great record."

On the Road Again

Stanley travels extensively to play a variety of clubs, listening rooms, and house concerts. He offers this advice for those wishing to do the same. "Get on the mailing list of every artist that you like who tours. And what you will see periodically is a post from where the artist is playing with a phone number. That's a goldmine for a young artist. Google acoustic venues, contact guitar stores in town, and ask them about clubs. Go online and check the local newspaper. And there are guides: *The Album Network* costs some money but it has every venue in it."

The house concert phenomenon has benefited Stanley. The first time he performed in one of these homespun venues, a residence that could seat 99 fans, he relates that he netted around $2,500 dollars between the performance guarantee and CD sales. The venue also took care of filling the house with music fans, few of whom had previously experienced the artist. "I was done at 9:30 and I thought, 'This is a good job.' Now, I do 10 to 20 house concerts a year, in addition to the clubs I play."

That said, for emerging acts, he doesn't recommend these venues. "At a house concert, the audience is very nice and accepting, kind and nurturing. They won't challenge you and they'll laugh at your stupid jokes and they'll be OK if you forget the words and the guitar is out of tune. It's not. None of those things makes for a great artist. If you're learning the biz and play nothing but house concerts, you think you're really something special. But if you play a club and the audience is there to find someone to go home with or they like drinking, dancing, and partying, and if you can turn that crowd into an audience, then you'll be a performer."

The Heart for the Art

"Winston Churchill said, 'Never give up.' The only people who make it are those who believe in themselves. One of the things that helps is don't measure your success next to anyone else's. It will make you angry and bitter if you think someone who isn't as good as you is getting more attention. All you can do is measure what you do compared to what you did last week or last year. Do what you do and aspire to be great. Remember: Everyone's job is as important as yours. Some guys think because they play music they're elite. John Coltrane, one of the greatest sax players of all time, would come off the bandstand and talk to everyone. Respect everyone and respect your gift."

www.jamesleestanley.com

John Legend

Songwriter/producer/guitarist Dave Tozer remembers this gig just a few years back. "We had a little rag-tag band playing on this outside back patio of a restaurant while people were having dinner inside. The maitre 'd came out and asked if we could have our singer stop because it was disturbing the dinner crowd—they wanted softer music." This shushed singer—John Legend—now performs for more appreciative audiences and the Grammy-winning Best New Artist also made a point onstage of thanking Tozer when he collected his award for *Get Lifted*.

The new artist accolade was flanked by two other Grammy Awards—R&B Album of the Year and R&B Vocal Performance—and to the uninitiated, it might seem that John Legend's ascent into the big leagues of modern R&B music has been a rapid one, but it took almost 10 years of total immersion into his craft as a songwriter and vocalist for John Stephens, gospel choir director and aspiring R&B star, to make the transition to

Grammy-winning John Legend. As Tozer tells it, Legend's is less a story of struggle than a mission of predestination. "John's a rare case, an overachiever. He's always excelled in all of his peer groups—that's what he's still doing."

Growing up in Springfield, Ohio, a Midwestern town often typified as an "All-American City," John Stephens' first musical influences were gospel. "There was a piano in the house and I learned to play and read music early on," he recalls. "By the time I was eight or nine, I was playing in the local church for the choir. My grandma taught me a lot of the gospel songs, and between lessons in classical music and singing and playing in church, I really developed my 'ear.' I always loved the feeling when people responded to my singing and playing so I was already making little gospel records in high school. I was ambitious and just loved being onstage."

By his teens, as Stephens added R&B and hip-hop to his repertoire, his piano chops flourished and expanded. He landed a regular gig as musical director at his church, directing singers twice his age. Home-schooled by his family, Legend was allowed to skip grades in school and graduate early, and at age 16 was enrolled in the University of Pennsylvania in Philadelphia as an English major. Gospel music remained a touchstone when he was enlisted to lead the music department at Scranton's Bethel AME Church. "As far as being able to put a choir together, I don't think you can find no better," said the Reverend Wilhelmenia Coleman, a former choir member who's now pastor of the church. "I mean, he can take anyone's voice and make you feel like you can sing."

Dave Tozer recalls that the church bought John a car for the commute from Philly, but the duo also put it into secular service. "A little Honda—we tore that car up, gigging." Tozer had first encountered Stephens when a friend invited him to drop by for an informal jam session. Stephens sang some Smokey and Stevie, and Tozer recalls, "I thought, 'This guy was pretty good.' I was used to being around a bunch of hacky rock musicians who couldn't really sing." Tozer hired Stephens for casual dates, including the infamous restaurant gig. Stephens impressed Tozer with his writing chops and the pair began collaborating. "I remember sitting down in my living room and saying, 'We should do your solo act.' I saw it was generating real interest right off." The two recorded their initial demos on a Tascam eight-track with beats courtesy of an Alesis drum machine.

When Stephens played on "Everything Is Everything" from *The Miseducation of Lauryn Hill*, it provided entrée to the record world. (Stephens had been introduced to Hill through a mutual friend from the church.) Armed with a voluminous music industry directory, Tozer set out making contacts. "Cold-calling labels and making demos. It wasn't there yet, but people knew it was going on. We had good songs." After Stephens graduated, he took a straight job as a corporate consultant, moved to Boston, then to

New York, and kept writing, gigging, and recording on weekends with Tozer plus leading the choir. "The four-song demo became nine songs and that became the first John Stephens disc to sell at shows," Tozer clarifies.

Two more independently produced live CDs, *Solo Sessions, Vol. 1: Live at the Knitting Factory* and *Live at SOB's*, followed. "We got the website together. I'd get checks and mail CDs out from my house: $10 for the CD and $2 for shipping," laughs Tozer. With Tozer as musical director and guitarist, John continued performing in and around Philly, and by 2000 he had expanded his audience base by doing shows in New York, Boston, Atlanta, and Washington, D.C., frequently appearing on bills with national R&B artists such as Musiq, Jaheim, Amel Larrieux, Glenn Lewis, and Floetry.

Through his college roommate and another collaborator, Devo Harris, Tozer and Stephens met Kanye West (Harris's cousin). West, who was emerging as a producer for acts such as Jay-Z and Scarface, was soon to be an artist in his own right. West came to see Stephens and his band, led by Tozer, in Harlem. Over time, Stephens was invited to sing hooks on West songs and West gave him beats for his demo. For one track, Stephens created "Do What I Gotta Do," based on a beat sampled from Aretha Franklin. West became a strong ally. By now, Stephens was clearly in the club: He played piano, sang, and co-wrote two tracks on West's blockbuster release. The next year, John dueted with Alicia Keys on "You Don't Know My Name," the lead single from the multiplatinum *Diary Of Alicia Keys* set, as well as co-writing, singing, and playing on the Kanye West remix of "If I Ain't Got You" from the same album. John's collaborations with West also include singing and playing piano on "Encore" and "Lucifer," tracks from Jay-Z's *The Black Album*. John sang and co-wrote "The Boogie That B" from the Black Eyed Peas' *Elephunk* album.

The name changed from "Stephens" to "Legend." Says John, "I originally was given the name John Legend by a friend from Chicago because he thought I sounded so much like an old-school artist," John confesses. "At first, I thought it was funny to be called 'Legend,' but then a lot of my friends started calling me that and it really caught on so much that more people were calling me 'Legend' than my real name. So I started to consider using it as my stage name. I knew it sounded a little presumptuous, but I figured it would definitely make me stand out from the pack. I figured it would make people pay attention to me. And once I have their attention, I hope to make them fall in love with my music."

They did. In 2003 and out in 2004 came still more guest appearances: He played keyboards on "Overnight Celebrity" (from Twista's *Kamikaze* CD); sang, played, and appeared in the video for Dilated Peoples' "This Way"; co-wrote and played on Janet Jackson's "I Want You"; co-wrote, played, and sang on "I Try," the lead single, featuring Mary J. Blige, from Talib Kweli's *Beautiful Struggle* album (which also features John's work as lead vocalist and pianist on the track "Around My Way"). In addition to singing lead on Slum Village's "Selfish," John played on sessions for Eve, Common, and Britney Spears. His own deal was eminent.

By late 2003, Kanye West had signed the multifaceted Legend as the first artist to his production company, KonMan Entertainment, and a deal with Columbia Records soon followed. After signing with the label, John narrowed down his repertoire and tracked his debut. Dave Tozer contributed to eight songs on the major-label debut.

"When the Kanye thing came into play, there was the thought, 'Is the rug going to get pulled out from under me?' But the key thing is I was banking on John's character. I knew him as a person the whole time. I knew he wouldn't let that happen."

Hauling a Fender Rhodes on the subways, tearing up a Honda, mailing out CDs, cold-calling record labels; it's been almost a decade's journey from the jams of Philly to the Grammy Awards. "You've gotta stick it out," advises Tozer. "It took a long time, but I knew this dude was the real deal." Adds Legend, "I never really got frustrated because there were always little 'victories,' plus the real people—the audiences—liked me. You have to have a lot of stamina to keep going."

www.johnlegend.com

3 The A&R Exec/The Label

Despite the well-publicized changes in record labels, the role of an A&R (artist and repertoire) executive is still about the most basic elements: signing, working with, and overseeing recording artists and their creative output. If one is blessed to be working with a magnificent singer like Celine Dion in an A&R capacity, the job is to help find the material and the producers who are best for the singer and the song. In signing a self-contained band that writes everything, the job is very different. You might bring in ideas for potential producers, but many times these acts know the type of producers they want. Sometimes there is little work to be done, but often there is a lot; in all cases, it is the A&R exec's gig to bring the finished product to the label. In many ways, A&R is considered a sexy job, but it is not just going out and signing bands and artists. It is an endeavor with varying tentacles, all of which must be managed.

The primary responsibility of any A&R person is to work with the acts they have already signed. You have made a commitment to the artist, emotionally and financially, and you must now do everything in your power to ensure that the act can be musically successful. The A&R responsibility is heavyweight: If the wrong act is signed and doesn't reach the ears of the public, jobs will be at stake—not just those of the person who signed the act, but many others at the company.

While many in the record industry are conscious of putting music and art in a box, it is often the most innovative music that turns out to be the gem. Although indie labels have less staff and overhead, they still have similar pressures as those of a major label. As you will read in this chapter, music companies can spin on a creative and/or a corporate axis.

Tony Ferguson: Attributes of A&R

"…we can't take any stray dog off the street, and we don't have the people to do it."

Like many executives in the music business, Tony Ferguson was first a musician, specifically a guitarist with the bands Christie and Unit 4+2. Growing up in his native UK, he absorbed the spirit of American music via Radio Luxemburg. "Black music was unbelievable to me," he remembers. It was the economic woes of the 1970s that drove Ferguson from the stage to the office. "The OPEC oil crisis hit Europe really hard. It was terrible to be a musician in England at that time." Initially Ferguson came to the U.S. to work in the East Coast office of Stiff Records (whose motto was, "If It Ain't Stiff, It Ain't Worth a F**k"). The label was home to Elvis Costello and other acts.

As an A&R executive at Interscope Records and its affiliate, A&M Records, Ferguson has worked with artists such as No Doubt, Bush, Tupac, the Reverend Horton Heat, and Butterfly Boucher. Ferguson continues to sign and develop talent. "Eighty percent of my age group would never listen to the stuff that excites me. It's still the same elements. To have hit songs and to get noticed today, that process has not changed. When I hear a rap song, I can tell if it's a hit or not. Pop songs? I hear them straight away. It is always the songs that drive the ship."

Raising the Scope at Interscope

Iconoclastic Jimmy Iovine, with a rich history as a record producer, is the high-profile chairman of Interscope/Geffen/A&M Records. "Jimmy was tired of making records in the studio. He knew the power was in the major label's court and he had always wanted to start a label," says Ferguson. "He started a management company first and that was active for three or four years until Jimmy didn't want to do it anymore. Ted Fields, of the Marshall Fields empire, had always been a lover of music. Jimmy and Ted hooked up. Interscope was the name given to Ted's financial holdings and the name just stuck."

Ferguson was on board. Going against the trend of grunge music, "Rico Suave" by Gerardo was the label's first hit. "It got our name on the map," he says. "After that, Marky Mark, Helmet, Primus, and Nine Inch Nails. Hip-hop was our biggest transitional change. Jimmy said, 'Why can't hip hop artists sell like Guns 'n' Roses?' And he proved it right with Dr. Dre's *The Chronic*. It blew everything out of the water."

A witch hunt concurrent with the rise of rap set sights on Interscope because of the messages engendered by its artists. "It was the Clinton and Bob Dole presidential campaign that got Interscope into hot water. Right-wing people pinpointed Interscope as the root of cultural problems in American youth. Yet we were signing the best poets available: Tupac, Snoop Dogg, and Dr. Dre. They were at the top of their game at that point with subject matter that was controversial. So Warner Bros. [who was distributing the label] said, 'Get rid of these acts, and we'll double your funding.' Jimmy said absolutely not. So Interscope went to Universal."

A&R Roles

Unlike some A&R reps, Ferguson prefers not to be engaged in the recording process. "I will make observations and suggestions, but I like to think artists can do it themselves. I don't tweak the knobs much," he says. But he is involved with the projects prior to the artists going into the studio. "B. B. King and producer T-Bone Burnett, for example, were great. When you work with professional people, you just can press 'play' and let them go. It gets harder to take developing artists and try to mold them. When signing an act, you're signing the potential of what that act can be. They're not exactly camera-ready. The more the artist understands themselves and their audience, the easier it is to make the record."

"Female pop artists are the dangerous ones. To make those types of records it is extremely expensive because you're often hiring multiple producers and musicians. At end of the day, if there is nowhere to go with the tracks, it can be disconcerting. You have to have a marketing and promotional vision in mind for once the album finishes. Otherwise, it just sits on the shelves."

Ferguson references a young female Australian guitarist, Orianthi, for whom he is "trying to find songs that will infiltrate the marketplace but will also showcase her prowess as an amazing guitarist. If the deal is realistic enough, with low expectations, we'd artist develop her as a live act. Part of the disease of the business is that the cost of making records is imbalanced by the revenue stream on the back end. Costs have to come down. In a general sense, they are, but very slowly. The cost of making records is still way too high."

Ferguson attests that he looks for music everywhere and anywhere. "I do a sh*tload of research online. It's a computer race where you go and hear virally what is generating interest in the artists. But by the time you find out, everyone else is on board. Because of this process, we don't have to get on a plane and travel halfway around the world every time to see a new band."

"We also rely on producers and production deals. Indie labels do the grunt work of independent development we can't do because we can't take any stray dog off the street and we don't have the people to do it. By then, artists know who they are, and they have a volume of songs under their belts. It works; it's been done for you already."

To the Bank

"Sometimes you go weeks or months without anything going on, but then there is a song that triggers something and connects. That's why we're in the business. This business is all about connections. It's networking more than anything else."

"For artists: Listen to the best music you can and dissect what makes a hit record. Understand what really makes a song popular. This involves production, performance, and the song itself. You may have a hit song but not have a hit record. Listen, learn, and pay attention to what everyone that you meet in the industry says. The basic creed I live by is respect more than anything. I try to be a mentor to give people advice they can take to the bank."

www.interscope.com

Diarmuid Quinn: Major Label Music

"Even though you need the songs, you especially need loyalty to the artists."

As president of Reprise Records and executive vice president of Warner Bros. Records, Diarmuid Quinn works with a notable roster of artists, including Metallica, Josh Groban, Michael Bublé, Green Day, Tom Petty, My Chemical Romance, and Neil Young. "I have an affinity for all of them," Quinn enthuses. "It's cool to work with your heroes and yet exciting to work with new acts."

The label has elevated many artists' careers from the ground up with original marketing plans, Quinn says. "Certainly Michael Bublé. We built him from zero record sales to 5 million. Josh Groban can sell 200,000 Christmas albums in one week. We're doing a lot of direct-to-fan stuff now. With Josh and Michael, we are paying particular attention to micromanaging our relationships online with fans to make sure they get anything about the artist first. Josh Groban had the biggest record in America. What really happened was six years of building up his fan base, so when the right record came along, the fans were ready and we could activate it quickly."

Marketing the artist is key, says Quinn. "Even though you need the songs, you especially need loyalty to the artists. The Tom Petty film [*Runnin' Down a Dream*, a documentary directed by Peter Bogdanovich] was a big deal for me because it put Tom Petty in the right light as one of our great American songwriters. Then he did the Super Bowl followed by a huge tour, and it all just proved how great I always believed he was. Helping him realize that is really rewarding."

Ozzy at the Gate

Giving fans of the artists what they need, Quinn says, is an essential element in building artist loyalty, vital to the careers of artists like Bublé or Groban. "I go after what I think they want and make sure they get it. The artist grows because of that. Ozzy Osbourne and AC/DC taught me valuable lessons. Ozzy stops and signs every autograph while walking through an airport. His philosophy is that every fan is critical to his success, and AC/DC believes in the same thing. They talk to every kid. 'We're only as good as the fans. If they go away, we're toast,' is the approach. If you 'superserve' that to those who are fans, you lengthen your career. If you don't, you risk everything."

Quinn notes that branding is something everyone at the company does on a continual basis. "You have to have a message that's clear, that cuts through everything. So the more we can get to people, as long is it doesn't compromise the art, is good. It is a simple rule: Success is directly proportional to the amount of work you're willing to put in. Michael Bublé worked his tail off, and he is lucky to get any days off. But everyone who works for him at the company will kill for him, and artists need that."

360 + 5

In referencing the increasingly common 360 deals, wherein a record company, in exchange for monetary support of an artist's career, can profit from touring, merchandise, publishing, and other income, Quinn changes the definition. "I like to call it '365'—working for the artist 365 days a year."

And he refers back to keeping fans involved with their favorite artists. "We are getting aggressive about ticketing. When tickets go on sale, the fans can get music with the tickets. So they know the new music, not just existing tracks. We want them to know the body of work. Real fans are at the shows, so we need to make sure that the new music is available to that captive audience."

The label, Quinn says, is developing its own merchandising arm as well and has a film and television music department. "We're adding experts and reinforcing the people we have. We do what the artist wants. But if we don't have great music, none of it really matters."

Major Clout

Independent labels can market effectively in a more nimble fashion, Quinn surmises. "But they can't take the risks that majors take. It's now an artist-driven business on the top end. Now they are more in control of their futures than ever before and if they are savvy about it, they can do whatever they want. There are no rules now, which is the best part of it."

"The advantage we have is we create a profile for them—we're a giant resource with experience from 200 people working on a record. Look at what we just did with Metallica. We had a dedicated nine-month plan called 'Mission to Metallica,' a website that had new content every week , and it built and built. That took a lot of resources, money, and time and indie artists would have a hard time doing that on their own. Acts need major labels to build their profiles so that all their other businesses are successful."

"Premium fans are willing to fund things if they get value for it. We work with Oasis and do their arena tours and their merchandise business in North America. Fans are not paying for recorded music like they used to. But it was the first time in a decade that Oasis was in the top five in *Billboard*. The reason they do business with us is that Oasis has control, they're partners with us, and we have constant dialogue. We are helping to rebuild their brand in America and we can't do that without them helping us with their other businesses."

"There are new acts we have deals with where we spend money marketing an album for two years. Mute Math are great songwriters and hard working guys. We are in business with them on everything. It enabled us, when we didn't sell as many albums as would have liked on the last album, to continue to fund them because we participated in touring and merchandise. Their album hasn't exploded, but the tours have gone from small clubs to larger theaters. Other businesses have enabled us to stay with them, so hopefully the next album does much better. It's hard to take the sizable risks without having the top end sales anymore. But we can do it if we work together on all levels."

Quinn offers two quick words of advice. "One: Don't forget that you love the music, and you will succeed. Two: Do what you say you're going to do when you say you're going to do it, and you'll be 90 percent ahead of everyone else."

www.warnerbrosrecords.com

Brian Postelle: The Urban Agenda

"A lot of people can sing and rap, but they've got to be able to walk in a room and light the room up. I'm constantly looking. You can be a nobody, but if you walk into a mall or a club at nighttime and you can catch my eye, like, 'Who is that person over there?' and if you look like a star to me, I'm going to ask if you can sing or you can rap. And we'll take it from there."

There's an old saying: No one starts at the top. For Brian Postelle, one of urban music's preeminent dealmakers, entry into the business began with a stint in a tape room, at EMI Music Publishing. "I stayed there for two years, learning the business and having fun—having more fun than learning, and not really realizing that by having fun, I was learning."

"I was making my contacts, never realizing that they would be valuable contacts—I was just making friends."

Two years later, Postelle received a call from Famous Music Publishing saying the company might be interested hiring him. Postelle recalls the initial meeting. "I went to the interview and it turned out to be a four-hour interview with president Ira Jaffe. Ira and I clicked from that moment until he retired. He asked me what I knew and what I didn't know, and he asked me who I knew. He said, 'Brian, don't worry about the rest. I'll teach you what you need to know." I went back to EMI and told them what had been presented to me. I'm a loyal person—a key in the music business is loyalty. You never know when you're going to cross someone's path again. And if you've done good by someone, it can benefit you later."

When EMI didn't match the offer, Postelle moved over to Famous Music Publishing, where he came into his element. "Ira said, 'Brian you're going to be so big you're not going to leave me for less than a quarter of a million dollars.' He was laughing at me; I was so young. He let me go to work. I went in with a vengeance and a chip on my shoulder, but I knew my stuff. I wanted to outdo EMI at this small publishing company." Signing publishing deals with Eminem, Red Man, and Irv Gotti, plus Fred Jerkins, Montell Jordan, and the writer/producers who were working with Nelly, Postelle was on his way. But he recalls one signing that got away.

"Ira, not yet knowing my judgment, wasn't willing to put that risk on Jay-Z. I was in there early. I got a phone call at 9:00 p.m. one night: 'Do you want to sign Jay-Z for $750,000? Let's close the deal.' I went to Ira and said this is the next guy—Tupac and Biggie had blown up, and now this is who we need to bet on. Ira, still wanting to teach me the business, wanted me to do all of the due diligence of clearing samples and checking back catalog and all of that. I said, 'This is fine and dandy, but we can do this later, let's close the deal.' Ira said we had to do it like that. Two weeks later, he realized my passion for Jay-Z and he raised the money to $950,000, but by that time Jay-Z was in bed with another company."

Eminem Eminence

Eminem first came to the attention of Postelle through his girlfriend—now his wife—who worked at Aftermath Entertainment, the company formed by Dr. Dre. "Dre was going through a transition period of figuring out what he wanted to do. I got a phone call from my girlfriend, and she said, 'Turn to this page in *Source* magazine—that's Dre's next signing.' People were saying he didn't have it no more, but I knew he did. I got in contact with Eminem's people, and they said I was the first (music publisher) to call. They sent me the music and I was in my office playing it and Ira walked in my office and said, 'What the hell is that?' I said, 'Would you let you son listen to this?' And he said, 'No, no way.' And I said, 'Exactly! That's why I'm going to sign him.' He looked at me like I was crazy. I said, 'Every parent in America is going to want their kids to not to listen to this, and the kids are going to be dying to hear it.' He knew we'd missed Jay-Z, and he wasn't going to lose this one. Ira gave me a green light to do whatever I had to do, and I did my damnedest not to let him down."

Postelle, formerly senior vice president, A&R Urban at Island/Def Jam Records, notes that often publishers do more in the realm of artist development than labels. "A publisher will sign a singer/songwriter and put her or him in the studio. They'll spend the money to put a demo together and cultivate the artist before a major ever hears them, then shop the demo to the majors. That's how a lot of artists get signed—the publishers were there first. I sit back and laugh: I remember seven years ago, I got a demo across my desk of Amy Winehouse. It was put together by a bunch of publishers."

Change Rearrange

From Famous, Postelle moved to DreamWorks in the A&R department, but the company was short-lived as it was "inherited" by Interscope. "At Interscope, it was good—I knew all of their prized-possession artists. I had signed Eminem, I knew Dre, I knew 50 Cent—the artists that were top dogs. I had relationships with all of them. Me going over there was a perfect fit, but I didn't feel it was a building that let A&R do what they do with artists. Jimmy Iovine [head of Interscope] is a producer, so he depends on his producers and his artists to bring him talent. Little by little, Jimmy started weeding out the staff and artists from DreamWorks. He came to me and said he wanted to keep me there and that I could work on the artists they kept from DreamWorks. Unfortunately, he had a head of urban music that, I guess, felt inferior because of my relationships, even though I tried explaining to him I didn't want to be head of urban music. The situation started getting sour. I made a call to my friend at Arista and to say I wasn't feeling the situation, and he said he wasn't feeling the situation where he was either. He was at Arista, and it got folded into Jive Records. He said, 'I'll get out of my job and you get out of your job and we'll go and do it.'"

His friend was mega-producer Jermaine Dupri, and the duo moved first to Virgin Records and then Island/Def Jam, where Dupri was installed as president of urban music. (He has since parted from the label.)

Signing Power

Postelle notes that in urban music, the gangsta, thuggish criminal identification that has been a trademark of so many artists appears to be passing. "I believe it's oversaturated. Before, with NWA and Snoop Dogg, even 50 Cent, it was believable and respected. I think now people think they need that to sell records, so they're going to that first. They're not focusing on the art, it's all about what the artist has done in the past rather than the music they are putting out."

And he attests that what draws him to acts first is their visual appeal. "It's a look. They have to have star power. A lot of people can sing and rap, but they've got to be able to walk in a room and light the room up. I'm constantly looking. You can be a nobody, but if you walk into in a mall or a club at nighttime and you can catch my eye, like 'Who is that person over there?' If you look like a star to me, I'm going to ask if you can sing or you can rap. And we'll take it from there. If you don't look like a star, it's hard to make you look like a star. We can put you in the studio with Jermaine or Dre and get your record and we can find a hit song, but can you deliver? That's the key."

"I think that people have to go outside of the Internet. People in the urban music world got lazy and they don't want to put in the work. They think they can get on the net and make people believe it and get a deal. They're not out doing shows, pounding the pavement trying to get their visuals up. Maybe I'm driving down the street and I see a poster or a flyer about you, or I'm at a mall and someone is handing out a flyer. It takes a lot of work, but it pays out. When 50 Cent first came out, he flooded the streets of New York with mix tapes and there was not one kid in New York in the urban community who was not talking about 50 Cent. I had friends in L.A. who went to New York and came back and told me to sign 50 Cent—in high schools malls, colleges, movie theaters, that's all people were talking about—the only thing. When you get that kind of buzz, there's no stopping you—it's on. And he could back it up with great music on top of that. Make sure you believe in your music, get the craft down to a science to what you believe in, then you have to get in people's faces: Perform at every possible showcase, every possible venue you can get to play. If you rap, do the other things à la 50 Cent."

"If you're a singer, you have to have a live show—if you're good live, you're marketable and sellable. Go to New York or L.A.; get an opening act on a tour. You have to hustle. There's a million people who want to be in the music business. How many acts become successful? This is worse than baseball. If you bat 300 percent in baseball, you're in the Hall of Fame. The percentage of people that make it in music is much lower."

John Janick: Using the Noodle

"I like stuff that has hooks. I want youthfulness and energy, and I like curveball things."

He was 17 when he began his career in the record business. Today, the company that John Janick founded in 1998, Fueled by Ramen, is less of a record label and more of a brand for a community of bands and fans that clearly embraces what the company signifies: the nucleus for punk and punk-inspired music. An EP release by the Arizona-based band, Jimmy Eat World was a significant early success, and a subsequent release by Yellow Card upped the ante. Fall Out Boy's *Take This to Your Grave* was an unqualified introduction for the band that has since launched a multiplatium career. As the company begins its second decade, Paramore (Grammy-nominated for Best New Artist), Panic at the Disco, the Cab, Phantom Planet, Gym Class Heroes, Cobra Starship, and Cute Is What We Aim For enrich Fueled by Ramen's roster.

Although he didn't play music, John Janick was fascinated by it. "Especially underground and punk rock. I was one of those people who was always excited and wanted to turn other people onto music. Around 11th grade, when I was mail-ordering records from my favorite record labels, I found some indie distributors that sold lots of different records. I ended up buying records for six or seven dollars from the distributors and would try to turn random people in my high school onto the music. Then I would end up selling the records to them for a few dollars more. I wasn't looking to make a huge profit off of it, but I got a little bit of money. I loved music so much. I loved the excitement of being around the shows, so I started interacting with the artists. When I was 17, the Internet was beginning. I reached out to bands I loved and began putting together some compilations. That was my entry point. It was the best thing I could do to be close to music."

Gaining in Gainesville

Blessed with an innate sense for sales, Janick said he also ran his compilation business strictly by the book by incorporating his endeavors and registering with the state. When he attended college in Gainesville, Florida, he accelerated his enterprises. "My first year, I ran it out of my dorm room. That was my office, where I did all of the phone calls. My sophomore year, I moved into an apartment and worked out of my bedroom, and I had a closet downstairs where I kept records for mail order. My third year of college, we actually moved into a small office space, and pretty much every year after that we moved to increasingly bigger office spaces as it continued to grow."

The label's name was distilled from a longer creed: "Fueled by Ramen, no food, no sleep, just music." Says Janick, "It was about not having much money but putting what we had towards music."

DIY Ethics

"I loved the DIY [do-it-yourself] ethic of punk and the energy that it gave off, how passionate and excited people were about the music. And even in punk music, there were bands with great choruses and very catchy songs, and I like that—everything I signed had to have great energy to it, and the people in the band had to have the right mentality of what they wanted to be and what they wanted to do." He says he found his niche when he observed that all of the big labels were capitalizing on a few hit songs and making people buy expensive CDs to have them. "I got into the Internet because I had to find new ways to market the music and turn listeners on. I didn't have radio or video, so I had to turn to the Internet and take advantage of it, to make sure the kids were hearing our music."

"We were working with developing artists who didn't have to have a hit single on their first record. We could develop these acts. These bands were going to be touring acts and selling merchandise and having careers, so they didn't have to live and die by the single. And because a lot of these artists we signed were so young, they had to find themselves."

Falling into Fall Out Boy

Janick first saw the name Fall Out Boy included on a show flyer for one of his bands. "I thought, 'Who would name their band this?' Two weeks [later] I saw another advertisement for a band from Chicago, and Fall Out Boy was on their bill too. I called our band and asked about them. I went online and listened to one of their songs and I loved it. I found their contact information. Three of the guys were living in the same house, and that first day I talked to all three. Pete Wentz and I talked for an hour, and in the next two weeks I signed the band without ever seeing them or meeting them in person. We just clicked. I believed in the music and the people. I had a good feeling about them."

"Panic at the Disco came in partnership with Pete, because we'd developed this great relationship with Fall Out Boy. Some kid had posted a song on his blog and Pete sent it to me. It was Panic at the Disco, and we signed them together. With Paramore, someone told me about them. I thought her voice was really good and the music was very poppy, but it didn't have that edge to it. I had lunch with Haley from the band, and I found out she did all different music; someone was pushing them in the wrong direction."

Swimming Upstream into the 360 Deal

There is a music industry term called "upstreaming." When a band is signed to an independent deal, if their indie label has such an agreement with a larger record label and that band becomes successful, the band might then be "upstreamed" to take advantage of the marketing dollars and resources of the larger entity. Fueled by Ramen works with Atlantic Records domestically and with Warner Music Group internationally. In the success of Fall Out Boy, upstreaming was beneficial for all parties. "Because I wanted to maintain a good relationship and to be partners. I didn't want the hold the band for ransom. We were the development process."

But the Fueled by Ramen reputation is imperative. "We built a brand signing good acts for 12 years. There are not that many labels out there doing this. All of the big labels used to be independent: Sire, Atlantic, Warner Bros., they were all known for their reputations, and listeners latched onto that. We want to be a quality place where people can look at a record, see our logo on the back, and know that this is music they will be into because of what we did in the past."

The current model of "360 deals," wherein a label, in exchange for its investment, profits from a band's touring and merchandising income, has long been a common role model for independent labels. "It's always been about careers. I wanted to make sure the band was doing well on the road and selling merchandise. I always had the mail-order business and web store. Then we made the shirts and did the tour merchandise. I thought, 'Why don't we go into retail and sell the music and merchandise together? Tie it in with touring and turn it into a well-rounded thing.' We naturally developed into it."

"Managers and lawyers didn't get it, because the labels were making millions selling CDs, even though the labels were the ones spending millions of dollars breaking artists who then did so well in touring and merchandise. Back in the day, the labels didn't need to do the other stuff, so people on the label side weren't doing good business. But you have to be artist-friendly, and to make sure the artists understand. It's a good thing, and I want this to be a feel-good thing because if it's not, it doesn't make sense. I've always been a good partner with artists. In this world, that is essential."

The A&R Ears and the Righteousness Card

Janick personally signs off on every band that his label signs. "I like stuff that has hooks. I want youthfulness and energy and I like curveball things. Fall Out Boy and Panic at the Disco are not the same. Gym Class Heroes is an alternative rock band with a rapper. I try to diversify, but I like bands that have great songs, are going to work hard, and have the right mindset. The right artists have a vision of what they want to be."

"I was going to college full time and working 60 hours a week trying to build a record label. There were times I wanted to give up, thinking, 'Now, do I have to get a real job?' I didn't, fortunately, because now I get to do what I love. There were hard times: I slept on an air mattress."

"When I was 19 and 20 years old, I heard the stories, that there were snakes in this business. I was conscious that I had to protect myself. I want to be a place where the artists are happy. I might tell them the truth, but my reputation is the most important thing. You have to treat the artist and the people you work with well, plus anyone you come in contact with. The business is so small that you can burn bridges very quickly."

www.fueledbyramen.com

Diane Meltzer: Winding Up with Wind-up

"You have to believe in your bands and stick with them."

Wind-up Entertainment Inc. is a privately owned company that was founded in March 1997. Wind-up Records, a division of Wind-up Entertainment, is currently the largest independently owned and operated label in the United States. Wind-up Entertainment Canada, Inc., Wind-up Nashville, and expansion across Europe reflect the growing global presence for the label and development of the company's repertoire to encompass most genres. The label's roster features Evanescence, Seether, Finger Eleven, the entire Creed repertoire, and more than a dozen developing artists, which include Company of Thieves, Thriving Ivory, Civil Twilight, Pilot Speed, and others. Wind-up Entertainment also houses the publishing concerns Sakyamuni Music Publishing, LLC; Bodhi Music Publishing, LLC; Renfield Music Publishing, Inc.; and Pronto Merch, LLC, a full-scale retail, online, and touring merchandising company. Wind-up Entertainment also operates Wind-up Artist Development Corporation and Wind-up Touring, LLC. Husband and wife Alan and Diana Meltzer are company principals.

Origins and Oracles

Diane Meltzer, the company's head of A&R, explains the company's foundation. "In 1993, Alan created Alliance Entertainment by combining CD One Stop with several competing distributors. Even though Alliance grew into a $700 million company, Alan was disenchanted with the music business because he felt it was too much about business and not enough about the music. He then established Wind-up Entertainment as a self-financed independent record label that could compete with the majors with the goal of 'developing career artists,' which is Wind-up's slogan."

Wind-up Entertainment also owns Wind-up Artist Development Corporation, which handles all of Wind-up's touring-related artist matters, and Wind-up Touring, which currently owns the rights to the Snocore tour; a popular music tour that has existed for over 10 years. Wind-up is relaunching the tour in 2009 and expects it to include Wind-up acts.

Seed with Creed/Rockers from Little Rock

Wind-up's first huge success was with Creed. "When I first heard the band, I literally dragged Alan and a few other senior Wind-up people to Tallahassee, Florida, where they were playing the next night. We met with marketing after that and concluded that the best strategy was to send them out as 'headliners' even if it meant headlining for 50 people. We worked the Internet with intensity, as well as radio and retail."

"Alan immediately saw the potential of the Internet from the first time he logged on," notes Diane. "Wind-up has always used the Internet to grow our artist fan bases, communicate with the music community, and promote our artists. In 1997, when we were launching the first Creed record, we provided fans with a prepacked website with music and their own exclusive Creed photo."

The band eventually sold over 30 million records worldwide. "When you find amazing talent, you cannot worry about how the artist fits in with the current music scene or how it will work at various radio formats. Current trends in music will quickly grow old, so you need to trust your instincts."

The Grammy-winning band Evanescence is another Wind-up success story. "A producer friend was playing demos for me of a new band he had been working on. When he played me their ballad "My Immortal," my instinct told me to sign the band immediately. We actually signed the band without seeing them perform live.

"I arranged to move them from their hometown of Little Rock, Arkansas, to Los Angeles, where we spent two years developing them and building a full band. While in L.A., they wrote their first two singles: 'Bring Me To Life' and 'Going Under.'"

Bringing Up the Band

Not all of Wind-up's artists are household names, but Meltzer believes in the lost art of artist development, as she explains when she references the Canadian rock band Finger Eleven. "They have been on our roster for over 10 years. I saw in them a great rock band in search of a commercial single." On their previous album, the band delivered "One Thing," and the new album *Them vs. You vs. Me* features the massive hit "Paralyzer." The song hit the top of numerous charts, including the Canadian Hot 100 and both U.S. rock charts, as well as reaching number 6 on the U.S. Hot 100 and number 12 on the Australian singles chart. The band also won a Juno Award in Canada for Rock Album of the Year.

"Seether is from South Africa, and when I heard their record, I knew we had to get them to New York. Despite the long trip and frayed nerves, Shaun Morgan showed us that his writing skills and ability to really rock were undeniable. Today, Seether is a franchise artist by any measure."

Listen to the Lions

Wind-up recently made a deal with Lionsgate, the leading independent film and television music company. Wind-up will share in artist publishing with Lionsgate in exchange for first-look placements in Lionsgate productions. Meltzer says that the company is already seeing more placement opportunities for the company's bands in both film and television, including a show on VH-1 titled *Scream Queens* that includes almost all Wind-up music. There is also a future possibility of artist appearances by Wind-up acts in Lionsgate television shows and films.

"It's all about development," Meltzer concludes. "Once you sign to Wind-up, the likelihood of you not getting three swings at the ball is slim. We encourage our artists to explore their creative instincts, collaborate with others, and give them the tools they need for success, especially extensive touring."

www.winduprecords.com

Joe Galante: Nashville Cat

"I'm appalled by the number of singers that you go to see live that are awful who have actually been successful. People see something on YouTube and flock to it because they're curious. Artists think that if they are on YouTube that they're ready for a record deal. They have no sense of how to entertain, and there is no way to build a fan base unless you perform."

Joe Galante ascended quickly from a budget analyst in RCA's New York offices to become the youngest head of a major Nashville label in 1982. When the former label, Sony Nashville, was absorbed by RCA Label Group and was reborn as Sony Music Nashville, Galante was tapped to head the company that now encompasses country labels Arista Nashville, BNA, Columbia Nashville, and RCA Nashville, as well as Provident Music Group, a Christian music company. Combined, the labels' rosters shine with a constellation of artists including Carrie Underwood, Kenny Chesney, Brooks & Dunn, Alan Jackson, Brad Paisley, Gretchen Wilson, Kellie Pickler, Martina McBride, Miranda Lambert, Montgomery Gentry, and Jessica Simpson.

"Everybody has their own level of development," Galante begins. "We have superstars and ones that are developing. The reality is the same for both: In all cases, it is about getting better in performance, appearance, and music. Kenny Chesney is constantly reinventing himself, looking at the competition and saying, 'I need to do this in order to be relevant with the audience.' We encourage all of our artists to look at different producers, video directors, and songwriters so we keep them fresh and people don't become disinterested."

Hit Chorus

Certainly, Nashville's reverence for the song form cannot be overstated. These days, it's not just country in Music City either; Christian, pop, rock, gospel, alternative—and especially alternative country and Americana—are also viable forms. In all areas, the caliber of songwriting talent is in the stratosphere. Typically, country artists cut "outside" songs, created by professional songwriters. Even if artists write themselves, Galante believes that it is essential for them to acknowledge their limitations as tunesmiths. "I think the really successful ones understand that. They realize they are writers, but they can't write it all. You wind up with artists like Brad Paisley and Alan Jackson who write probably three quarters of their hits. No one else can write the way they write. Same with Kenny Chesney; two out of five singles will be his. But not everybody is 'a jack of all trades.' But Alan Jackson can write 'Where Were You When the World Stopped Turning,' and then come back and do, 'Remember When,' both different moods and styles of which there are very few folks who are that capable of capturing."

That said, Galante notes that having one great song does not make a career artist. "People have access to songs that allow them to get on the radio, but I've not seen the success from the sales side. I see people who have hits singles but do not have successful careers."

The singles phenomenon, well noted in the iTunes world of pop, is an immense factor in country music as well. "People are buying singles more than albums," Galante points out. "So if artists want to have careers, they have to let people participate in those points of revenue. Otherwise, we are making decisions on singles not based on careers because there's not a return on the money."

And referring back to YouTube and similar channels, Galante notes that immediacy does not always work in the emerging artist's favor. "People are conscious that things get out immediately. That's good, but it becomes more complicated too, because now there are so many more channels. What bothers me from an artistic standpoint is that you can pick apart an artist's work and download the single and it's all you ever know about that artist. Although it gives people the jukebox effect, it doesn't make them into fans."

And country artists still meet their fans in grassroots situations. "This whole format is about 'relate-ability.' They spend time doing meet and greets, and sign autographs in booths, and play for free, and there is a lot of charity work. It's very much about being with their fans."

Image and Integrity

Like pop music, country increasingly relies on independent labels to develop artists, which are then released and distributed under the umbrella of the larger record label. "We recently signed Craig Morgan, who had been on the label Broken Bow. Independent labels are set up to provide certain development, especially in radio. Other aspects of it, including digital, international, accounting—all those channels that you have to work—they don't have the staff or the muscle in place."

For aspiring country artists, Galante offers this perspective on who he would sign and how they can ascend. "Do you really believe this person will be a star?" he says. "If you don't feel that, I don't know why you would move forward. Artists have to look around at the competition and make some honest assessments. I would encourage a new artist to play around as much as possible; it needs to be in front of a live crowd. If you're a songwriter, you need to work with a performing rights organization (ASCAP, BMI, or SESAC) or to find publishers to help build your craft. It's all about work before you get here. Because when you get here, we expect certain things to happen. We can spend a year of development, but at some point, it needs to be ready to go."

And a telegenic image is a huge part of the equation. "From when he signed until now, Kenny Chesney is like night and day. He came in looking like George Strait, and then channeled more of Jimmy Buffet and John Mellencamp and built a business because people love that combination. It took him a while to get there. People weren't buying him as the young George Strait but fell in love with him as the new beach guy. Image is super important; consumers want their stars to look better than they do."

"At the end of the day, you sign the artists, then it's their repertoire; everything after that is about their look and the choices we make. The first and second singles? Which touring partners? The image of the video? The image on the album cover? What are they doing live? Is there a live coach that we can bring in? Should we improve their interview skills? We spend a great deal of time doing that with our artists. We're looking at the process and working to always make it better."

www.songbmgnashville.com

Steve Greenberg: Veering on the S-Curve

"Make a record you want to listen to in 20 years, even if it doesn't sell."

From gritty soul to smooth pop, as a record producer and a record executive, Steve Greenberg's musical and business savvy have both served him exceedingly well. From 1987 to 1991, Greenberg was in the employ of Warner-Elektra Asylum International before becoming an A&R executive at Big Beat, where he was responsible for shepherding projects with the Grammy-winning Inner Circle and dance artist Robin S. He moved over to Atlantic Records to continue his A&R career under the auspices of company president Danny Goldberg, but Goldberg was moved out of the position to affiliated label Warner Bros. Records, leaving Greenberg high and dry. "I was a dead duck at Atlantic," Greenberg recalls. "I was in the middle of signing Alanis Morissette there in 1994. I was friends with her producer, Glen Ballard, and we had the deal. She wasn't talking to other labels. And Danny got moved without any warning. I get called into the office of the new president, and he didn't want to sign that girl whose deal I thought had been finalized. I had to tell 19-year-old Alanis that her record deal was being pulled. I left the label. I was unemployed, but I then became the music supervisor for the TV show *Central Park West*. Eight months later, Danny Goldberg called me up and said, 'Congratulations: Your act is number one.' Alanis was on Maverick Records, distributed by Warner Bros. Goldberg said, 'I'm leaving Warner Bros. Wherever I go, you're the first person I will hire.' He became president of Mercury Records, hired me, and I signed Hanson."

Greenberg served as executive producer of Hanson's debut album, *Middle of Nowhere*, which sold over 10 million copies worldwide and was nominated for three Grammy Awards. "Their manager gave me a cassette with 'MMMBop.' The guy's voice was really great, and the song was amazing. I went to a county fair in Kansas. I wanted to check them out, but I had a hunch that we shouldn't do it; back then, we didn't do kids. Then I saw them and they were just great. So I signed them."

Hits from the Doghouse

Asked to identify the 10 most annoying songs of all time, readers of *Rolling Stone* magazine ranked "Who Let the Dogs Out" by Baha Men third. After Mercury Records was sold to Polygram, Greenberg left the label with the idea of writing fiction. But the hook of "Who Let the Dogs Out" from a song he had heard was an insistent thought in his mind. The song, created by Anslem Douglas for Trinidad and Tobago's annual carnival, had been recorded by an ad hoc band, Fatt Jack and His Pack of Pets. Greenberg thought it was perfect for a group he was promoting, Baha Men. "I said, 'Let's do it right, and it'll be great.' I begged the group's lead singer at the time and told him that we'd have a hit with this song. He left to be a backup singer for Lenny Kravitz. We went down to the Bahamas and had open auditions."

Anslem Douglas and an original Baha Men member, Stephen Nunez, were sued in 2001, and lost the lawsuit with regard to full authorship for the song. The chorus was originally composed in 1995 by Patrick Stephenson and Leroy Williams of Just Platinum Recording Studios/Action House Studios in Toronto, Canada, for a radio jingle. It was proven that at this time, Douglas was a client of the studio and had used the chorus to compose the song. The lawsuit was settled for an undisclosed financial payment.

"I didn't know who originally wrote it or performed it, so I went on the Internet to the Ask Jeeves site," Greenberg discloses. "Up pops this link to a message board of people vacationing in the Caribbean, and the site said it was on this particular compilation record. Tower Records couldn't keep that record in stock. We knew we had a hit."

No Stone Unturned

In 1999, Jocelyn Eve Stoker, age 12, sent an audition tape to a British television talent show, *Star for a Night*. "I wasn't really thinking that I was going to do it," she says. "I didn't even know a whole song—I sang half of 'Amazing Grace,' half of 'Jesus Loves

Me,' half of 'This Little Light of Mine.'" Apparently it was enough for the producers, who invited her to a live audition. She passed and performed on the show, winning with a version of Donna Summer's "On the Radio." Two London-based producers, the Boilerhouse Boys, Andy Dean and Ben Wolfe, saw Jocelyn's performance and forwarded the videotape to their friend and associate Steve Greenberg. The Boilerhouse Boys have been at the forefront of the British music scene for over a decade, as award-winning songwriters, million-selling producers and remixers, major label A&R consultants, influential DJs, and now innovative soundtrack composers. When Greenberg received a call from the Boilerhouse Boys telling him that they had just heard the greatest singer they'd ever heard from their country, he was wise to heed their enthusiasm.

One of Greenberg's closest associates is New York–based producer, engineer, and songwriter Mike Mangini, who recalls Greenberg's first response to the videotape of the young British soul singer. "Steve said, 'It's got to be like Milli Vanilli. There's no way this girl sounds like this.'" Greenberg was impressed enough to bring Jocelyn to Mangini's studio in New York. "In the studio, we downloaded some karaoke tracks off the Internet, and with no preparation, she sang 'Midnight Train to Georgia' and '(Sittin' On) The Dock of the Bay.' And I signed her on the spot."

Mike Mangini recalls, "We were making a little EP, a critic's thing so people could talk about her until she put out a real record." *Soul Sessions*, the demo project, ended up selling 2.5 million records for the artist, now recording under the name Joss Stone. "It was cut in four or five days, live, no overdubs. I'd never cut a record like that," marvels Mangini. With the success of the project, Mangini relates that it was the artist who made it all a reality. "Joss is always amazing, it's just what version of amazing you want. She'll go in the studio for eight to 10 hours—in the booth, no break, no dinner. I produced the record with Betty Wright and Steve Greenberg, but Joss is her own biggest critic. In this project, I didn't have to be a dictator. *Soul Sessions* was truly a live record. The band played live, and we didn't manipulate it at all. And all of Joss's vocals were live takes. She just went and sang it a few times, a take was picked, and that was it."

The One That Got Away

In 2005, Steve Greenberg placed S-Curve in hibernation in order to take the position of president of Columbia Records. During Steve's tenure at Columbia, the label released hit albums by such established recording artists as Bruce Springsteen, John Mayer, Barbra Streisand, System of a Down, Neil Diamond, and the Dixie Chicks, while developing new talent including John Legend, Anna Nalick, Boys Like Girls, the Jonas Brothers, and others. Throughout Steve's Columbia period, S-Curve's catalog continued to sell briskly, leading to the label's placement on *Billboard*'s August 2006 list of

"The 20 Biggest Independent Labels" for 2005–2006, even though S-Curve at that point had not been operative for over 18 months.

"At Columbia it was a weird time. I was in marketing. I was only there for another four months when they gave me a pile of Christian pop—one was an artist named Nicholas Jonas. I heard it and thought he had the best kid voice. He had two brothers. I went and checked them out. They had written and co-written great songs. I wrote a few as well. They had a number four track on Radio Disney, and they headlined a Radio Disney tour. Then Columbia dropped the band and gave them back their record. They wanted to drop my act because it was my act. That same day they dropped One Republic and Katy Perry."

S-Curve Curves Back

S-Curve has been revitalized as a full-service music company. In its new incarnation, the company has broadened its business scope by adding music publishing, artist management, and complete digital capabilities to its original business of selling master recordings. The label counts two initial artists on its new roster—alternative pop/rock band We the Kings and music icon Tom Jones—and returns with much of its original staff, including Greenberg and Steve Yegelwel, who rejoins the company after serving a stint at Columbia Records as senior vice president, A&R. Greenberg describes the management arm of the company as "the classic 360 model of management. People use music in different ways now, while watching a TV show or playing a video game. Music is in more places than ever before. Whatever new technology emerges at the moment will affect how people hear music, and there is a lot of competition."

S-Curve's first venture in the world of online marketing is its equity stake in Nabbr, a company which creates and distributes dynamic viral video players on the social web (MySpace, etc.), which are spread from fan to fan, providing a steady stream of programming and consumer goods, including video, audio, tour dates/personal appearance information, contests, merchandise sales, and chat with fans. Nabbr currently provides its services to numerous record labels and has done campaigns for major artists, including Justin Timberlake, the Beatles, 30 Seconds to Mars, Amy Winehouse, and many others. S-Curve's own artists will be working closely with Nabbr's development team to create cutting-edge applications of its technology. Greenberg serves as chairman of Nabbr.

But Greenberg, whose extensive career is proof of his business acumen and intuition, says that although marketing tie-ins might be a seductive invitation to enterprise, the music is more important than what it may be attached to. "Don't get seduced by the fact a song was used in a TV show but it may not be a particularly good record. Don't jump on the bandwagon, make it really unique, and try to do something a little differently. The best defense against wasting your time is making music you love and believe in. Make a record you want to listen to in 20 years, even if it doesn't sell."

www.s-curverecords.com

Doug Howard: Branding the Country
"A guy with a guitar case, a legal pad, and pencil can change my life...."

Doug Howard wears two hats: as senior vice president of A&R for Disney-affiliated Lyric Street Records, label home to Rascal Flatts, Bucky Covington, SHeDAISY, Josh Gracin, and Billy Ray Cyrus, and senior vice president and general manager of Disney Music Publishing, Nashville. "There was an open door at Disney for somebody to build something down here because there wasn't any presence. And the Disney brand is so respected. Most country music fans have been to Disneyland or Disney World; as kids we grow up with that brand of respect. So when I was asked, I didn't hesitate."

"On the publishing side, I have an open-door policy," Howard says. "If someone e-mails me and wants me to hear something, I will. I have an iPod that is dedicated only to the publishing company. And I love songwriters. On the record side, I still listen to artists that are submitted."

Getting Tan with Rascal Flatts
Producer Mark Bright cut demos with the band Rascal Flatts and played them for Doug Howard. "I asked if the guys could play for me. It was one of those deals where I loved the CD and studio work, so I wanted to make sure they could sing live."

With his background as a music publisher, Howard was instantly aware that Rascal Flatts was the real deal. "I always knew when I heard something that I believed in. I remember situations where someone didn't really take the time to listen. Sometimes it takes me longer to get back to people, but if it's somebody I know, I will somehow make time to hear a new artist. With the Rascal Flatts guys, I heard them and made that decision. Most of our acts were presented by them bringing in a CD and us saying, 'Man, can they come in and just play live?' There's such a relationship between artist and radio and we know part of the gig is that you go to radio and probably will have to play a set. And that's the first step I always take. If someone can blow me away with guitar and vocal in my office, then I know we can make a hit record."

"I can't stress this enough to new artists, but when they came in, they all looked really rough. Like they hadn't seen sunlight in the past year. But (lead singer) Gary LeVox was just beautifully tan and looked healthy. I said, 'What's up with you?' and he said,

'I clean pools in Nashville.' He was out all night playing clubs and in the day cleaning pools to pay the bills. He was willing to do things he didn't want to do, which made the story even sweeter for me. In the past three and a half years, they've donated $3 million to Vanderbilt Children's Hospital. Their spirit hasn't changed and they haven't forgotten where they came from."

SHeDAISY: Musical Gardens

The group's name, pronounced "Shuh-daisy," derives from a Native American word meaning sisters. Like the Carters, Everlys, and Judds before them, the three sisters who comprise SHeDAISY share a harmonic blend born of common blood.

"SHeDAISY, when they were very young, were signed to RCA Nashville but never put out a record," Howard notes. They had a record deal, it didn't happen, and were probably too young for the format at the time. They waited for Cassidy (the youngest sister) to graduate from high school, then they came to Nashville and did formal demos. "Their harmonies blow you away. Kristen, the oldest sister, has written everything they've done. There's a genius that she has."

With their Utah-born good looks, a trio of sisters is not exactly an unwelcome visage. "In the past, everyone talked about how videos changed everything. I'd be lying if I said it didn't matter to me. For me, 'intriguing' is a better word. In the same way that I like a style vocally. Even though an artist may not be the best singer, perhaps they don't sound like anybody else. In that same way, beauty is one thing and distinctive, compelling looks that are mysterious and dark are interesting. It's not about model beauty."

Blinded by Beatles

Inspired by a certain Liverpool foursome, Howard played in bands throughout high school. "I had the opportunity to work at a radio station in the summers. I'd do station IDs and commercials, so I'd just sit and read *Billboard* magazine all the time. I'd be reading about management companies, and when I graduated, I wanted to go to Nashville because it was a music center. I got my degree, came to Nashville, and worked in a bizarre mastering facility. This led me to get hired by the Welk Music Group, which had an incredible staff of songwriters."

"If you're working for a publishing company and you know the catalog, it's giving you the keys to eventually set up a company. The Welk family sent me to Vanderbilt to get an MBA degree. The old publishing companies were about that. They hired someone and built companies from within. How do you repay that? I'll always admire those guys for doing that for me. I ended up running Polygram Music. Someone said, 'Boy, they must like you a lot to do that.' But if you make somebody money, they'll remember that too."

State of the Country

Howard says changes might come slower in the country, but changes do come. "I think traditionally that the country audience held onto 8-tracks and cassettes longer than everyone else. There's always been that lag in our audience. I know that the bulk of Rascal Flatts' audience is 15- to 30-year-old women, so we've seen that change happen. With the Flatts' albums, about two are stolen for every one legal download, and that has skyrocketed. If you look at bigger country acts, they're approaching those higher numbers now, so downloading is definitely affecting our market. We've accepted that, but we've been hit that hard."

"When we're used to looking at traditional charts, we're heartbroken. You see it's actually being consumed but not purchased by thousands of people. All of us in business should say, 'We're closing the door for music and artists,' but that would be defeatist. Lots of people are actually consuming this music even if it's for free. With Flatts' records, if we see a spike in some city where the record is being downloaded illegally, then we have to assume that we don't have product there. So we're using illegal downloads as a tool to see where there are holes in the market. A lot of people want it to be free; they are not buying, but they're consuming it more than they ever have in history. People are going to find a way to get their hands on good music. Outletwise, you have ringtones, etc., and it will all continue to evolve, but there has to be a way to compensate all those composers and artists. And that's a chore for a generation. As an A&R man, I've got to make some money. We have to change our rulebook."

"We're so dependent on radio. Even a few years ago, we had '15-week records' going up the charts. And the writer and artists were looking at two or three singles a year. What has happened, with the exception of superstar acts, most of the developing acts, their records are taking 40+ weeks to go up the charts and peak. We're lucky to get through one single and start another in one year, and that's affecting everything. If you're on the record side, even if it's top five but it's taken another 20 weeks [to climb there], retailers are already starting to ship that record back. Everything is changing."

"Country radio is still our number-one driver over video, which is now considered insignificant. I will say that word of mouth is a real contender."

No Heels, These Flatts

Despite every downturn Howard mentioned, Rascal Flatts have sold, worldwide, in excess of 20 million records. Clearly the band's powerful combination of accessible songs and authentic spirit inspires huge legions of music fans. "A lot of it is the 'X-factor' and if something moves me as a fan of music. If it doesn't move me, how is it supposed to move anyone else? Many times your heart sinks because it's just not there. I can never judge or pre-judge where an artist or a songwriter comes from, small town or big town, but a guy with a guitar case, a legal pad, and pencil can change my life, and it can change their lives. I'm always open to that."

"When Mark Wright was producing Lee Ann Womack, he asked if he could come by and play me something. He came over and played me her song that would become a hit, and I played him Rascal Flatts' 'I'm Moving On.' We met in college, and 20 years later we were playing each other these potential hit songs. And that's why we came here: It wasn't about the money, it was about great music and moving myself and sitting across the table from friends."

Michael Laskow: Fueling Up on Songs with Taxi

"I see time and time again people don't spend enough time concentrating on writing great material that intersects what the market wants. That's the key to success in the music industry."

It was in the claustrophobic confines of a one-bedroom apartment in Woodland Hills, California, that Michael Laskow initiated Taxi, what was to become the world's largest independent A&R service. A veteran music business pro, Laskow had engineered in studios in Miami, New York, and Los Angeles, and at the time of Taxi's inception was working in audio post-production. "I was sitting in my office and thinking about the dilemma of unsigned musicians not being able to get their music listened to by A&R people. I had just learned about AOL, and I thought, 'Wouldn't it be cool to use an online service to disseminate info about what the record labels and publishers are looking for?'"

Today, Taxi is a membership organization, roughly 11,000 members strong. Record companies, publishers, managers, producers, and music supervisors call the company directly to find new artists and bands to sign. They also call to find hit songs, instrumentals, and tracks for TV and film placements.

"Basically, we will do anything we can to help musicians, bands, artists, and composers in any way we can to get their music under the noses of the people who are looking," Laskow says. "The industry identifies its needs; we put the word out to our 11,000 members in 100 counties around the globe. And they send their music they think fits the need."

When Taxi receives a request, it provides its members with the exact details about what type of music is called for. The company or person requesting the material remains anonymous to protect them from being bombarded with truckloads of unsolicited material. Once received, all material is reviewed by Taxi's A&R staff: 200 highly trained industry veterans who carefully listen to each and every song. If the music is on target for what the listing company has requested, it is forwarded directly to the person who requested it. "We filter it down to that group of songs, then send it back to the industry person that asked for it. If they're interested, they contact writer, artist, composer on their own, say, 'Let's make a deal,' and Taxi is out of the picture at that point." If the music is not ready, the writer or artist receives a detailed, constructive critique on how to make the music stronger.

Oiling Up the Ideas

"A taxi is something that gets you from where you are to where you want to go," Michael Laskow explains. "It is a service vehicle. Back in the day of Checker Cabs in New York, they were strong and secure and friendly as well as helpful—all those good connotations. I invented the term 'Independent A&R.' Prior to that, A&R reps only worked at record labels and were not independent. Because we made it past our first few years, we have remained and thrived and we are the leader. Not only were we the first, I think most people would agree that we're the best."

And Laskow pointedly notes that Taxi is a business, not a charity. "We have a $299.99 annual fee plus a $5 submission fee per song. This prevents people from 'shot gunning.' We've had people send 100 songs for a $500 expense the first day. We don't encourage it; if we see someone do something foolish, we pick up the phone and strongly recommend that they just send their very best material. We've always looked at everything we do in terms of what our customers need, but make a little money along the way."

Statistical probability, Laskow confers, is a determining factor for artists in obtaining record deals regardless of Taxi affiliation. "We have had a few people get record deals. Obviously having a hit is way out of our hands; that's up to record company, the artist, the public, and radio. The truth of the matter is a big manager who has five unsigned artists may only get one of those artists a deal. In today's climate, it is harder to come by. We've been successful with publishing deals from staff writer deals to multiple-song deals, but the majority is getting our members' songs placed in hit TV shows, all over cable and big time movies, and not-so-big stuff. Quirky music is always good for indie filmmakers, they love our stuff. Thousands of members have gotten deals. One of our biggest success stories, Adam Watson and Andy Dodd, had a song forwarded to Carole King's daughter, Sherry Goffin, who was developing Jesse McCartney. Adam and Andy had a hit song, 'Beautiful Soul,' cut by him. The record went platinum and that led to Disney publishing deals for each of those guys. From one single connection with Taxi, their song was on 25 million albums."

Convention Attention

The annual Taxi Road Rally brings together Taxi members from around the world for pitch opportunities, classes, workshops, and one-on-one mentor sessions with industry professionals. From an initial attendance of 350, the rally now boasts attendance of over 2,500 songwriters and artists from around the world. Best of all, for Taxi members, the event is free and they can bring a guest. "The price tag of other conventions is around $600 a ticket. I've spoken and mentored at many of them. I scratch my head as panelists pontificate about how cool they are and the great stuff they've signed and here's their resume and how good they are. I didn't think people were getting any value from this. The first step in creating value is to give it to them for free. That way, they have nothing to lose and everything to gain."

"I didn't invent the format; it existed many years before I came up with it. What we do differently is this: We just don't parade industry big shots and say, 'Look who we know.' We design every nuance of the rally around what our members need. Because we're so close with them, we know what they want to know. We ask industry people the tough questions. They are not as forthcoming at other conventions. Our members are given the keys to the kingdom. They know where the bar is set for the quality of songs. They know how this business really operates and not the fantasy of how they think it operates."

"Our goal is consistently to make it the best," says Laskow. "I wouldn't care if it shrunk in size as long as it gets better. People who have no access because they live so far away in a remote area can come and have a drink with a legendary music pro. People at all stages in the career trajectories are on equal footing and it has resulted with people ending up with deals. A guy from Oklahoma met Brian Howes, who produces Daughtry and Hinder and big acts of the day. I have little doubt that someday our member from Oklahoma will get a song cut as result of the relationship he built with this industry powerhouse at the Road Rally."

Taxi Fare

Laskow believes that the days of artists selling 10 to 30 million albums are behind us. "The majority of the consumers will just steal it. The Internet has leveled the playing field, but nobody has found the magic formula that puts money into the pockets of musicians. Taxi is giving more and more tools to members that dramatically improve feedback and give them specific info to move forward to become better songwriters and artists faster. But everything starts with a song. People ask: 'What does a great bio look like? What kind of picture do I need? Don't hear my stuff, it's not mastered, we have another guitar part to add.' But none of this will create a hit song for you. If it were an amazing song, it could have nothing more than an acoustic guitar. It's our mission to make sure everyone writes the best songs that they can."

www.taxi.com

4 The Producer

The recording artist/producer relationship is often akin to a marriage: A married couple might fight like hell, but they should be in love! A producer is the objective voice, the one who says to the singer, "Put a little twist on this phrase," or to the guitarist, "Something is not working well. Let's approach this line in another way." Since the producer is accountable to both the artist and to the record label, diplomacy is often a virtue.

Some producers are musicians who can play instruments, some are not. While new technology makes "perfection" achievable, perfection does not always make for a real musical experience. A skilled producer will know how to capture the performance, and the recording engineer will create the sonic moment in time.

Rick Nowels: "Green Light" and a "White Flag"

"I still believe people want real and meaningful art, even with a disco beat. That's the world I try to live in."

"I can't say that any one song defines me," begins Rick Nowels. "I've written a lot of songs since the age of 13! I remember Madonna said to me, 'it's about the body of work.' I agree. Of course, the hit songs are the most exciting because they will hopefully live on. For me, the standouts would be 'White Flag' [Dido], 'Heaven Is a Place on Earth' [Belinda Carlisle], 'You Get What You Give' [New Radicals], 'The Game of Love' [Santana/Michelle Branch], 'Body and Soul' [Anita Baker], 'Green Light' [John Legend], 'Rooms on Fire' [Stevie Nicks], and 'The Power of Goodbye' [Madonna]."

Nowels has often written with artists, and the list includes such well-known luminaries as Madonna, Stevie Nicks, Nelly Furtado, Dido, Jewel, Sinead O'Connor, Carlos Santana, John Legend, and Keith Urban. "I like to work with naturals," he notes. "I was a solo songwriter for 15 years before I started collaborating, so I'm most comfortable working with others who come from the same place. They are usually quite capable of writing a great song on their own but choose to collaborate because it's fun and kind of takes you out of yourself. It can be quite liberating with the right partner. It's great to get a song done on inspiration before it becomes work. When you write a strong song with someone, you get a collective ego as a songwriting team. That is a powerful place to come from. You set a bar for yourselves as a writing team."

"The best artists know who they are and are really comfortable creating something from nothing. They are confident melodists and lyricists and have something to say. A song is a short story. I love writers who can say something profound or poignant in a simple way. Language and message is everything as an artist."

"My simple rule is that I want to look forward to the artist walking through the door. I don't really try to write with singers who don't write. There's a lot of that happening these days. Someone said a song is only as good as its weakest writer. Most artists have a strong point of view how their record should sound. There is always a fair amount of experimenting and mixing before you get the final thing. Two strong aesthetics are usually better than one. I'm perfectly happy to co-produce in the right situation. The best rule is to work with people you respect."

End of the Era

"With today's technology, making records is far more democratic than it used to be. You can make really good sounding records with fairly inexpensive gear, so the playing field has been leveled. Having said that, there will always be a small number of producers and writers who rise to the top and consistently make hits. That's true in any artistic field."

"When I started making records in 1986, many of the legendary record people and producers were still working. I got to meet a lot of them. Label executives like Ahmet Ertigun, Lenny Waronker, Clive Davis, Rob Dickens. They set a tone for artistic excellence in the artists that they signed and supported a really high standard of record making. For the most part, if you had a record deal, you had something pretty special as an artist. Then MTV made music a visual experience and image became more important than talent. Technology changed the culture and the marketing followed."

"The whole business has completely downsized, literally from a peak in 2000 to an all-time low in 2008. That's a huge fall! So many good and passionate music people have lost their jobs. That is sad. Money has really gotten tight. The result is that the labels are playing it very safe. They can't afford to stumble on any act, so it makes the signings more conservative. 360 deals have created acts like the Pussycat Dolls, where it's all about tie-in revenues. I don't find this very inspiring for music or culture. But the Internet is leveling the playing field, so we'll see what happens. The major labels won't have a monopoly on music culture anymore. I still believe people want real and meaningful art. Even with a disco beat. That's the world I try to live in."

Nowels currently has two studios, one in Los Angeles and the other in London, where he currently lives. "I like to write and produce in a big, comfortable room with lots of natural light. Like a living room with keyboards, guitars, basses, and percussion. I go to proper studios when I track drums and grand pianos. Over the years, I've worked in most of the legendary recording studios: United Western, Ocean Way, A&M, Conway, Gold Star, Village Recorders in Los Angeles; the Hit Factory, Record Plant, Right Track, and Unique in New York; Mayfair, Sarm, Abbey Road, Olympic, Townhouse, Whitfield Street, and Air Lyndehurst in London. Plus many, many independent studios in many cities and countries. Many of the classic studios have closed down in the past few years. Artists and producers are a little more isolated these days working in their own private spaces. I used to love the random meeting of other creative people working in the bigger studios.

www.ricknowels.com

Howard Benson: Heavy Music

"I was recording a singer who had been through the 12-step process, and he wasn't singing very well. I said, 'You were a better singer when you were a f**king drunk.' He got so mad at me that he threw a Coke bottle across the room and shattered the vocal booth—all the glass."

The All-American Rejects, My Chemical Romance, Relient K, P.O.D., Papa Roach, Hoobastank, Daughtry, Kelly Clarkson: Howard Benson—Grammy-nominated for Producer of Year, one or rock's most prolific producers—has been behind the board for all of them. He makes his decisions based not only on the band or artist, but also on the team around them. "I used to base it on star power and if they had the songs, but now I've added that they need strong management and the record company has to believe in them. I've had experiences where the management has been weak and it's a struggle from beginning to end. Or worse yet, having no management. Obviously, I have to like the music and the artist and there has to be some potential commercially. But I won't produce if there is a problem with the A&R person—that's a huge part of the equation. It can come back to bite you later when you're trying to get the record worked. If the band doesn't have direction, I won't be there. If they don't know who they are, that's a real problem. As far as the songs, I have a lot of say in that. I put pressure on the A&R person and I'm not recording a single note until they have the copyright. I'm not saying the songs have to be finished, but I have to know I can make the record. Maybe it's portions of songs, but if they don't have them, then I'm not going to go into the studio."

The Intimidation Room

Benson notes that one of the most important milestones in his career occurred early on, after being fired by a band, their A&R rep, and a manager. "They wanted to bring in their own people, but I begged them to please let me stay. I wanted to learn. I didn't have any process, was doing it by the seat of my pants." He observed how the band's new producer—an industry heavyweight—got things done. "He didn't take any sh*t, he did it his way. He made songwriters come and background singers come in, and the band that thought they were going to get more now saw that it was now his record. With the way he carried himself and the confidence—he was the man. He had a room called 'The Intimidation Room.' When conflicts came up, he would bring people into this room, with gold records literally from wall to wall, and then he would say, 'But what do I know?' It was hard-core. I learned that if you're going to be successful, you've got to be the man. That was the best moment for me."

While many successful acts eventually co-produce their own project, Benson avows that if a new act requested this, "That's not going to happen. I would only co-produce with artists that have sold platinum or multiplatinum. They would have to want the leadership role, and to understand the process of making records. They might come in as performers, but once they want to be producers, I hold them to that; they might realize that's not a job they want."

In the process of making records, Benson says that the process of creating the final mix can be the most painful. "This is where the artist can be the most anal. In some ways, the important part is done for me: the songs. I've delivered the rough mixes, but that final process, unless you have a confidant mixer, the whole thing can go to sh*t." Among Benson's most trusted mixers is the legendary Chris Lord Alge. "The last thing you want to do is overthink it," Benson concludes. "Sometimes people reinvent the whole record in the mix."

Open Ears, Open Wallets

"I think that overexposure hurts—it's almost like there is no mystery anymore. You can't start a rumor about anything because there are no new rumors anymore," Benson observes. "Record companies are going to sign what they can to make money and create value. I think they're still looking for music; most of the A&R guys I know are really out there looking. But the question is, Is it there? Could the Seattle scene ever happen again? Would people get on airplanes and trek up there to see the next Nirvana or Alice in Chains? Right now we wouldn't do that—we would search in Google: 'Seattle—bands.' And then we would find out if there were any bands up there, and we wouldn't have to even leave our bedrooms. I think that's damaging, but maybe not. To kids, these are the good old days for them—that's how it is—when kids surf on the web, they find things we could never find, things that their friends found, sites we're not aware of. I think the next generation of artist is going to come from this."

"Discovering something on our own and thinking it can be yours? Maybe you grew up on the East Coast and remember when you heard Springsteen—and he was a hometown artist. Now you hear the artists immediately. It's a change of perception whether these guys are special or not. The Beatles landing from Liverpool was a cool thing. If Coldplay landed from Liverpool, it wouldn't be an event because everybody would have heard their music already."

Breaking the Band

Despite the changes that Benson notes, he believes that radio play and touring still exist as fundamental elements in a band's career. "They still have to survive at radio. It's the mass marketing, a passive listening experience, you don't have to be in front of the computer, you can be walking around the house or driving a car. And that's still a way to break bands. Playing shows, having people come out and fall in love with you like Jason Mraz does—that still works, but you have to be great at it. There are a lot of ways to get famous, a lot of apparatus. A group I'm producing now based their entire thing on the Internet—they had 1,000 people at their first show. You have to have great songs; worry about vocals and guitar sounds—that's that—worry about songwriting and your band. Don't get caught up in things that aren't going to affect the final outcome. I see artists get bogged down in the production with ProTools. I don't think it's a fundamental concern. You have to have great songs. It's like a broken record."

Breaking Glass

Finally, what happened with the now-sober singer who tossed the Coke bottle and annihilated the glass in the vocal booth? "Then he sang the sh*t out of the song, and that's the vocal you hear on the record," concludes Benson.

Richie Zito: Behind the Glass

"How can you possibly guide an artist through a career if you haven't done it before successfully? It's like going to a doctor and having her do surgery on you because you think she might be good someday."

Richie Zito doesn't shy away from telling tales and naming names. "I think the statute of limitations has expired—I'll tell you anything you want to know," he chortles. Zito knows a lot: Having been signed as an artist to Atlantic Records at age 15 by the legendary Jerry Wexler, he eventually made his first major impact in the business as a guitar player. "I came to L.A. when I was just shy of 21. I played in a band with Rick James; I was on the road with Bobby Hatfield from the Righteous Brothers, then I joined Neil Sedaka's band when he had his comeback with Elton John's label and won a Grammy with 'Love Will Keep Us Together.' I was in Elton John's band, on movie soundtracks like *Scarface*, *Top Gun*, and *Flashdance* and on Tina Turner's land-mark comeback, *Private Dancer*. I had the good fortune to be successful, and it was through Giorgio Moroder that I transitioned into a record producer. I've always felt that producers came from one place or another—writer/producers or engineer/producers or musician/producers. I'm in the last category."

"What has always inspired me and excited me and made me want to work with artists is the same as when I was a kid buying records. I'm a big fan of voices, of songs, and charisma is a wonderful thing too—that star quality, the X factor, if they can wrap you up in the aura and essence, they can do it to a lot of people." Zito feels that with the current technology, there is a tendency for artists to record long before they're ready. He uses a cooking metaphor: "All the ingredients in the world, but if you take it out of the oven too soon, it's not going to taste good."

Founding Fathers

Zito doesn't believe that developments in recording technology have advanced the sonic craft. "Nobody's put a mic next to an amp today any better than Tom Dowd did—in fact, they don't do it as well," he pronounces. "I was at Atlantic when they signed Led Zeppelin and Cream; the Stax/Volt crowd with Otis Redding, Wilson Pickett, and Aretha Franklin. It was incredible the amount of talented artists who were around that company—it was very A&R driven. Later, I was around the legendary A&R staff at Warner Bros. When those guys said you might want to consider changing the pre-chorus, it was like getting it from the founding fathers—Thomas Jefferson and George Washington. It was a different world; they had the good fortune to allow an artist to develop. That pressure to make sales quotas really handcuffed the creative folks. No one can afford to give artists three records to develop—it's all, 'Now, now, now.'"

Still, Zito says, the search for significant artists is always on. "Everyone is always looking. Teaching at Musicians Institute in Hollywood, I meet a lot of 19 and 20 year olds, really gifted kids. They're not always completely cooked, but they get closer. But it's a rare thing to find that talent. Things have changed with MySpace, digital work, the peer-to-peer networks. Before, the labels always had the advantage because the artists were going to them. Today you can find artists through other artists."

Live Nation

Zito is adamant about one significant requirement for an aspiring artist. "The artist should perform live. It's like the famous showman, P.T. Barnum—an artist has to draw a crowd. I don't care if you're standing on a pier somewhere with a hat and people throwing quarters—you have to stand in front of people and play. And you have to make them come back and you have to make them tell their friends to come see you. I think this is the number one thing that separates the men from the boys and the girls from the women: You have to be able to do that; it's not something you can learn later after you've had success. I saw Billy Joel when I was a kid with his band the Hassles. They were playing every club on the East Coast. So when they did their album, they were able to back it up. A lot of that is God-given, but a lot is experience and hard work."

"Doing it on stage, learning what works with a crowd—the best way to a long career is writing great songs, honing your craft, and not rushing to the studio. Look, I can put you on hold and record a song. But play out and see what works, what doesn't work, what excites people. It's harder in New York and in Los Angeles, where you do one show and A&R is there the next week. The bands who have the opportunities to grow are in the smaller cities. The whole indie record business can help like crazy—the indies serve as farm clubs. Make a record yourself, as long as you have someone who can help you thorough the process, that can really make a difference. Playing live is a real big deal. The difference between now and when I started making records is that back then, everyone could perform. That's why we don't have that many artists now with a full body of work and full careers. Being able to back it up live is really the ticket."

Trick Tosses the Tape

Zito's widescreen production on Cheap Trick's *Lap of Luxury* is a highwater mark in rock records. *Lap of Luxury* also shot the band back into the public consciousness and delivered Trick's only number one, "The Flame." "They hate it to this day," recalls Zito. "They needed some rejuvenation."

Author's Note   "The difficulty for Cheap Trick at that point in time was that they had some major selling albums but now weren't selling many records at all. The label was wondering whether to continue with the band, and naturally the band blamed the label for poor record sales. I was a big fan of theirs. I had just joined Epic from Capitol, had major success with Heart, and believed they could have the same type of resurgent success. They were a proven band, had a definite image, and were a great live act. I felt they could make a great record, and we needed to address that.

I found "The Flame" in England. We played it for the band, and they hated it. It took us a few weeks to convince Robin [Zander] to go in to do a vocal/piano version of the song, and that became the focal point for the whole album. Robin got it! It was a brilliant vocal performance by him. The others were reluctant, but they finally got it, too. The company freaked, and it became a massive number-one record. They hadn't had anything even close to that, and it revitalized their whole career. To this day, they really don't like that song. I understand; it's a fine line. You cannot force things. But I just believed in my heart and soul—and Richie did support it as the producer—that this was a great song and that it would be good for them. It turned out to be great for them. They didn't turn down the royalties that it brought."

—Don Grierson

Zito remembers it this way: "Rick Nielsen took out the tape and threw it against the wall. They refused to do it, but we knew it could be a smash. I went into the studio with the singer, Robin Zander, an engineer, and a keyboard player, and put together a mock-up track. We did one line, he learned it, and then sang and we pieced together a vocal. We thought this was worth fighting for. I dragged the band into the studio. One by one they came. We played the song and at the end of the day, it was a number-one record. They still hate me to this day. But they got what they'd never had: a top record. And I'm proud of the fact that they don't like me."

"When you look at what's selling today and that *American Idol* roster, which is responsible for so many units, it's TV-driven. The Disney crowd? Those records are coming from another medium. It's not like finding an artist in a garage somewhere and saying, 'I found a gem I think is going to have an impact on our culture.' I don't think that exists. Companies can't afford the A&R staff and I don't think too many of them have been involved with successful records. And there's no way to learn."

Dave Sardy: The Producer and the Paradigm

"There will be a new paradigm, because music is more vibrant than ever. People ask me, 'Aren't you scared?' I'm ecstatic. I've had to work with some of the worst, biggest, most arrogant no-talent f**kers ever at record companies. It's frustrating. Seeing them no longer having jobs doesn't bother me."

Brooklyn-born Dave Sardy (aka D. Sardy)—who has worked with luminaries including Slayer, System of a Down, Marilyn Manson, Jet, Wolfmother, and Oasis—came to his current career as a producer and mixer as an offshoot of being a musician. "I played in punk bands and started touring at 14. When I went in to the studio with my second band, I was trying to convince the engineer that punk rock isn't supposed to have reverb on the drums, and he was looking at me like, 'Shut up, little kid.' And I vowed I would never go back into a studio until I knew what every single knob did. I taught myself while I was playing in bands; I started recording stuff in my basement in the days of the cassette four-track. There was a great magazine called *Option* and in the back of the magazine they had people reviewing each other's cassettes. I started making recordings, sending them to other people who also made cassettes. They started sending me their stuff, and I eventually started selling my cassettes to [New York City record store] Bleecker Bob. I'd sell 10 cassettes. It was all very homespun and DIY."

Barkmarket was the name of Sardy's band. He toured with them for almost a decade and the group was signed by producer/executive (currently co-chairman of Sony Columbia Records) Rick Rubin to his Def American label. "There was a great underground scene. You could get in your van and go, and a couple of thousand bucks would get you through." The band, Sardy says, did better in Europe than in the states. "They have a concert and festival culture. They discover a band and become die-hard fans. They bring their children and say, 'I met my wife at your show.' That's supposed to only happen to big bands!"

Inspiration Mediation

What inspires Sardy in the artists he works with is a sense of fearlessness. "It is when you hear something so completely and utterly bold it gives you the impression of, 'What were they thinking and I'm so excited I'm hearing this now, I can't imagine someone was so committed to how insane this idea was that they put it down on tape.' And that's really hard to get across. To go through recording, mixing, mastering, and pressing something up, putting it through so different mediums and experiencing it in a whole other place. By the time the listener hears it, how many steps has it gone through? And for it to have any impact is amazing. Anything that does that, that gives you the hair-standing-up, emotional twist, that's the goal."

Author's Note   When a listener hears music, he or she does not generally analyze or question how simple or complex the recording process was; they simply respond to the end result.

—Don Grierson

Sardy says he begins the process with dialogue, as he explains his vision for the record. "And if they're on the same page with me, then it's a great fit. If not, there's no point in doing the record because we're just going to argue. The fun part about having been an artist—when you self-produce yourself, it helps you produce other people. It's hard to change your perspective so you're actually hearing it, not just doing it. Making a different-sounding record when you make records every day is hard. Artists who don't sound like someone else are few and far between."

"I like records that are three quarters of the way there songwise because the songs are more important than anything else. It's more important to spend time in pre-production than to spend weeks tracking. I'd rather be in the rehearsal studio working on songs than to be in the recording studio with the clock ticking. A song that has the potential to be great has to get to that next plane. Some of the biggest artists I've every worked with are some of the most stubborn and unwilling to take their songs up the hill any further. On some level, it is like admitting that they, or the songs, need help. Almost all songs need something. That is what a great editor is—a great writer has an editor. Part of the job is to be the audience before the audience gets to it and say, 'Hey, this part is boring' or it's not."

80 and Counting

Sardy sends out this challenge to those with whom he communicates at record labels: "It used to be there were more experienced people at the labels and the producers were up and coming. Now I'm talking to people at labels who have made six or seven records while I've made 80. Thirty years ago, all of the artists who are landmark artists didn't have huge first records. Every band I've worked with who had a huge first record has self-destructed. It's almost like it's better to have a huge third record because you now know what you're doing. But the system doesn't allow for that. I'm noticing that more of the new bands I work with who have budgets are a hell of a lot better than they were 10 years ago. There has to be a little bit of a 'This has to work,' as opposed to, 'They look great—this is one good song, let's do it.' My manager, Sandy Roberton (Worlds End Management), and I have turned down hundreds of albums with one hit song. Since I'm the guy in the studio, I'm thinking, 'I don't want to sit around for months and listen to those nine terrible songs.'"

The producer, Sardy says, is the only one in the creative chain who can be brutally honest. "You're up inside their creative process, and you're the only one sitting 'round not hoping to get fired. The manager doesn't want to get fired, the A&R person doesn't want to lose his gig. With young bands, I have to tell them how the business works. I tell 'em I spent 10 years in a van on tour—you're not talking to someone who is imagining how it is out there. I don't know that a lot of people are honest with the band. I believe it's important to be honest all of the time. I guess that's why I'm on this side instead of on the record side."

Out of Tune, Out of Time

Sardy speaks of working on a record with a very successful band and realizing he should have walked away from the project. "They didn't listen to me. I said 'You're making a fateful decision here, this is the wrong way to go and it's not going to work.' And they said 'We're the band and you work for us.' Since then, I've learned to say, 'Find some-one else.' You get to a point where you know what's going to work. Since that moment, every time it's gotten to that point, I've said, 'I'm out,' and people back down. Every huge f**k up creates an incredible lesson. Without them, you get nowhere. Making every single record is like taking a graduate course. Each one has told me so much about something, and it's usually something I'm not expecting it to teach me about, whether it's musical or personal or psychological or creative—it's nonstop, constantly pushing the edges of something."

Dandy Warhols and Marilyn Manson at the Oasis

Sardy's production of the band the Dandy Warhols on *Thirteen Tales from Urban Bohemia* was an immense step up in his career. "I still get checks; it's one of those licensing recordings that keeps on living," he notes. It was the first in a long string of credits, including Jet and Wolfmother, whose debut album Sardy produced, and which won a Grammy for Best Hard Rock Performance; and OK Go, a project Sardy remixed in his home studio, which won a Grammy for Best Video. He has also produced the last two Oasis albums.

"Jet and Wolfmother sound more American than American bands," Sardy says of the two Aussie aggregations. "The Jet guys loved the Dandy Warhols record I did. They did demos and sent me songs. It was one of those 'light' moments: A garage rock record hadn't been made and we had great songs. You can always learn to be a great live band. You can't learn to be a songwriter."

Marilyn Manson is another major Sardy credit. "Marilyn is a culture hound more than a songwriter. He takes what's going on in the world, flips it inside out, and spins it back out. That's art. He's a performance artist within his whole persona. He's one of the smartest, funniest, quickest guys you'll ever meet. We spent nine months in a mansion in the Hollywood Hills. Some days I'd roll in and it would be, 'We can't work until five. Manson is doing a full body cast of himself for some website idea.' We had great people coming by all the time. People were fascinated by him. Insightful, smart, and a nonstop creative lunatic. That's the guy I know."

New Dues

Sardy recently scored the Kevin Spacey film *21*. "I got to a place creatively where, if I didn't do something brand new, I'd bail on music because I have made so many records. In being a composer, you go from being the head honcho to being 29th in line—which the composer is. You're nowhere near the boss—you're trying to serve the movie."

"There was something incredibly positive about the studio system for making movies and the major label system when it was right—you had to be at a certain level to get these very talented people to pay attention to you and then to help you with your craft. It put the game up so high. Just having a program on your laptop doesn't get you anywhere near that. Your favorite classic records had multiple A&R people and managers and arrangers and incredible players. There was this level of the game being raised by that system that made some of my favorite records. We know what goes into great art. That's the job of the producer and the A&R person and the manager. Not just because they're getting a big check."

In all musical journeys, Sardy believes that making music should be making art. "And making art is an internal journey about the external world. If you're not looking at any of that, 'I play guitar or sing because I have a good voice,' you never get anywhere. It's not about the talent level, it's about the intent. Sometimes millions of things get in the way of you thinking how to be a successful person. The role of the producer, the bandmates, or people in your world is to give you those tips every day. To me, it's so obvious. When someone steps in front of a microphone and is in touch with that person inside themselves, for me, coming from a band, I know what it is like being on the other side of the glass."

Ted Bruner: The Long Road In

"You might see some slow years, but if you keep your integrity high and you're putting the pieces together in your head, you will notice all the little signs."

Ted Bruner was in a group that smoked a lot of herb. "Colony was the name of the band. We wanted to be R.E.M. We toured, but our album didn't translate to radio. We would record in Vancouver and be stoned from when we woke up until we went to bed. The album didn't sound how we wanted it to." After another record deal didn't pan out, Bruner moved to Los Angeles to write, produce, and, as he says, "slowly start to build." After co-writing songs for Miley Cyrus, Bowling for Soup, and Plain White Ts, Bruner has achieved major breakthrough success with Katy Perry's *One of the Boys*, co-writing and producing two tracks on the release.

He says that as a producer, he's often in the line of fire. "Producers have the hardest job. They're the ones that get the blame from all sides. If it doesn't work, they get the guns pointed at them from label and the artist. And if it isn't a hit album, they get blamed and have to put in the long hours to fix it when it's not working."

As a songwriter/producer, Bruner allows that even if an artist doesn't have outstanding technical chops on an instrument, their vibe might still be an integral part in the sound. "I love when somebody has their own style and sound, and often even if they aren't that great on guitar, how they play it is part of the personality of the song. In general, I'm pretty lazy. I don't use MIDI, I don't like the idea that I can switch the sound infinitely once I put it down. This gives my recordings a bit of an edge—if I want a sound, I just have to figure out how to make it."

A Co-Writing Kiss with Katy Perry

Viewed as one of pop music's hottest new artists, Katy Perry, given her young age, has had an extensive career in the music business. Ted Bruner recalls his introduction to her: "She originally came in to sing a demo for a song that a couple writers and I were pitching to a Disney project. When her manager heard this song, he said 'Let me bring in Katy, because she needs one more song to seal her deal. She came in and sang it, and she was looking at me crazy the whole time like, 'Wow, this is what I have to do to get a record deal?' I asked her what she liked and she said Daft Punk. I asked, 'Why doesn't your music reflect that? I'd rather break new ground with you, you seem fascinating.' So she came in and we did a couple of songs and finally I kept pushing her to get a bit more emotional. She had been through hard times in the studio and this business; raised to the top so many times, then dropped on her head. If she wrote about that, it would be gold. No way she would just phone that one in. It would capture what she had gone through, what she was feeling."

Respect and Renewal

Bruner maintains that enlisting a supportive team of collaborators is a key component to sustaining a creative buzz. "And that's pretty much up to you, you manage your managers; you build a team and hopefully it's a bunch of people who keep that same mindset, the same energy, and are all hungry enough. I think that as a writer, I know how I write and who I want to work with. I go online trying to find artists on my own. But it's a team effort for sure. My publisher will hook up some stuff, or someone I've written with will tell people about me. The ball gets rolling; if people respect you and know you work hard, then your name gets out there and slowly builds."

"Keep in mind that this is your life—I try to remind people of this all the time. Nothing was happening for me. It was hard, my girlfriend said, 'Who cares? Let's just move to Colorado and live the life we want to right now. Let's just write about this kind of life, instead of why we're so sad that our careers aren't working.' The next day, I wrote a song that got this band a deal overnight. It sets an amazingly bold step. People lose that when money gets involved. Music is a rebellious path; it's all about freedom, and if you lock down and listen to people who are worried about making a buck, that will shave off all the reasons you got into it in the first place—to have an adventurous and exciting life. If you keep that mindset, then the music will keep coming to you."

"After being in the business and not making whole lot of money, the hit allows me to live my life the way I want to. This thing with Katy, that's a big deal, but whatever. It will make a few bucks, but I'm in the same boat I always was in, and I have to get back to work.

"Then my girlfriend and I went to Sedona, Arizona, and were in the middle of nowhere at a gas station, and two girls came driving in and blaring out of their speakers was my song. I thought, 'This is a pretty cool business; now I get it; there are people listening to my song.' It was an overwhelming moment."

www.tedbrunermusic.com

Rodney Jerkins: Soul of the Darkchild

"When I was 17 or 18, I did this remix and it came out pretty decent and everybody liked it. But I remember playing it for someone and they were like, 'You did it once, but can you do it again?' And so I did another remix—it was Gina Thompson, one of my first artists—that blew up in the clubs. I said, 'They said I couldn't do it again, but I did,' and that became my little slogan, my little trademark."

And he certainly keeps on doing it. As a producer and songwriter, Rodney "Darkchild" Jerkins is a soulful powerhouse who aligns himself with a seemingly endless list of platinum-plated acts: Britney Spears, Beyonce, Ciara, Jennifer Lopez, Toni Braxton, Brandy, Monica, Kirk Franklin, Joe, Whitney Houston, Mary J. Blige, Will Smith, Blackstreet, Tatyana Ali, Deborah Cox, and Marc Anthony, among others. If there is one distinctive urban backdrop that illustrates this particular piece of the millennium, it would have to be Rodney Jerkins' stuttering soul grooves under dense, syncopated keyboards with soaring string lines, all seamlessly tied to tight, reductive melodies.

He has been a major player in the music business since his emergence while still a teenager in 1996. His first production gig was for his own self-produced album, a gospel effort recorded when he was just 15, titled, appropriately enough, *On the Move*. He's a self-taught producer; at age 10, he would sneak into his brother Fred's room and play his drum machine and Yamaha keyboard. Both of his parents play piano, an instrument that Jerkins began performing on at age five. He also sang in the choir of the Evangelical Fellowship Church in Pleasantville, just outside Atlantic City, where his father is a pastor. At 17, Jerkins signed a worldwide publishing deal with EMI, to which he is still attached. He currently has his own production company, Darkchild, for his projects and the development of new acts. When he was 18, he bought his parents a house in New Jersey, where he spends time when not recording in New York, Los Angeles, or Miami. He maintains his own studio nearby.

The Gospel Road

Despite his prowess in the modern urban arena, gospel music continues to be Jerkins' most enduring touchstone. He explains, "In my life, I've seen gospel music evolve from traditional to contemporary to very contemporary, and I'm actually happy to be of this era of gospel music. I've worked with the Winans and Commission, and I've seen gospel music actually change, and I've been with some of the artists I've looked up to when I was a kid. I feel like right now it's our time of music, and gospel is going to a whole new direction. It's allowed us to minister to the youth with this full sound."

Still, ever since the days of Thomas Dorsey, there have been accusations that gospel music is too worldly. "Of course," says Jerkins, "but they all stem from each other. R&B wouldn't be R&B if there was no gospel. And gospel is the root of all music. Now, you have a lot of gospel music taking the R&B things that have been happening, with the tracks and the music. And gospel music is saying more now. When Kirk Franklin came out, gospel was competitive against R&B music on the charts. And then it went number one the way it did. Gospel music is moving up in all spectrums of music—not just gospel, but even on the R&B charts, gospel music is getting recognized. And I'm waiting for the day when people recognize it even more."

To what would Jerkins attribute this recent revelation? Are audiences digging deeper for spiritual truths? "I just think at the end of any day, even though I'm writing love songs, Jesus is still closer than any brother. And when you get home, you need some noise that's actually going to speak to your heart. Certain gospel songs hit home and people want to hear that now, they want to hear the Word, the reality, what it is, and that's what gospel is."

Bring in the Singers

Given the weight of Jerkin's track record, are there other established artists that he'd like to work with, but has not yet had the opportunity to do so? "You know, I've worked with everybody I'd ever dreamed of working with," muses Jerkins. "Hopefully, there will be some new artists that evolve in the future. It's funny: Every time I say it, there is another artist coming along who sold 20 million records; you say, 'I want to work with that artist.' Now, you've got people like Christina Aguilera, who is an incredible vocalist."

Jerkins himself is also involved in developing young artists. "I'm excited about it; I really like working with new artists because everyone is always expecting a score with the giants in the industry, but sometimes you have to help make that giant." What are the qualities that Jerkins looks for? "Just something fresh and new," he says, "a style that's different and has got a ring to it that people like, and doesn't necessarily sound like anything out there. Sometimes you come across mediocre talent, an okay singer or whatever or a great image—I've worked with those kind of artists— but I like to find real singers; that's my mission, to find the best artists that can sing."

"Everybody can't sing everybody else's song. You can write a great song, but it may not be meant for someone because it doesn't match their voice. What we may do for a Joe or a Michael Jackson may not be meant for Lionel Richie. So you have to come up with songs for the voice. We craft songs for Brandy, but those songs can't necessarily be for Britney Spears; that's just the way it is."

And although Jerkins works with Joe, Will Smith, and Kirk Franklin, it's his sonic affinity for female artists that has become a distinguishing trademark of his career. "I think it's because the minute that me and the writing team sit down and start writing, we say a female name first. 'Who do you want a write a song for today? Oh, let's write a song for Whitney or Brandy.' We go for a female first. I don't know why—it just happens that way."

Jerkins' brother, Fred, and Lashawn Daniels are key components in the crafting of songs and tracks. But Rodney is deliberately vague when discussing their mutual creative process.

Vague, but not deceptive, because ultimately music seems to be something Rodney Jerkins feels and does, rather than something he intellectualizes or is comfortable talking about. Consequently, there are no lofty metaphors, no long, confiding stories. Witness this sparse testimony on the craft of songwriting: "Basically what I'll do is I'll build a track, then my writers will go in the room and start pounding away on melodies, and we'll try to come up with the best melodies possible. Whoever comes up with the best melody wins. And," he concludes, "that's just the way it is."

A Shot of Brandy

Jerkins is now reunited with Brandy, having first worked with the singer on her 1998 multiplatinum sophomore set, *Never Say Never*. Jerkins, the executive producer of the singer's latest full-length release *Human*, also produced the first two singles: the uptempo "Right Here (Departed)" and "Long Distance," a ballad co-produced with Bruno Mars.

"Right Here (Departed)" is a co-write between Jerkins and a Los Angeles–based songwriting collective known as The Writing Camp: Evan "Kidd" Bogart, Erika Nuri, and David "DQ" Quiñones. The song is an ideal example of what TWC does best, as it taps the collective consciousness of modern-day pop, infuses it with soulful overtones, and delivers an irresistible melody and snappy, precise lyrics.

Some artists, the trio avow, prefer hearing tailor-made demos; others prefer something more generic. "Sometimes if they hear a demo singer that sounds like them, they won't respond," says Nuri. A&R reps, Quiñones believes, often prefer to hear demos that sound like the artist. "But the artist might not like it." Having the artist come in and demo the song avoids this pitfall. "Men, in general, will hear a guy vocal and think, 'I'm going to come in and crush that vocal,'" says Quiñones. "If there is a female demo that kills it, it can be intimidating to a guy. I would advise songwriters to represent the song the way you hear it," he continues. "You can always tame it down if you need to. It's always harder to add on to it. Let them hear your vision. When we demo, the backgrounds are full out, but the lead vocal won't be as crazy. We want the artist to hear what they would do with it." Nuri says it's about having the right voice on the song. "Because if you get the wrong voice, it can totally change the song." Distinctive artists, Quiñones concludes, can define a song. "Think about it—there are certain hits that wouldn't have been hits for other artists." Bogart says he prefers it when artists make the songs their own. "Our songs are just blueprints for other artists to come in and say, 'I want to build on that' or, 'I love the house as it is; I'll just take it move-in ready.'"

Mississippi Ministerial

Clearly, Brandy has control over the recording process, and nowhere is this more evident than when she cuts vocals. She avows that the solitude inside the studio is her favorite creative space. "I don't have the huge belting type of voice where I'm blowing everybody out of the water. I'm more of a stylist. I love creating different moods. I'm so serious and focused in the studio. That's my favorite place to be. I wish I could just put out albums and go back in and do more, that's how I wish my career would work. Unfortunately, you've got to get out there and do other stuff. But the singing and creating is the most fun—that's when you can see who you really are, in the studio."

Born in 1979 in McComb, Mississippi, Brandy began singing in church at age two. She relocated with her family to Carson, California, when her father became a minister of music for the Southside Church of Christ in Los Angeles. In 1994, at age 15, she recorded her first album. She was cast on the television series *Thea* before she assumed the title role of *Moesha*, a show with a huge audience that became the most-watched show on the UPN network. Whitney Houston, the teenager's idol, requested that she take part in a remake of *Cinderella*, in which Brandy would star as the mistreated princess-to-be. The made-for-TV Disney film, a first-ever with color-blind multiracial casting, captured over a million viewers and maintained its popularity by becoming the most-watched Disney TV movie ever.

Following her debut, Brandy didn't return to the recording studio until 1997, and her second album, *Never Say Never*, included a single recorded with Monica, "The Boy Is

Mine," that earned the singer a Grammy and sold over 14 million copies worldwide. 1998 also marked the year that Brandy made her big-screen debut in the film *I Still Know What You Did Last Summer* with Jennifer Love Hewitt. The film grossed over $40 million at the box office and officially crowned Brandy as a movie star.

Her next release, *Afrodisiac*, marked the advent of the grown-up Brandy, and recently *Human* extended that maturity. In R&B, the role of the producer is crucial, she affirms. "The legendary musicians had the great producers they could create with. It's about finding people you can shine with rather than someone overshadowing you or making the track too strong for my voice. Hopefully you have the same passion, vision, and voice when you're creating. I have a great chemistry with Rodney Jerkins."

But she's not about impressing the suits. "The industry isn't that important. People are going to like you or they're not. You can't always impress the industry; it's a hard industry to please. I just have to pay attention to what I do and make great music for my fans, and that's what it's all about. The industry is just an avenue to get my music out there."

www.darkchild.com

Kenny Aronoff: Brilliance in the Beat

"I'll never be as good as I want to be, but I'll spend the rest of my life trying to be as good as I can be."

If there is one rock drummer whose presence on the modern-day throne is truly ubiquitous, it would be Kenny Aronoff. Although he is best known for firing the gunshot backbeat for John Cougar Mellencamp, he has also toured with Bob Seger, Smashing Pumpkins, Joe Cocker, Melissa Etheridge, and John Fogerty. His equally impressive studio gigs include recording sessions for Bob Dylan, Elton John, Carlos Santana, Ray Charles, Waylon Jennings, the Highwaymen, Meatloaf, Jon Bon Jovi, Kelly Clarkson, Michelle Branch, Puddle of Mudd, Alice Cooper, Toni Iommi, Black Sabbath, and Ricky Martin. "I always wanted to be diverse," Aronoff says, "and it's paid off immensely."

Aronoff surmises that he was born with an immense amount of energy. "When you're a kid, what do you do with that energy? I grew up in Massachusetts. I remember seeing a marching band come into my small town on Memorial Day, and I was so blown away by the drumline. I would follow them on my bike. I took piano lessons when I was 10, but what got me into playing music was seeing *A Hard Days Night* in the movie theater, and that sealed the deal. A week later, I had a band. All I had was a snare drum and a cymbal."

The Swing Thing

Although he's a rocker, Aronoff observes that jazz drummers provided a key influence on his style. "My biggest influence was Mitch Mitchell [the Jimi Hendrix Experience]—a jazz drummer playing rock 'n' roll. I play rock 'n' roll, but I have this swing thing in my playing. The greatest drummers have influences of jazz and swing, because that came before rock 'n' roll. In between the beats comes this feeling—the swing element. I can relate to drummers that are musicians who are listening to other musicians, and that's what makes them sound amazing, when they place all the notes against the other musicians. This feel comes from listening."

Stage to Studio

Since Aronoff is notable both as a live and session musician, he indicates that there are striking differences in the approaches. "Recording is focusing on one song. Live, you're focusing on an entire evening—a lot of songs put together into one big song and so much more to remember. Both can be very intense: The studio is like looking through a microscope and a show is like looking through a telescope. Both are very complex."

For the microscopic world of the studio, Aronoff reveals what makes a magic session. "In some cases, musicians are creating the music to a large degree. Some of the great producers are the ones that step in and hire great musicians, then shut their mouths and let the musicians create. And that's what makes those situations amazing—when musicians are extremely creative and make a huge contribution in everything that's happening. You could have a great song and a producer, but the genius comes with guys who play the instruments. The feel, the hook lines that become melodies and make the song forever recognizable."

In the modern recording scenario, where ProTools and similar studio gadgetry often supplants the live recording process, Aronoff believes that creators are cutting corners at the expense of the music. "People are throwing the baby out with the bath water. They end up looking at a computer screen and not using their ears enough. It's not all black and white. In general, a lot of music today starts to sound the same because they cut a lot of creativity out. The energy of great musicians into one room—you can't compete with that. Basically, by human nature, we are creatures that like to touch, engage, and feel things and interact with people, we're not supposed to be by ourselves. Tech music might sound great, but it's more robotic and not human. You leave the song feeling lonely because you are not engaging in human nature's biggest attributes. New equipment today has all these features and effects, but it doesn't represent honest human interaction. Music is a reflection of that."

Educated Notions

Aronoff credits his educational background with making him a stickler for preparation. "I am classically trained. I learned to read, write, and conduct in college at Indiana University. I would prepare solo pieces and work under a conductor. I spent one year working two hours a day to prepare for one performance. This gave me the tools to know how to prepare, but mostly I have a desire to do a great job. Learning how to read and write music helped a lot. When I go into a studio, I will not record until I have the form down exactly from beginning to end. I can write out every note if I want to. At a more casual session, I go out and play through the song and it's 95 percent right. This then allows the director to work with me; he doesn't have to worry whether I know the song or not, which allows the artist and producer to be more creative. I was just asked to replace a drummer for Styx. I spent 35 hours just studying his drum fills—every note in detail. This will make the other musicians feel comfortable, as if that drummer was still there."

Pick Up the Sticks

For aspiring drummers, Aronoff offers this straight-ahead advice: "Practice technique and practice to be good on your instrument. I call it 'punctual practicing.' Practice what will make you sound good today, and what will make you sound good in the future. Longevity comes from doing the things you love doing. Play music you love and it will keep you wanting to work hard and you will be willing to make sacrifices, but you have to be able to take care of business too."

And odds are that as you are reading these words, Aronoff, somewhere, is prepping for another gig. "I'm a workaholic; I would rather play music than not. It's not about money, it's about an experience that could be amazing. I don't remember ever saying no."

www.kennyaronoff.com

5 The Mixer

Hip-hop, R&B, rock, pop, and dance: A mixer's forte is that he understands the sound and feel requirements of a specific genre. There are mixers who are brought in to create the appropriate sonic mix for radio formats or to do remixes for dance clubs—that is, to create an enhanced or alternative version of a song that already exists.

The hot guys get the big bucks. Remixes, from a cost factor, can be very expensive. And although the music can't be "fixed in the mix," a creative, knowledgeable mixer can hear the song with a fresh set of ears and ready it for the marketplace.

Manny Marroquin: Above Board

"This is about learning as much as you can and leaving the ego aside. Music changes constantly, and if you don't keep up, you won't be in demand."

Manny Marroquin, one of the most in-demand mixing engineers in the industry, has worked with artists such as Carlos Santana, Whitney Houston, LeAnn Rimes, Tupac, Biggie, Alicia Keys, Craig David, and Pink. His talents are equally in demand for hit producers such as Babyface, Soulshock & Karlin, Warryn Campbell, Kanye West, Brian Michael Cox, Tim & Bob, and many others. With numerous Grammy nominations, Marroquin is in possession of two of the golden statues: for his work with Kanye West (Best Rap Album) and Alicia Keys (Best R&B Album).

Born in Guatemala, Manny moved to Los Angeles with his family when he was nine. His musical talents became obvious at age 11, when he began playing drums. A few years later, at the prestigious Hamilton High School for the Arts, his love of drums was replaced by his passion for technology: "They had a MIDI studio, and I became really interested in electronic music. By 11th grade, I was pretty much in charge of the studio and knew that after graduation I wanted to be in a studio. I didn't really know what a mixer did, but I knew that I wanted to mix."

Master of the Mix

"My first real gig was being a runner at Enterprise Studio," says Marroquin. "I was 19 or 20 when I started being a runner [the low man on the totem pole of studio employees, often a "go-fer" who fetches coffee—or other libations—for the clients]. I became really aggressive and tried to not to become a career runner. I went from a runner to an assistant. I did that for a couple of engineers; whenever they had engineering sessions, they'd call me. Eventually, I did a rough mix for a client who was really impressed, who then called his partner and said, 'We found someone to mix the whole album.' The album never came out, but I had a lot of experience working on it. Then I did Japanese and Taiwanese records—I could mess them up and no one was going to judge me."

From there, Marroquin says his career advanced steadily. "It was a very gradual thing and I'm glad I went through it. I started to do hip-hop records and then remixes. Producers from Denmark paid me to mix, and from that came a lot of remixes and then a couple of big albums. Before I knew it, people were calling me. I didn't really know why—there wasn't a specific hit, it was just gradual."

Dance to the Music

Among the songs remixed by Marroquin are "Waiting on the World to Change" and "Gravity" by John Mayer, plus tracks by John Legend, Brandy, Ludacris, Duffy, and Jennifer Hudson. He compares being a remixer to being a sonic interior decorator. "I get the files and a rough mix. They give me a road map, then I do my thing. I analyze what they're trying to go for; I want to make it sound like their vision, but with my touch. They might say, 'I want the couch against this wall,' but then I pick the couch and the fabric."

"I don't ever forget what I was hired to do. I wasn't hired to write or give an opinion, I was hired to mix, and I have to be a professional. Anything that affects you personally will affect the mix. I will try to find something in a song, and I put all my emphasis on that and build from there. Maybe after I put my flavor on it, the song that I didn't like originally I eventually like better. I try to put my focus on the positive stuff in the song and to not concentrate on things I don't like. Sonically, I'm a drummer, so I like to concentrate on drums. In pop music and rock, it's about the rhythm section."

The Mystery of Music History

Marroquin stresses that possessing a strong musical sense and having a deep knowledge of music history are prerequisites to becoming studio-savvy. "Listen and analyze records in different genres. You have to have a good sense of the song and the vibe from your favorite records. So study music; and there's no right or wrong, it's simply your interpretation of it."

"This business is about rejection, and you have to be aware of that. I always say, 'What doesn't break you will make it stronger.' They may not like my first 10 mixes, but I'm going to learn from every mix and try to get better. I still consider myself a student. You have to keep learning and not stop. This is about learning as much as you can and leaving the ego aside. Music changes constantly, and if you don't keep up, you won't be in demand. See rejection as constructive criticism. You have to stay open-minded to new things, because you don't really know when the next thing will change the business of recording."

www.mannymarroquin.com

Phil Tan: Golden Faders

"It's a matter of chemistry and relationships and what have you done for me lately?"

As one of the most highly respected mixing engineers in the business, Phil Tan has created mixes that have appeared on over 220 million albums and singles sold to date, for artists such as Mariah Carey, Gwen Stefani, Jennifer Hudson, Ne-Yo, Usher, Nelly, Snoop Dog, Jermaine Dupri, Alicia Keys, Killer Mike, Janet Jackson, among many others.

A two-time Grammy winner, Tan frequently works with producers StarGate, J. R. Rotem, Polow da Don, and the Neptunes. He maintains close ties to hit producer Jermaine Dupri. Tan, who is based in Atlanta, relates that he originally met Dupri at a TLC session at Soundscape Recording. "Atlanta was a pretty small town at the time, from a musical standpoint." Tan, who was born in Singapore and came with his family to the U.S. when he was 18, says he was bored in college and wanted to do something that would be fun. "Things just kind of worked out. When people ask how I got here, I say 'luck.' I arrived in Orlando, Florida (where he attended recording school) and made telephone calls for internships." Tan says that he and Jermaine Dupri clicked instantly. "Being in the right place and right time is important."

New School and Pro Tools

Tan confirms that what a mixer does is to "make things sound a little better. Technology has come down in price. Back in the day when I practiced, I had to go into a real studio, whereas today, if you have a couple grand, you can buy a laptop and Apple Logic and have a lot of the tools that professionals have already. And you can work on your own. Producers and artists will come in with a close concept of where they want the song to be already. Sometimes, there's someone who wants a reinvention of a song. They don't know where to go with it, and they ask me to take it somewhere else. And then I'm acting as a producer."

As far as equipment is concerned, Tan says the simpler, the better. "I mostly work with Pro Tools. We basically convert everything to audio and import it to that. With speakers, I was an NS10 [small reference speakers] guy for a long time, but they got to be more fatiguing for me, so I switched."

Tan says that he bases his decisions on what project to do primarily on the people involved. "I will work with anybody. If someone comes and says, 'We have a new artist, we don't have a Mariah Carey budget,' I will take a listen, and if I think I can help, I will say, 'Yes.' Knowing that they are a new artist and they don't have the same budget doesn't matter to me. With most established artists, typically they will pay you more up front. International acts are most likely to say yes to remix royalties. It's weird to say that one thing is more successful than another; I don't look at things from a commercial standpoint. I want to make a good product, but the relationships with the people are what I take away from the experience more than how well something does."

"Because of my long relationship with Jermaine, I almost never say no to him. There have only been two mixes I haven't done of his since 1992. One was an All Saints remix in London, and my mom had surgery, so I couldn't go." Tan says Dupri prefers to work closer to home. "He has his own facility here. And he's a creature of habit and he knows all the different places he wants to reference his mixes. That's where he feels comfortable. When he has to mix in the different location, he never really enjoys the project."

In the Mix

Keeping everyone in on the process of hearing the music, Tan says, is crucial. "The songwriter, producer, artist, and artist management will have a lot to say, as well as A&R executives and radio people. And with film work, you have the music supervisor and chief sound mixer who will comment as well. It can get pretty weird sometimes. Typically, hardly anyone shows up to mix sessions. I have done work with producers StarGate, originally from Norway. We've done plenty of records together, but I've never met them."

For aspiring mixers or engineers, Tan says his advice depends on the person and what they're after. "If I'm directing this towards a younger group, I would have to say get rid of any sort of sense of entitlement that you may have. You will have to work for everything that you want. Nobody is going to just give it to you. I see that from a lot of kids. They think things are going to happen just because, and it really doesn't work that way. I don't know if I would recommend this industry to most people."

"There is something which is killing the creative part of the industry. Delusion is a major part of it. You have to be honest with yourself—if a record isn't good, then start over. Have a point of reference, and if you're not sure what you want to get, then find a similar song that has same general tone or energy or vibe to get a point of reference and try to re-create that vibe in your own mix. I never just go in blind and start working on something without a plan."

DJ Escape/DJ Johnny Vicious: Fire on the Dance Floor

"The straight boys were looking for a piece of ass. They found what they were looking for and were out by 3 a.m. But the gay boys knew the music, and they stayed until the lights went up in the afternoon. The music was part of their lives, just as it was mine."—www.djescape.com

"I haven't found a really good artist—a diva. If I could meet a Loleatta Holloway right now, I'd love it."—DJ Johnny Vicious

DJ Escape is a DJ/remixer/producer who cut his teeth in the hallucinogenic gay dance palaces of New York. "A lot of my stuff was played by legendary DJ Junior Vasquez and was driven by my relationship with Salsoul Records. I used a lot of their vocals. From there, it got picked up in Europe, where everyone loved Salsoul. My records were promoted in Europe and my name got well known. As a DJ, no one knew who I was—my productions got me famous. As they spread out in Europe and all over the world, I was invited out to DJ. I played Ministry of Sound in London. After I played there, agents called me to book me all over Europe: Germany, Italy, and England. From there, I got booked by the actual promoters in Australia. The same promoter from Sydney had the other cities. Back then, there was no e-mail, it was a phone number on your record. They would contact our office and book me here and there. Now it's all e-mails, your website, and MySpace."

DJ Johnny Vicious relates that dance pioneers like Frankie Knuckles influenced his sense of direction. "When I was playing records as a DJ, it got to the point I was playing for the same people every weekend. I was playing a place where there was hip-hop and house music and I needed to make a segue between the two. So I made a record that went from hip-hop to house and back and forth. It was my production, but I took other people's music to do it. The mash-ups you hear about today? I did the same thing to make a segue back in the early nineties. That got me into doing music and making remixes."

"I knew Johnny even before I started doing dance music," says DJ Escape. "I was into hip-hop and we had a lot of mutual friends and we became close. A couple of years ago, we got together and collaborated. He brought his style that matches my style—a cross between what happens in the gay clubs and the straight clubs. When we get together to mix, we feel like we hit everyone."

Anatomy of a Remix

A remix is an alternative version of a song, created through the studio alchemy of audio mixing to compose an alternate master recording. Often the remixer will add or subtract elements of the song, alter the equalization, dynamics, pitch, tempo, playing time, and other musical components. While some remixes involve substantial changes to the arrangement, many are subtle, such as creating a "vocal up" version of an album cut that emphasizes the lead singer's voice. Remixes can give a song that was not popular a second chance at radio and club play or make it more suitable to specific musical genres or radio formats—especially dance clubs.

DJ Johnny Vicious says that a remix supports a record, but in essence, there are many key elements to breaking one. "Right now in the U.S., it's a matter of radio breaking the song and us supporting it with a mix. Nowadays, with the Internet, anyone can get anything. You can get something from someone's blog—anything you want. Now, if a listener has it on an iPod or computer, you're breaking a record. When you're in a club and you're playing to 2,000 people and you play a song they've heard on the radio, you're breaking a record in the club. Before there was a handful of people going out after hours in New York and if a record played and everyone went nuts, you'd break a record. Now everyone is spread out, with so many genres, the mash-up has taken over. There's a good house scene here, but I think radio needs to support a record and we need to support a record to break it."

"The only way to break it in the club scene is if there is a real good mix on it. There's no breaking into radio from the club scene anymore, unless it's a dance radio station. What the major labels do is use a remixer to have support in the clubs. For smaller acts on an indie label, it is very important for us to play that record in the club so they'll be played on BPN, the satellite dance radio station. It's a weird vibe right now, it's not like it was 10 years ago. People are making their own decision on the radio stations; they don't even go to the clubs, and if they do, they're there for an hour, and they're probably not going to the right clubs. But they're looking at other playlists. And as a DJ who compiles a lot of compilations, I know the A&R at the labels do not go out and party at the clubs. They're looking at radio playlists, *Billboard,* and chart sales. When you do find a record being broken in the clubs and on the DJ playlists, you know you're going to have a successful artist."

Bodies on the Dance Floor

"I always want to introduce new music, but you can't do that without playing things the audience knows," says DJ Escape. I always drop 'Sweet Dreams' in the middle of nowhere. I could play an hour of new music you feel you're connecting with, but as long as they hear things they know, it will keep the dance floor happy. The new music is very exciting, but for me, it's hard to play a set of unfamiliar music. My crowd needs to hear something they can sing along to. I can feed them 12 new songs and then I play a bunch of oldies they were dancing to 10 or 15 years ago."

DJ Johnny Vicious qualifies, "The straight scene is the mash-up between the house and hip-hop and electro and hip-hop. Everyone samples rock records and puts in vocals. In Atlanta, for example, there are big straight clubs. You'll always get the house club in the after-hours scene. People go to clubs to hear house music and their hands are going to be in the air all night. With the Internet, everything has come together. Everything is being played west to east, Florida to Canada, and that's a really good thing. Ten years ago, there was a big difference: San Francisco was hugely house and New York City was banging. Then trance spread, and they were playing that until three years ago, then electro, that is now big from coast to coast. New York, I have to say, loves the tribal: the Portuguese sound, the Colombian sound, and sounds from Spain."

From Beat One
DJ Escape offers this advice to DJs aspiring to create an identity as a remixer: "Find a sound you like and find your own niche in that sound to make yourself special and stand out. Anyone can be a DJ and put your record together, computer programs can do it, but it's the sound you create and the vibe that gives you an identity. For anyone starting out now, pick a style of music, express yourself, and be different from what's out there."

www.djescape.com

www.johnnyviscious.com

Karmatronic: The Big Beat from Budapest
"The most important thing we believe is that you have to love and believe in the art that you are making with all your heart. With that, success is born!"

Karmatronic, a remix duo founded by Achilles Sparta and Peter Krajczar with the help of their New York–based manager Moe Cohen, made their name producing remixes for major labels. A huge hit, Beyoncé's "Ring the Alarm," upped the duo's profile considerably. Since then, they have established themselves as major mainstream remixers, working with such artists as the Pussycat Dolls, John Legend, Michelle Williams, Kelly Rowland, Amerie, Tiffany Evans, Jennifer Hudson, Mary Mary, and many more. The duo's first *Billboard* radio hit was "We Break the Dawn" by Michelle Williams, and they have since chalked up numerous number-one Billboard club-play remixes. Among their recent projects are "I Hate This Part" by the Pussycat Dolls, "Single Ladies" and "If I Were A Boy" for Beyoncé, and John Legend's "Green Light."

Achilles Sparta is also a managing director at the top dance radio station in Hungary, Roxy Radio. Now, Karmatronic plans to record and to release their own debut.

Borderless Sounds

The origins of their collaboration began when Achilles, with profits from his enterprises in the business world, built a studio. Meanwhile, Peter had been working with electronics and keyboard manufacturer Roland Europe S.p.A. and producing beats to be featured on the company's equipment. Both Peter and Achilles, who met on the DJ circuit, were looking for a way to take their skills to the next level. "We bring two very different styles to the table," says Achilles. "Almost 'Beauty and the Beast'–like, with Peter bringing the beauty of the keyboard and me with the beast of the bass."

The duo also have a label, Karmatronic Records, an outgrowth of their remixing career, a vehicle to bring other DJs and Eastern European artists together and give them opportunities in the West. "Music without borders," says Achilles. "We produce almost all the music on our label, but have recently picked up a few bands and artists that have current music, but we look to produce any new tracks here in our studio in Budapest."

Label Copy

"I think where we are a little different, we actually were producers first, remixers later," continues Achilles. "Our first group had a break-beat musical style. At the same time, we also produced a hit in Italy called 'Radio Deejay' (which hit number one on the radio), and from there our network began to grow. After that, we came to my very good friend Moe Cohen. He had family in the music industry in New York and he was able to get us a Beyoncé track on spec. This was 'Ring the Alarm.' Columbia Music purchased our first-ever remix. We didn't believe Moe at first, but then he sent us the CD with our names on it. We were in shock—amazed! We finally made it. Where we come from, to work with someone like Beyoncé was unheard of."

Clubland

With their successes, the duo entertains a number of offers, both business and social. "Once you establish yourself and become known, it's true you do get invited everywhere, but we find our name alone is not enough—we still need a good booking manager. For now, we are working in the studio a lot during the day, visiting as many clubs as we can at night. To us, our music is more of a spiritual event, feeling the karma in the room, if you may. It's not enough to be a DJ and to play what is hot at the time. You need to feel a room out and to channel the vibe you are getting from the floor."

In Eastern Europe, the underground clubs are key to breaking music. "When you get that feeling, the screams of a crowd that send shivers through your spine, you know you have a special hit. It usually takes almost a year for that hit to get to radio, and by then the clubs have moved on," says Achilles.

Working with major and minor labels, the duo notes a decided difference in philosophies for the remixes they create. "The majors need and want you to use most of the vocals in your dance track to give it a more mainstream feel. When you work with independents, you have the ability to be a lot more creative with the track. These are two extremely different approaches."

Since dance music is global and relies more on beats and production than lyrics, it can capture more listeners. "What is great about the UK and Europe is that for the dance remixes, the majors seem to be more flexible there. If they feel the dance mix has a better feel for their audiences, then there are times that they go to radio with it. I think dance tracks have a much higher success rate in the UK and Europe than in the U.S."

While the duo receives requests worldwide for their talents, they pick their projects carefully. "It is not about the money. To us, it needs to be qualitative and quantitative. There are times we do multiple remixes so the artist has options depending on the market."

For aspiring remixers, Karmatronic offers this simple directive: "Do it because you love it and have the passion for it."

www.karmatronicrecords.com

6 The Manager

Although the struggle of a fledgling manager attempting to launch the career of an artist often seems overwhelming, consider the opposite position, when a manager represents a singer or a band who everyone wants a piece of: TV, news outlets, magazines, radio station appearances, record company promotion, domestic and international touring, and other various aspects of exploitation. The manager oversees all of these elements and works with all of the varying entities involved.

A manager must possess more than just an unwavering belief; he or she should have a widescreen view of the possibilities and certainly a career vision. It might be said that a manager doesn't know everything, but he or she needs to find answers and deal with a diverse cast of varying entities.

Whether a dictator, a babysitter, or a confidant, the best managers are rare. As you will read in this chapter, the artist-management bond is one of the most fundamental links in the music business.

Jim Guerinot: Managing the Music

"The sale of pre-recorded music has diminished, but there's so much more that's going on. You can't focus on what's not working when there are so many other opportunities. There are more opportunities for music than ever before."

A corporate gig with a record label and the freewheeling career of an artist manager: disparate pursuits to be sure, but Laguna Beach–based Jim Guerinot (Rebel Waltz Management) has handled diverse enterprises with equal aplomb. Today, as one of the most respected managers in the music business, he represents superstars No Doubt and Gwen Stefani, Nine Inch Nails, Social Distortion and Mike Ness, Offspring, and a young Canadian band called Hot Hot Heat.

Guerinot was general manager at A&M Records when he also managed Social Distortion. "I was a manager before I worked at a label. When you are starting out, you don't realize the many hats you will be required to wear. When you get older, you look back; it's then that you realize, 'I was a booking agent, graphic designer, and I was a record company.' I was all of those things before starting at A&M. I had in fact booked national tours for bands acting in a booking agent capacity. I did artwork on a weekly basis for [concert promoter] Goldenvoice. I'd never taken classes, and when I ran out of ideas for advertising, I would laugh and say, 'Just put more skulls in the ad.' I had to rub out letters before I had the first Mac Plus computer in '85 or '86, and I'd try to make it look quasi-professional."

"I had a number of different areas of experience because basically I was willing to do whatever I could to not have to put cheese on shelves at Vons. When I could quit my job at a supermarket was really one of the most successful moments of my life. I was doing something that I loved and was thrilled to be able to do it and pay my rent."

The general contractor of the remodel is the way that Guerinot views the management capacity. "We're not plumbers, but we have our hands in the plumbing, we're not landscapers, but we make sure that it's working. We oversee all the subcontractors and the timing of the subcontractors. We're not looking to have the guy paint the house before the drywall or the plumbing is in. It's our job to stage the activity to maximize the opportunity. I love that. When I went into A&M Records, my management experience was a tremendous asset to me because I was able to think like the artist. The artists are not thinking exclusively of their recording careers. It is a huge part of it, but it's not the only part of it. But the ability to think along the lines that the musicians were thinking with a broader scope definitely helped me."

Hands on the Talent

Signing acts with the potential of career longevity is Guerinot's priority. "Neil Young is a perfect example. I love him and all that he stands for. If you're going to end up with the time and trouble, you want it to happen for a long time. I recently celebrated my 10-year anniversary with No Doubt; Nine Inch Nails put out their first record in 1989, and Social Distortion and I put out our first record in 1979. Offspring's been around since 1984. There's something about that that's appealing to me. They have careers, and if you have careers, it means that on a financially mercenary level you can sustain periods where there's no income and make better creative choices. For Bruce Springsteen, *Nebraska* was a reasonable career choice because he already had a long body of work, whereas that kind of record for a pure pop artist can be career ending, and all the time that you've spent with that artist means, 'Wow, it's over and now we have to start from scratch again.' It's not as interesting to me musically and doesn't make sense businesswise."

Guerinot says he has made a real effort not to sign additional acts. "I don't want a large roster. As we say in the office, you don't want to find yourself an opportunity to sign incredible talent, then all of a sudden realize you can't because you have such a large roster that you have time issues. At the end of the day, I like to have a very personal hands-on involvement with each one of my clients. That's part of why I love the label business—I felt like I was managing from above. I still like to design the flier, if you will. I really enjoy the hands-on experience. And as you become more of an exec, you get paid more but you get more removed from the day-to-day stuff that got you in the business in the first place that you still really enjoy doing. I wanted to bring that more in balance, and the only way I'm able to do it is to keep my roster small so I can plug in and comment about a band's set list and possibly write down the sequencing that I think works, as opposed to just kind of managing the process, but actually managing the client."

"With my clients, I have a personal stake and a personal part of each and every one of them. I like that and I don't want to get away from that. I don't want to have 20 clients and just be managing managers who are managing managers managing bands. That doesn't mean it's wrong or not effective, but it's just not for me, personally."

Truly liking the act, Guerinot says, is also a necessary part of the equation. "I've had a tremendous number of opportunities to sign multiplatinum artists that would generate a lot of money that I choose not to do, because I'd feel like that's just punching the clock to make a buck, and I'm making a buck, I don't mind being competitive with the financial side of it, but I'd rather be doing it with something where I feel I'm investing my time and my company's time in something we believe in that will last a long time."

After No Doubt sold an astonishing 17 million copies of their watershed CD *Tragic Kingdom*, they were in the market for new management. "They met with virtually everyone in the business. And it just came down that: I just got the gig. I convinced them that I would best serve what their interests were. Same thing with NIN. Trent [Reznor] met with everybody, and there were capable people that were interviewed, but I definitely didn't have the scale of roster that the others have. I had the ability to say, 'I've been waiting for you, and I don't sign a number of acts; I wait until the great ones become available and I sign them, and you're one of them. And I've got the time to do this job the way you'd like it done.'"

Image Consultant

The Beatles' haircuts, Elvis Presley's sideburns, Bob Marley's dreadlocks, Gwen Stefani's stage set: all essential elements of style, and the way that an audience is allowed access to the artist. "All of this is presenting oneself in a particular way. Part of Gwen's image is that she is the creator of that image. And that's specific, whereas some people might have certain clothing styles or hairstyles, one gets the sense that with Gwen Stefani, they were her choices. And that's a very accelerated point on imaging and creates a level of reliability and authenticity that plays in part with everything in terms of long-term career standing. What it boils down to is, do we feel that this individual is authentic?"

MySpace Is No Place

A keen focus on songwriting and performance, Guerinot stresses, is integral to a young band's potential. "And that's it. First and foremost, be sure you're writing the best songs you can write, and that you're a phenomenally great live band. Don't tell me about your MySpace page and the graphics on it. That's not as interesting. Unfortunately, the contemporary music press is more interested in the business aspect than the creative aspect. And as young bands start out and start reading these, their focus becomes on the business. Keep writing and keep playing. I've said this to every artist I've ever worked with. When artists write their first record, frequently the saying is they've had their whole lifetime to write it. But they've started with a groundwork of the greatest music of all time, which is what they learn. They don't start writing songs, they start covering songs, but what do they cover? The greatest music of all time."

So You Wanna Be in the Biz?

"Kids going to school and getting ready to graduate ask, 'How do I get into the industry and what do I do, or how do I manage?' And if you open the [Los Angeles free paper] *L.A. Weekly* and look at the club section, I'd be guessing that there's hundreds of bands listed. I don't know if any of them are any good, but, hey, all of them need help and they all are more than willing to have someone come in and help, whether it's to pass out fliers or to help grow their business, whatever it is. In the event that you can find a way, which I was able to do with Social Distortion, I'd say, 'I can help out here. I'll try to get to get you a show in Phoenix; I'll try to get you a show in Santa Barbara.' You're actually in the music business. You might not be making any money yet, but that was what it was for me, you know, having local hands-on experiences."

"I don't think there's a music business monster.com that's going to say 'Wow! We're thrilled with your experience and education.' People have a need to help promote music and artists like crazy. As long as there's a need, that means you can have a job. It might not pay, but you're in. You have a legitimate reason to call the *Los Angeles Times* for a music review and to call every club in town. You have some reason why you can be on the phone."

www.rebelwaltz.com

Sandy Roberton: Piloting Projects to World's End

"I've had A&R people that refer to artists in colors. 'Make it a little browner.' And that guy is hugely successful."

Sandy Roberton knows from huge success. Commencing his career in his native country, the UK, first as an artist in the duo Rick and Sandy, signed to Fontana Records and then as a solo act with a cover of Neil Diamond's "Solitary Man," Roberton eventually found his surest footing on the other side of the desk: running the London Division of Chess Records' music publishing company. "By that stage, I got the bug to produce records," he relates. "I went off producing 60 albums back to back in the UK. I went from artist to publisher to producer, and then invented producer management. We had producers working with Robbie Nevil, Duran Duran, the Cure, and Thompson Twins. In 1986, I moved to the states. The company became so successful, there was no point in having an office in the UK. I bought out my partner, and we've been here for 22 years. I've got my own little 360 company going, with a booking agent and artist management division, but film and TV is the business that's building up the most. My daughter runs a label here, signing cutting-edge UK acts for America."

Among Roberton's client is The Matrix, three hugely successful songwriter/producers—Lauren Christy, Graham Edwards, and Scott Spock—known for hits with Avril Lavigne, Jason Mraz, and many others. "Lauren Christy was an artist signed to Mercury and she had made two records. Then she started to record new demos and was involved with *HITS!* magazine. They called and asked if I would meet her. The songs were really fantastic, and I tried to shop it for them. She was at that age, though, 30, when it was just a little too late timewise," Roberton recalls.

"We almost did a deal with BMG in London. Mark Fox said, 'I'll do this if I can sign her to my publishing company.' I got back to LA and thought, 'I also have a publishing company.' I worked out deal with Lauren's lawyer and signed her. She said, 'Why don't you meet my husband, Graham Edwards.' I went to west Los Angeles and saw a production team with a studio. I asked to represent them as a production team and they came up with a name—The Matrix. Then it was knocking on doors for nine months trying to get songs cut. Ron Fair (then A&R at RCA Records) loved one of their songs and cut it with Christina Aguilera for her Christmas album."

It was at a meeting at Arista that Sandy Roberton first heard a young artist who, although being developed for the country market, saw herself as "young and punky." It was Avril Lavigne. The Matrix co-wrote and produced five songs (including "Complicated" and "Sk8er Boi") for the album that yielded three number-one hits and became a smash.

"Every track on that record was an incredible major success story," Roberton avows. "It sold 15 million copies in the U.S. That's when I realized how new recording works. That recording was made in-house in the San Fernando Valley, and there was no sound-proofing in there. Although it used to be about rich expensive studios, it's just not about that so much; it's about the people behind the music. Every producer should see the Wrecking Crew movie about musicians in L.A. in the fifties and sixties to see how it all worked on Phil Spector or Beach Boys records. The musicians, producers, and engineers had to get everything working in the room to get that sound."

Signing the Perfect Storm

Roberton maintains a strong presence representing songwriter/producers. "I have to hear magic in the writing. One guy from Denmark, he's been writing with tons of people, and now it's the perfect storm. Two publishers want to sign him. It took all this time to start, but I just knew from his songs. But established successful songwriters don't need someone like me. I like taking something from scratch. With The Matrix, for example, we would go to the 7-11, buy horrible, cheap champagne when we got the first cut, and we all celebrated."

Although Roberton can identify alchemy, he states that his daughter is the sound-savvy partner in his enterprise. "I'm more business affairs and the checkbook. We work mainly with digital distributions labels since physical distribution is very expensive and you have to be absolutely certain that there will be so many sales. Majors will only approach me when we have a huge record. It's funny: They will spend more money picking up an act once it's successful than picking it up cheaply from the beginning."

And the new industry standard of 360 deals—where, in return for an investment, a label profits from touring, publishing, and merchandise—is something that Roberton avows can work for certain artists. "I can see both sides. The labels are putting the investment in and they see from the sidelines that the acts are making millions from playing live when they did all the heavy lifting. At this stage of the game, I think bands should probably go ahead and do a 360; at least they get that investment. Paramore is not suffering from their deal with Atlantic, and I know that's a 360-type deal. When you get more successful, you can renegotiate."

"Labels have to be careful. They're getting more into the publishing business and getting a piece of the action there. But they have to prove, 'This is what we did for you.' A big difference from when I started to now is the lack of quality control. There's so much music, I'm just overcome by the choices. Anybody can put out a record, and there's so much crap out there. A&R has become computer-based, with YouTube and MySpace. You don't even have to go out and see a band. But there will be a time when this settles down and quality control will come back."

Thunder Down Under

In addition to his presence in the U.S. and the UK, Roberton works extensively in Australia. "I've been there 17 times, and I've got my producer clients with every Aussie act I can think of. With Savage Garden, I helped do their deal with Epic. Wolfmother, INXS, Jet, Silverchair, Midnight Oil, all these acts came from me going down there every year getting to know the community, the managers, publishers, record companies, and going to shows, and then sending my producers to meet these Australian acts. And it's all about relationships. I got to know people as they got established and as they came up. I've kept those relationships going over the years. There is fabulous talent in Australia and so many venues where they can play, so they can really perform live."

Advice and Consent

Roberton advises industry aspirants that a powerful way to enter the game is by writing with an artist, rather than just co-writing with other songwriters and hoping the song will get cut. "Shopping songs is hard. A lot of artists are looking, and they all want a piece of the song, even if they only wrote a couple of words. You have more chance of getting a break if you work with an artist. People don't spend enough time on their songs. Where's the chorus, the bridge? The Matrix had a big hit with Jason Mraz with a song of his that had no chorus. They came in and finished it up. Writers need to create a lyric where someone else can actually feel that that lyric is about them. Carole King did that. Although her songs are personal, you can actually sing those songs and think that you are that person singing. So the lyric really has to be the most important thing."

www.worldsend.com

Jeff Rabhan: Career Orchestrations

"Many labels and management companies don't accept unsolicited material, which for me is the most comical aspect of this business. We're in the business of discovering new talent, but we won't allow them to reach out to us. I welcome unsolicited material. It's truly how talent is found, and most talent needs to be developed."

Los Angeles–based manager Jeff Rabhan was a journalism major in college, but it was music, not print, that inspired him the most. "Ninety-nine percent of people in the music business love music, whereas the majority of people in the film business love money—they don't really love film. We eat, sleep, and breathe music, which makes it such a great business."

After working at *Rolling Stone* magazine in the PR department and later as a writer, Rabhan moved to *Spin* magazine before relocating to Los Angeles and taking a position with Atlantic Records. Later moving to Elektra Records, he was involved in film soundtracks. As an independent A&R consultant, he worked on the hit Wes Craven film *Scream* and shopped a band of fresh-faced brothers—Hanson. "I wasn't compensated for that, and it turned into a drawn-out lawsuit, which was eventually settled. I never wanted to put myself into the position of having to sue anybody for what was rightfully mine."

The Talent Vortex

Visiting Sedona, Arizona, Rabhan was roped into taking a time-share tour, where he met a woman who told him about her goddaughter, a fledgling singer named Michelle Branch. "The rest is history," says Rabhan. He subsequently launched his career as an artist manager. For artists seeking representation, Rabhan says the following questions are applicable. "What can we do to further your career, and where do you, as an artist, want to be? There is no shortage of good managers, it's just finding a good fit. It's putting together the plan. Management is not 10 big decisions, it's 1,000 little ones. You have to be like-minded with the artist. Making sure that before you sign an artist everything is laid out and is perfectly clear. I handle my clients like they're my children. I try to make sure clients are appreciative, respectful, kind, and treat others they way they want to be treated."

As Rabhan's management business became more successful, he teamed up with The Firm, a major management company in Beverly Hills, California. Next, Rabhan launched Three Ring Projects with a team of partners. The entertainment company has a management roster that includes Everlast, Lil' Kim, Jermaine Dupri, Kelis, Haikka, and Elliott Yamin, among others. The company is based in Los Angeles and Nashville and has a record division, TRP Records.

In Rhyme with the Times

Music, Rabhan believes, is in tune with the epoch in which it exists. "What's going on in our business follows what goes on in the country. What happens musically is what is happening with kids: from the summer of love, to Kurt Cobain and grunge, to mindless pop, which has taken control. But music is moving to more substance. I think fans want to talk to the artist, they don't want to put them on a pedestal. It's difficult to be a diva today and be untouchable. Image is important, but substance over style is the direction that we're heading in. *American Idol* is representative of that. People are like, 'I chose you,' and the majority of people that have won aren't ones that majors would go after. Kelly Clarkson, for example, who is one of the most talented people I have ever had the pleasure of working with—she wouldn't have been able to get majors to listen to her. Major record company people don't live in the real world."

Closing Chorus

Whether an artist is seeking management, a label, or a publisher, Rabhan believes that self-examination is in order. "Look at yourself and your music as objectively as possible and find the people that have shown a propensity in that style and really narrow down the field of who you're trying to reach in terms of doors opening. And do your homework."

www.three-ring.com

Michael Lippman: A Manager's Enduring Faith

"Record companies don't care—they just want profit."

Mega-manager Michael Lippman relates that he began his career with Arista Records, working under the guidance of legendary song man Clive Davis. "I took people out to lunch and dinner for a living," he observes. "It was like my post-graduate education. Record producers would cry and bitch about how difficult Clive made it for them to finish a record. They were always taking my advice, and I realized that record producers had no one to talk to. They didn't have managers, so they talked to the A&R guys at record labels or nobody. I said, 'These guys need to be protected.'"

And protect them he did, forming a company with producer Ron Nevison, lyricist Bernie Taupin, and songwriter/artist Melissa Manchester, and then enlisting an illustrious roster of producers who have created some of the biggest-selling records in pop history, from such artists as U2, Michael Jackson, the Rolling Stones, Guns 'n' Roses, Mariah Carey, Barbra Streisand, and George Michael.

Michael Row the Boat

Expanding his management role to include artists, Lippman became a key figure in the careers of David Bowie, Terence Trent D'Arby, Matchbox Twenty and, most famously, George Michael. Lippman, who was at the helm during Michael's massive success with *Faith*, has now, after a 17-year hiatus, reunited with the artist and overseen Michael's record-breaking 25 LIVE tour, commemorating the artist's 25 years in the business. "It is an incredible thrill to be asked back," Lippman says. "And to have all the success we had again, it was amazing. He's a really good guy. I went to countries I'd never heard of—he's gigantic overseas. He even reopened Wembley Stadium in the UK. Everything sold out in record time." With 80 shows in 12 European countries and gross sales figures estimated at over $200 million, Michael performed for a staggering 1.3 million fans. The 25 LIVE tour broke ticket sales records, most notably in Copenhagen, where Michael's concert at the Parken Stadium sold over 50,000 tickets in a matter of minutes, shattering the previous ticket sales record at the venue, formerly held by U2. (He subsequently achieved massive sales figures on the U.S. leg of his tour.)

The globalization of music media is a huge factor for the artists Lippman references. "I have relationships in most parts of the world. It's important for artists to be successful everywhere in the world where they can be. It's a worldwide business, just like Coca-Cola or cars."

Lighting Up with Matchbox Twenty

As manager of hit artists Matchbox Twenty and lead singer Rob Thomas in his solo career, Lippman was instrumental in extensive artist development. "In the early days, Matchbox Twenty used to lock me out of the dressing room because I was trying to help them with their live show. A lot of times you voice an opinion, you go away, and they make that change. They at least consider it."

The day that Matchbox Twenty's first CD was released, their record label went out of business. "And they sucked anyway as a live act. They then spent six months learning their craft. So they were ready when Atlantic Records (who had since signed them) said, 'Go on the road, and we'll give you the money you need.' Rob Thomas wasn't inhibited about being onstage, but he never knew how to move—he would just stand there and sing—and he eventually learned how to work an audience. It's important."

Rob Thomas' solo debut shot to number one on the album chart. This marked the first time that a male artist from a rock and/or pop group had debuted at number one with his first solo album in the history of the *Billboard* Top 200. This solo career, Lippman says, yielded unexpected results. "We were all worried if Rob went solo it would adversely affect Matchbox Twenty, and now they're bigger than ever. His success helped their success." The band has sold over 45 million albums worldwide.

Indelible Images

Lippman points to a cross section of artists who he admires. "My heroes Sammy Davis, Jr., Prince, James Brown, and Elvis—you don't see those artists happening today." In addition to being great showman, all of the luminaries he references also possessed immediately identifiable images. "Image is vital! It separates you from the rest of the artists out there."

And specific criteria interest Lippman as far as future clients are concerned. "They would have to have the potential to be worldwide superstars. I like singer/songwriters. I don't seek out people that don't write their own material. You see *American Idol* and Disney artists, a lot of people selling lots of records are collaborating with many people. It's not a bad thing, but it doesn't excite me."

Perseverance Platitudes

"Never take no for an answer as an artist because you'll run into a lot of roadblocks," Lippman advises. "Find people to work with that you trust and respect—the lawyer and accountant—but also learn your craft. Try to be special. Learn to work an audience and hone your songs."

And management, he avows, is now more important than ever. "We are always looking for new, alternative ways to market our artist and their records. For example, it is very important to make sure that you're on the Internet in the right way. Record companies don't have the same amount of money they used to have to build the artists. So it's up to us to do it."

"You have to love it to stay in this business. It's always good to have your vision accepted by the public. To love a song, hear it on the radio, and have people want to buy it is the greatest feeling. I get off on the success of the artist. And if you do a good job and the public likes you, the money will come."

www.lippman-ent.com

Kelly Curtis: In and Out of Pearl Jams

"The normal person, when they look at complaining rock stars, it's hard to understand what pressures there are with being a super-famous person. You can't do anything without drawing a crowd."

In 1988, Kelly Curtis met Stone Gossard and Jeff Ament—two members of a band called Mother Love Bone—and he helped the band seal a deal with PolyGram Records. Curtis was also in the hospital room on March 19, 1990, when Mother Love Bone's singer Andrew Wood, who had overdosed on heroin, was taken off life support. And he was there when Ament, Gossard, Mike McCready, and a 25-year-old singer named Eddie Vedder played their first shows as Mookie Blaylock.

Since its inception, Pearl Jam has sold 30 million records in the U.S. and an estimated 60 million albums worldwide. Pearl Jam has outlasted many of its contemporaries from the alternative rock breakthrough of the early 1990s and is considered one of the most influential bands in rock history.

Broken Bones

Ament and Gossard were devastated by the death of Wood and the resulting demise of Mother Love Bone. Gossard spent his time afterward writing harder-edged material than what he had been doing previously. He began rehearsing with fellow Seattle guitarist McCready, whose band Shadow had broken up; McCready in turn encouraged

Gossard to reconnect with Ament. The trio sent out a five-song demo tape in order to find a singer and a drummer. They gave former Red Hot Chili Peppers drummer Jack Irons the demo to see if he would be interested in joining the band and to distribute the demo to anyone he felt might fit the lead vocal position.

They sent him a tape of the songs that would eventually become "Alive," "Even Flow," and "Black," and Jack said, 'I can't do it, I'm committed, but I know this surfer kid who is an amazing singer. Can I pass the tape on to him?' Eddie Vedder sang over this thing and sent it back, and we knew immediately—we were like, 'Jesus Christ! Where did that voice come from?'" Within a week, Vedder had joined the band.

With the addition of Dave Krusen on drums, the band took the name Mookie Blaylock, in reference to a then-active All-Star basketball player. When they signed to Epic Records, concerns about trademark issues necessitated a name change to Pearl Jam.

Corporate Climates

"The band always believed in keeping t-shirt prices lower," says Kelly Curtis. "Venues take 30 to 40 percent of the t-shirt revenues. We took a stance that we would never sell t-shirts at a venue that took more than 20 percent. It only took a couple of times for us to not sell t-shirts that word got out. It was smarter to cut a deal than fight us on it."

"Sony was pretty respectful of us for the first 10 years. I know we were difficult and we were learning as well. There were fights with the record company, but they weren't too terrible. There were people we disagreed with or didn't like, but we always ended up getting our way. It's been said that we were good corporate citizens. We fulfilled our contracts and then we left. We didn't try to screw anybody beforehand."

From the onset, Pearl Jam attracted immense media attention. "The first record blew up so big, Eddie was on the cover of *Time* magazine, we'd had three or four singles, and the label wanted to go for one more. The band said, 'No.' Tommy Mottola [then label chief] said it was going to be the biggest mistake in my life. The normal person, when they look at complaining rock stars, it's hard to understand what pressures there are with being a super-famous person. You can't do anything without drawing a crowd. In order for us to survive, we stopped on that first record and said, 'No more.' Ultimately, that was probably the best thing we could have done."

The J Way

After seven releases with Sony, Pearl Jam left the label. "We had no real relationships—everyone we knew there was gone. We never got a call about the future. Everyone we'd worked with had left. It was new people, new battles, and it was hard to get anything done. We saw the light at the end of the tunnel. We made that clear to Sony. The band decided to do a "one-off" release with J Records, a label helmed by the legendary executive Clive Davis. "The Clive thing intrigued us; historically, he seemed like one of the last real music guys. We had some concerns, of course, that he would have to be hands on. He was smart enough to understand that, very respectful of the band, and very knowledgeable. He knew a lot of things, someone had done their homework. We liked the idea that we would know everybody in the record company again."

But when J Records came under the Sony BMG umbrella, the band was back at square one. "It was great to be at a smaller label. We thought J was that and then the merger was announced. We're an international band, and it was hard to get anyone on board. We played in Europe six weeks once and four weeks the next time and we never saw anyone from the company. They did a fine job in America, but it was a mess overseas."

Live

Pearl Jam released a whopping 72 live albums in 2000 and 2001, each one a complete concert. "I introduced the bootleg idea to Sony and said, 'We want to release every show we do.' They thought we were out of our minds. No one got it there except one guy—Mel Inberman. He said, 'This idea is genius.' But they were not into it. So instead of asking for an advance, we did a joint venture and licensed them so we would get them back. We now own all of that live stuff. We sold 3 million of that first release. In seven countries, we hit number one. The Lisbon show was number one in Portugal, the Rome show was number one in Italy. Funny, to say the least. Our whole plan was: there was no plan. But we were being bootlegged so heavily with sh*tty quality, why not have better-sounding records, charge less, and create another level of connection with the fans?"

"One of the great things about this band—growing up in the sixties and having heroes like John Lennon and having moral boundaries and things you believed in—like humankind—was for me to find a band that was carrying that flag. It was awesome. We've made people mad—Eddie Vedder was anti-war from the day the war started. We were getting booed, but Eddie held his own. This band has walked the line for so long that there's new-found respect for them—that they're the real deal."

www.pearljam.com

John Greenberg and Bryan Coleman: Dollars on the Nickelback

"I know a few bands in the Rock and Roll Hall of Fame that I personally can't stomach. And some people feel these are the most brilliant songs ever written."—John Greenberg

Along with partners Tim Heyne and Bryan Coleman, John Greenberg helms the Union Entertainment Group, a management firm who counts multiplatinum rock heroes Nickelback among its clients. Greenberg looks back at the legacy of rock music in America with this conclusion: "You had people who ran ABC Records and signed Tom Petty. Subpop signed Nirvana. Enigma distributed the Motley Crue records. A&M had the Carpenters and everything from Styx to Soundgarden. Metallica was on Metal Blade. These were indie labels that believed in artists and believed in songs. To me, it's amazing that the majors don't understand that they have to treat their artists like something special."

"Most of the successful music came out of U.S. or the UK. Now we have a Japanese company that owns Sony, a French water company who owns Universal, and Warner Bros. is owned by Seagrams, an alcohol company. What are we doing here in America? With our musical history—Little Richard and Motown, the seventies with Ted Nugent and Aerosmith into the eighties and the metal movement and the nineties with Nirvana, Soundgarden, and Alice in Chains—now it's more like *Top of the Pops* in the UK."

Careers can't be built on single songs, says Greenberg. "We're not building catalogs anymore. It's okay to introduce kids to music. It's like I used to do when I was a kid, buy a 45 and hope that the B-side would be as cool as the A-side. Then, if you liked it, you saved up money to buy the entire album and take a chance on it. I'd ask for advances on my allowance to buy records. I got locked into it and became a huge fan. The problem now is that labels want one song and they think it's enough. They forget that you can't build a brand for an artist that way. You have to give artists opportunities to grow and write and to nurture them, to sit down with their managers. We don't have that today at the major labels, so at management we try to do the best to supplement that. That's what we're missing, not giving artists or bands the opportunities to grow anymore or write a catalog of songs. Now it's what do you have, and how can I make money off of it immediately?"

"Bands aren't getting the care that they need. Less music is selling and fewer good songs are being written because of this lack of attention for the artists. Companies are coming in and buying catalogs. They're bidding on the past, they're not bidding on the future. They forget the next huge artist is the next new artist. You're not going to come back and get Bob Dylan to become bigger than he was. Imagine if you could find the next Guns 'n' Roses, the next Nirvana, or the next Pink. Then you would be looking to move forward."

Majors in the Shadows

Major labels, notes Greenberg, are mere shadows of their former selves. "They don't have real music people. They may fancy themselves as such because they're fans, but they have never studied it, or had opportunities to make records, so they're not musicians. Some of these hirings—you have to scratch your head because they're outside the music business. Bankers and corporations, what do they have to do with understanding? They're not producers or musicians who have made records. And now they want to take over."

Greenberg notes the power of the global economy. "People love melody and it doesn't matter what language it is in. If you have enough great melodies, you'll find fans that want to purchase that music. If it works in the U.S., it will work in Canada. Nickelback, for example, as they grew they become successful in Europe and Australia and there were requests to go into Asia. We hook up with the right promoters, and I go to meet with them. A lot of things in America come and go."

Tuned In

Greenberg offers this thought: "It starts with a song, but it has to be an artist with vision, drive, focus, a starting point, and a clear understanding of what they want their end game to be. Once that's established, they then have to find a manager to take them from their first gig in a coffee shop to a publishing deal, to possibly do a demo deal or a record deal if someone believes in them enough, and then turn that interest into the momentum for finding a booking agent to get the band out there performing. The hope then is that the audience reacts and goes out and buys their songs."

Nickelback: Change from the North

The now massively successful band Nickelback are Canadians who relocated to Vancouver from their hometown of Hanna, Alberta, where they recorded and released their inaugural EP *Hesher* and followed with a full-length release, *Curb*. The band sold 10,000 copies of their indie release without a record label or management and were still unsigned when they embarked from Vancouver on bare-bones van tours. The band's singer, Chad Kroeger—a former telephone sales employee—hammered the phones on his band's behalf and asked his friends to fax and phone radio stations to request Nickelback's single. Vancouver rock station CFOX provided radio support, and the group cultivated a grassroots fan base in Vancouver. Nickelback embraced the DIY ethic and kept track of the radio exposure they were getting in each city they traveled through, often using Kroeger's sales chops to pitch their wares to various record shop owners and DJs themselves. The strategy worked. The band was eventually signed to Roadrunner Records.

Bryan Coleman, Nickelback's day-to-day manager at Union Entertainment Group, notes that Nickelback's work ethic was very appealing when he first encountered the band. "They were promoting themselves and doing everything." He says Roadrunner

Records also shared the band's drive. "Everyone bled for this band and worked really hard for them—seven days a week, 24 hours a day, for months—to make their platinum album happen."

"They're a heavy rock band, but they can be played on pop radio too. We went to every radio station that would have them: Saturdays, Sundays, nights, and mornings. The band members are friendly and super genuine good ol' boys from Alberta. They have hospitality, people loved them and saw the work ethic and recognized that they were good songwriters. People can relate to the stories in their songs, and they're just real guys. It all developed and it all clicked—it's not just one thing that we did because we did everything. We played every night and would fly from Miami to Seattle for a show if necessary."

One component of the band's strategy is to limit releases to one CD every three years, on average. "It takes that long because one song will be a hit, so we tour as long as possible for that single," Coleman notes. "We have multiple hits, so it takes a long time to tour that out. And Nickelback's last single, "Rockstar" took two and a half years after its original release to go number one in the UK. We added a whole other leg of the tour because we had to promote and tour over there. Australia is a huge market for us, so we go there at least once every cycle. Germany is fantastic, as is South Africa, and we do well in Japan."

One Nation Undersigned

Nickelback recently inked a three-album, three-tour 360 deal with Live Nation, joining a roster that already includes Madonna, Jay-Z, and Shakira. The contract is estimated to be worth between $50 to $70 million. "It's a partnership with Live Nation for the future," Coleman says. "We see eye to eye on the vision they have for the future of the music business in uncertain times. It's not one specific plan this way or that way; they'll adapt to the times. In five years from now, if there's no physical product [CDs, DVDs, etc.], we'll be okay because we will have other ways of growing the Nickelback brand. The Live Nation agreement covers all aspects of the band's musical career, including future recordings after the Roadrunner deal. This is the new way, a new mentality, breaking from the old mold with no set rules. We can decide on anything."

Coleman says that with his growing family, his time has become very precious. Still, he says, it would be hard to turn down managing a band or artist who is truly monumental. For those aspiring to Nickelback's stature, he would advise the following: "It's great songs, but really it's the whole package. This includes a strong work ethic and passion about both work and art. We want to bring in good people who we're proud to have with the company and who we are happy to bring to our family BBQs. My advice to

A&R guys is to look for good music, not what's cool right now. Find a good band, you hang onto them; do good things, and good things come back to you."

Nickelback Has Left the Auditorium

Nickelback's Chad Kroeger confesses that the band knew they'd conquered the states when they appeared live on the American Music Awards. "These are your peers, those people in the audience, those are the hardest critics everywhere, the same people who do the same thing every single night. We brought the explosions and pyro, and when we got finished playing, with all the explosions and the fireworks, everyone stood up and gave us a standing ovation. I just could not believe it, rappers, country artists, rock artists, everyone was there and everyone got out of their seat and was giving this massive applause to Nickelback. You literally could not kick the grin off of my face."

www.uegine.com

Edwin Morales: Blazing Beats from Mean Streets

"Even though we're from the ghetto, there's no reason we can't present ourselves in a way that shows we respect the audience."

He might be a young man, but he has big ideas and even bigger ideals. As one of the principle founders of the Los Angeles–based Last Few Artists, Edwin Morales is involved in the career of a new artist, BE-1, and a company that encompasses a breadth of artistry and philosophies. "Last Few Artists started as an idea from Brian Quezada [BE-1] and myself. We had been involved with this since we were 12 years old. This is a company that caters to all kinds of media and outlets. We were so versatile growing up that we knew we could excel in music, theater, writing, or art itself. We went on to Los Angeles County High School for the Arts, where we had a culture shock, coming from South Central, where it was 99 percent Latino and one percent black. But we dove into the world of arts, and it opened our eyes. People in the arts, they interact, it is so easy. Eventually, when we were 16 and 17, we recorded our first album, put it out ourselves, and made a little money."

A year later, the duo got a bit more serious, Morales says. "We put together another project with more production, packaged it, and had a whole team, photographers, and put together a real CD that we could distribute. And we started doing shows. When I enrolled in the Music Business Program at Musicians Institute, we went full force. I'm probably the only 20-year-old you'll meet who is 100 Gs [$100,000] in debt. But that's what it takes—a full commitment." To raise the funds necessary to launch a label and build their recording studio, Morales and Quezada invested their own money and arranged long-term loan contracts with family members and family friends.

"If artist development existed today as a crew, what we did with BE-1 would be an example. We brought in someone to do beats; we got a photographer to work on the image, a creative advisor. At 17, I had a team of eight people working on BE-1. Last year, I was ready with the product. We had to test it; I had to be honest and say, 'Is this going to work, or is he just another rapper?' As a kid, I was doing it for a hobby, but my mind switched to business. We started analyzing every aspect: Are the music and the image strong enough? Is his personality and background worth anything? We needed structure. We did shows, and at the shows I watched the audience: Do they like it, receive it?"

Track Records

Morales and company recorded 150 pre-production tracks and cut the number down to 20 with full production. "Then I brought the project to Daryl Swan [Macy Gray producer]. After being with the project for three years, there's only so much I can add to it. Daryl is the objective ear. It's the difference between knowing how to make music and making a hit. I think only a person who has made a hit can hear a hit."

BE-1, Morales says, brings a new edge to hip-hop. "The genre originated from turntables the DJ and the MC. We believe it's time there should be an evolution where instruments are a big part of it. Rock has evolved; why can't hip-hop? We have a new project, *Coming Back Home*. BE-1 moved out of South Central and said he wouldn't go back until he had something to show." His illuminated lyrical and musical debut will mark BE-1's reintroduction to the community where he grew up.

And the visuals are a huge part of the vibe. "What I want to do with BE-1 is show the style. He wears suits. We're involved with youth. If we can inject a message with the music and have them copy a look, then we're going somewhere. No disrespect to the Game or 50 Cent, but take away their $5,000 chains and they look like average Joes. We want BE-1 to have class, to show even though we're from the ghetto, there's no reason we can't present ourselves in a way that shows we respect the audience. When you dress up, you feel good. It gives you confidence. A lot of kids lack confidence, direction, and objectives. Just something as simple as putting on a suit or tie will build them up."

Morales' family emigrated to the U.S. from Nicaragua, and BE-1's people are from Mexico. They are both aware of how culture impacts art. "There isn't a Latino rapper who has been effective," says Morales. "There are those who have been successful, Fat Joe and Immortal Technique, but there hasn't been anyone who has been explosive. It's an African American–dominated culture. We think BE-1 can penetrate. When he raps, he raps about people in general. Latin hip-hop always stays with the 'Ese' and the culture itself. We see our culture as an advantage: We're just people, and we're here with our music to represent all of them."

Sounds from LaLa Land

If an artist can connect in Los Angeles, Morales believes that can break worldwide. "Los Angeles is a big city. One man explained it like this: 'You're born in the United States. You can have any meal you want, when you want it. He said, 'Look at the state and look at the city—the most famous city in the world. If you don't make something out of yourselves being a native of Los Angeles, you've done f*cked your life.' We are in the entertainment capitol of the world, the center of what people are supposed to dig. I believe that if I can win the L.A. crowd, I can win the world. The crowd is very honest. Performers are welcomed in other places. In Los Angeles, that sh*t better be hot or it flops."

"It's commitment: If there is something you believe in, you go for it all the way. Before I go to sleep at night, I think, 'What's the next thing?' You have to pay your dues, go in debt, and go full out. When you are starting out, no one wants to listen, you have to make people care. When the artist goes on stage, he had better look like a star. So I go to the club, go up the sound and lighting men and pay them—that's something I have to do. Once my artist goes on, he looks like somebody, and the audience thinks, 'Damn! Look at those lights.' Also, it shows how theatrical you are. It's not enough to grab the mic and rap two songs. It has to connect. When people don't know you, they want to hear what you have to say. You have to let people know what it is just from the picture of the artist. You have to network, to be certain places, know where the industry people are, and communicate. Be approachable and presentable and make people like you. It's an inner circle. If you're not strong-minded, it is going to be hell."

www.lastfewartists.com

7 | Film/TV

For artists and songwriters, especially for those who are emerging and independent, having a song in a film or on a television show offers crucial exposure to a key market. The sync fees of varying amounts, and back-end payments from a performing rights organization—ASCAP, BMI, or SESAC—can represent a considerable income for songwriters and music publishers.

The good news is that network TV, as well as cable television and independent films, now affords an unprecedented bounty of music placement opportunities. In this chapter, you will see a wide cast of expertise offered by those who place music in film and TV, as well as those who create it and oversee it.

Can You Picture This? The Film and Television Music Overview

In the relatively brief history of American popular culture, the marriage of music to picture is one of its most successful couplings. Originally, piano music played in the cavernous silent movie theaters to provide reassurance for audiences fearful of the dark. With the advent of "talkies" came music recorded especially for the screen. World War II brought an influx of illustrious exiles from war-torn Europe, among them classical composers who composed for, and conducted, grand orchestras on Hollywood sound stages.

In the fifties, filmed Broadway musicals coupled songs with live action, and the resulting songs translated easily into hit records. The first rumblings of rock—via Bill Haley and Little Richard—only hinted at what was to come. In the sixties, films including *The Sterile Cuckoo, Midnight Cowboy, The Graduate*, and the granddaddy of all rock pictures, *Easy Rider*—integrated songs and film. This tradition has continued through the next five decades.

Owing to its origins as both a video and audio format, songs have always been a part of television. In this era, with the invention of the home theater and the multiplication of cable television channels, this need has dramatically expanded.

For an independent artist, a new band, or a rising songwriter, contributing music to a television show has become entrée not only to new audiences and industry credibility, but a lucrative pursuit in its own right. Indeed, many working musicians attest that they can potentially earn more from one strategic placement than they might see from a couple of months worth of grinding gigs.

Although the playing field has become increasingly level in an era of affordable digital technology, achieving the necessary mix to compete in the high-stakes world of top-line television placements means more than just buying the requisite gear. More significantly, it means knowing how to use it to create music with the elusive emotional content.

Karen Lamberton: Perfect Placement

"The more people you know, the better off you're going to be. It's about not necessarily calling someone when you need them, but before you need them."

Senior Vice President, Film/TV, Licensing and Strategic Marketing, RCA Jive Label Group, Karen Lamberton, born in New York, graduated with a B.A. in communications from Pennsylvania State University. After moving to Los Angeles, she "pounded the pavement to get an internship." She eventually began working for Thorn EMI. Later, as a vice-presidential assistant at the Gorfaine/Schwartz Agency, she worked with such top composers as Ennio Morricone, Hans Zimmer, and Michael Kamen. Her other stints included being an assistant to Capitol Records president Gary Gersh and being a coordinator at Worlds End Management, whose roster included producers Steve Lillywhite, Larry Klein, and Don Gehman. In 1998, Lamberton was hired by Quincy Jones' music publishing company as a creative director.

In 2001, she returned to New York City to work for Clive Davis at J Records, to create opportunities for the label's roster in film and television placements. "Working for Clive was tough, as it should be, because he demanded a lot. So it was challenging, but life would be boring without challenges. When I first began, we only had 20 artists, so it was very manageable, and I could devote time to individual artists and individual songs. The directive was so clear: If I didn't get something for Alicia Keys that week, I sucked! With so few employees or artists, it was based on what everyone had or had not done. These days, you have tons and tons of artists, and you don't feel like you have enough time to work on anything. Then I started working for RCA as well. A year ago, they gave me Jive Records also."

Lots of Slots from Sony

In her current position at Sony, which now encompasses the aforementioned labels, Lamberton says she and her staff are running from the second they arrive at the office. "There are so many artists and so many songs. I get passionate about helping the younger, developing artists. A lot of it is balancing, saying 'Okay I need to focus on this artist today.' It's impossible to describe a typical day, but at least once I will be putting out some kind of fire in addition to doing my regular job. Some days, I might read an e-mail from a music supervisor that could say, 'We have this situation in a show and we're looking for a song. We prefer male vocals,' and I will go through my entire roster of artists to find songs that fit. Then I might send them five songs through e-mail and set up a chart. They could contact us and say 'I like track two, but I need approval today.' Then, I have to get the artist's approval and get even more info on the project so that I'm confident that it fits with that artist. If everyone is on board and I have the artist's manager's approval, then I go back to the music supervisor and say, 'You can use this track.'"

Lamberton maintains close relationships with selected artist managers. "I've had opportunities to work with some artists when they were tiny and they have stayed with us for years. I became close with Ray LaMontagne's management, and we talk weekly. And they make sure folks in my area are serviced properly. I like to include management because it helps build our relationship. Later on down the line, when I get a request for a song to be used in a show but the supervisor only has $500 dollars, if I think it would be really important for the artist, that relationship I already built up allows me to make that call and say, 'Please trust me on this,' and they do."

Lamberton won't take credit for breaking any specific artists, but she relates that placing singer/songwriter Gavin DeGraw's song "I Don't Want To Be" as the theme song for the television show *One Tree Hill* gave the artist a significant boost. "One year on a popular teen TV show gave us a lot of attention. When we finally worked that single, people were already aware of it. We have some artists that haven't sold, but if we have the right texture for supervisors, we might be able to recoup our investment in them on licensing alone. And those artists are incredibly appreciative."

"The more people you know, the better off you're going to be. It's about not necessarily calling someone when you need them, but before you need them. Make friends first, then later on down the line, if there's a problem, that person is already your friend and you can work through a situation. We had a brand new artist working with some unknown writers. We were just clearing something on the master side, and they had to clear something on the publishing side. I had a feeling they weren't familiar with how this is done. So I said to one of the women that works for me, 'Call them and introduce yourself. Tell them if they have any questions to have them call you. Offer it to them now, they'll appreciate it.'"

Although the deals must be done rapidly, payment for usage in a film and television show might take years. "The problem is there [are] so many people involved in a studio or network and so many approvals to get. Then there is the cue sheet [a listing of all music used on a show], and if there is a mistake or someone leaves their position, maybe the studio or network can't find the paperwork. We have a hard time keeping up with all the paperwork that there is to do to back up every single deal. But that is just the nature of what we do. The folks who work for me do more of that than I do anymore. My time is taken with meetings on really big deals—advertising or trailer deals that are a lot of work and a lot of money. I handle these and they are generally very complex and take weeks to negotiate."

Fees, Please

It is no secret that television and film placements mean major exposure for all types of artists and bands. As a consequence, placement fees have been reduced because of the law of supply and demand. "There are so many different mediums now to participate in that you need exposure everywhere to hit everyone, assuming that the exposure is taste-ful," Lamberton observes. "It's become more financially challenging in last couple of years," she says. "Now there is more competition from independent labels and artists, but budgets at studios and networks have gone down for music also, because of that competition. In just seven years, the fees went from medium to really high back down to medium. If we're dying for a placement, it may be worth it do it for very little money. In general, superstar fees too have gone down, but there are exceptions."

While Lamberton demurs on naming numbers, she does make this general assessment: "There are so many things to consider. Is the song currently a single? Or if we find out there's new artist debut at number five [on the charts], then that might boost the fee up a third. I only handle front-line artists. If you come to me looking for an Elvis Presley track, I'll send you to a different group of people—I represent artists on the roster who have released a record in the last two to two and a half years. But the back-catalog people really need to stick to their guns and charge the right fees, because that's mostly all the company is earning for that music for the moment."

Perpetrating Passion

Being a music lover first, Lamberton says, is a primary consideration in the high-pressure, high-stakes arena in which she operates. "There are so many possible ways to fail that you absolutely have to have a passion, because some days that is the only thing that keeps you going. You have to have that underlying deep desire to be in this business and to love music. Otherwise, I don't know why people would do it."

Monica Benson: Writing the BOK

Monica Benson has run BOK Music, her own successful independent publishing company, since 1990. BOK has placed songs with a wide range of artists, including Whitney Houston, Daughtry, Misteeq, and the classic Motown act The Temptations and in the films *Bring It On*, *Miss Congeniality*, *The Hot Chick*, *Birthday Girl*, *Soul Plane*, and *Barbershop*. TV placements include *Lizzie McGuire (and on the show's soundtrack)*, *The OC*, *One Life to Live*, *The Young and the Restless*, *Charmed*, *South Beach*, *The Ghost Whisperer*, *Related*, *The Bold and the Beautiful*, *CSI*, *Darcy's Wild Life and Reunion*, *Beverly Hills 90210*, *Melrose Place*, and many others. "It is difficult, but every day I make money at it," says Benson. "If I'm pitching to artists, I can't say that."

Benson says that researching and analyzing the shows is essential to pitching. "I watch a lot of TV and see a lot of movies. I study it. There is a website where you can go on and see what songs are used on what shows. Before I contact a music supervisor, I get as much information as I can—because it's hard to watch every television show. There is a lot of legwork."

www.bok-music.com

Michael Eames: The PEN Is Mightier

Michael Eames believes that there has never been a better time than now to be an independent publisher, label, or artist. "For so many years, it's been about the corporations, the gatekeepers. The Internet leveled the playing field." Eames, who advises that PEN Music Group regularly places tracks and songs for television projects, adds, "These days, unless a writer is being asked to write something, there is an unspoken assumption that anything we'll pitch will be of a certain sonic quality. They know we'll pitch something that sounds like a record. If we were to pitch something that sounded like a demo, we may never be asked to pitch something to them again." And Eames says that in addition to the sonic sheen, the emotional content of the song is equally crucial to the recording. "You have to filter who is the character and what is the voice of the show. We had a song in *Grey's Anatomy*, and they use female vocal artists because many of the characters are strong women."

www.penmusic.com

Line of Fire: Music Supervisors

The music supervisor oversees all aspects of music in a particular production and plays a key role in the development of the entire musical landscape. This may include facilitating a show's creative needs with artists, songs and score, handling all licensing and contractual elements, dealing with the technical aspects of on-camera and studio production work, soundtrack solicitation, and more.

Alexandra Patsavas: Cuts at the Chop Shop

Alexandra Patsavas—owner of Chop Shop Music Supervision—obtained her start in the music business as a rock promoter in Champaign, Illinois. She moved to Los Angeles in 1990 and worked in the Film/TV department at BMI. In 1994, she went to work for Roger Corman at Concorde Films, where she was music coordinator and supervisor on over 50 B-movie classics (*Caged Heat 3000, Piranha 2, Bucket of Blood,* etc.) all in a three-year span.

After her stint at Concorde, Alexandra started her own company, Chop Shop Music Supervision, where she music-supervised the TV shows *Roswell, Carnivale, Boston Public, Fastlane,* and *The OC,* and the films *Happy, Texas; Wasted; Dancing at the Blue Iguana; John Tucker Must Die;* and *The Invisible.*

Alexandra and her staff at the Chop Shop are currently working on the TV shows *Grey's Anatomy, Private Practice, Chuck, Gossip Girl, Without a Trace, Rescue Me, Mad Men, Supernatural,* and *Numb3rs.* She recently supervised the feature film *Twilight.*

"It is a much different landscape now," says Patsavas. "Music supervision wasn't in the eye of the storm as it is now. I was always interested in new music, music from past eras and in films."

Chop Shop on the Block

Patsavas says she chose the name Chop Shop because of an interest in Western swing culture and the car culture of East Los Angeles. Each day at the business is different, she says. "I might be asked to help define the signature sound of a show by hiring a composer and picking the theme song. I read the script, then send compilations of music I feel are appropriate for the show. It's always a collaboration, working with different creators. The final say for the musical content is by the executive producer."

With an immense number of musical submissions to her office, Patsavas notes that she relies on professionals with whom she maintains relationships. "It's my job to go through so much music a week, but at this point, I have developed an instinct for what will work and what won't work, and I have come to trust individuals and companies that handle music and what they say will be top quality."

Label Stable

As an offshoot of the company, Patsavas formed Chop Shop Records. One of the company's first releases is the soundtrack to the very successful vampire teen romance she supervised, *Twilight.* "We have four acts signed," Patsavas explains. "It is a label venture with Atlantic. I was approached by few labels around the time of the [hit series] *The OC*, and Atlantic seemed like a great home for me. Chop Shop will always be small and focused with a few soundtracks and indie rock. I don't foresee it growing huge.

Chop Shop Rock

A recent Chop Shop venture is a web series, titled *Rockville,* that takes place in a live club. "Each episode has a different band, and I select the bands," adds Patsavas. "We shoot it at the Echoplex, a venue in Los Angeles, and it does present the essence of a local club. All the bands perform live and we have captured some great moments. I am looking for compelling live performances that keep a club alive—that's what I'm going for. Most of the acts are signed. I will see which bands are going to be in town, and then I go about booking them for the show. We have 20 episodes."

For artists and bands that would like to achieve similar exposure, Patsavas offers these words: "Work at your craft and don't expect overnight success. Perfect a live show and maintain a local fan base that you connect with. All those things will make it possible for other opportunities. One song in a show doesn't omit a need for good live show and a connection with your fans. All these things need to line up together."

www.myspace.com/chopshopmusicsupervision

Andy Hill

After teaching film music at Columbia University in the eighties, Andy served for nine years as Disney's VP of Music Production, overseeing the composition and recording of music for five Oscar-winning scores, including *The Lion King*. Following this, he worked as an independent music supervisor and executive music producer on films such as *Ed Wood, Hoodlum, Anastasia*, and *Message In A Bottle*. He was honored with a Grammy Award as producer of the music for *The Adventures Of Elmo In Grouchland*.

"As a rule, it's a non-starter to send out totally unsolicited material," cautions Hill. "Not because the supervisor doesn't want to listen, but he'll receive this package, and if there's more than one track, he won't know where to go or where to start. He's probably listening to the latest box of product from Warner Bros. or EMI. I always advise that you contact the person first and find out what kind of material they're looking for."

Does an indie songwriter or act have a realistic shot? "Absolutely," he emphasizes. "The majors rarely are prepared to make the big concessions on prices that are required, particularly in the indie film sphere. I just finished work on a feature, and we began with the expectation—as always—that there would be a big soundtrack advance that would underwrite the cost of all the licensed music. And because the distributor was so uncertain about the release plan for the film, no label was willing to commit that money up front. We were left with little money for licensing and 30 songs in the film. I was asked to get quotes for major tracks that were as low as $2,500—for both sync and master combined. Major publishers and major record companies stand by their quotes, and negotiations are a very painful process. That's where the independent writer, or independent artist, can get in."

"Unless you're dealing with a $30 million plus studio feature, there's always going to be a point where the music supervisor hits the wall of pain. It will happen sometimes late in post[-production], maybe even in the two or three weeks preceding the final mix of the film, where he finds he can't afford the music the director has chosen and he has to pull out of his hat material of a similar style and quality that can be licensed very cheaply. If the supervisor had in his hand targeted material from outside the sources of the major record companies, you'd find a lot more new songwriters and artists being exposed in films."

Like anything else in the music business, the key is to network, especially with up and coming producers and directors who may be working on no-budget or low-budget independent features. "Generally it's fine to contact the music supervisor directly from the Film and Television Music Guide or another Hollywood directory," says Hill. "Be prepared to know about the nature of the film. Even when you contact the supervisor and he says, 'We're covered. Try me in a few months,' it pays to stay in touch with him. Inevitably, he's going to hit that crunch point, and that's when he's going to need your material."

Miles of Styles

Music for film and television often mirrors what's happening on the charts sonically. But with the variety of shows airing, there are many calls for diverse styles. "There are more TV and cable stations now than there have ever been," notes David Quan, director, Music Services, NBC/Universal. "If you're a subscriber, you know you've got hundreds of them. All of the stations and shows need music. It's all over the board. If you watch television shows, you will hear everything from hard alternative rock to country, depending on what shows you're viewing—even Hawaiian music."

Music, Money, and Success, penned by Jeffrey Brabec and Todd Brabec, notes these numbers for major motion pictures. "The synchronization fees charged by music publishers are usually between $15,000 and $60,000." The authors also note that record companies normally charge an additional, similarly structured fee for the use of an existing master recording.

For indie artists in television, the fees for placing songs are not enormous: $150 up to $1,600 for a track. But it adds up and the back-end performance fees from ASCAP, BMI, or SESAC can be substantial. Plus, it's huge visibility and viable credibility.

Robin Kaye: Placements with a Purpose

With credits including country juggernaut *Nashville Star* and *The Singing Bee*, Los Angeles–based Robin Kaye is an influential executive who creates opportunities and places songs in television shows. "I came from the management, artist development, and label sides before moving to L.A., where I wanted to get into film and television music," Kaye says.

"My first film and TV job was at MCA before it became Universal. Then I went to Polygram to start the film and TV department. There wasn't one, it was part of special markets in New York, but they had such a huge catalog that it was really needed."

Clarifying the extent of her duties, Kaye continues. "The responsibility is to generate income for the label and the artists by exploiting the catalog for film, TV, and advertising and other ancillary avenues while protecting the integrity of the catalog. It's managing staff, overseeing the aspects of business affairs, projecting budgets, dealing with the politics of the label, pitching artists and products, looking for new areas of exploitation, creating and maintaining relationships with clients, and dealing with the new industry rights of emerging technology."

Everything in television is time-sensitive, says Kaye. "Every show has different requirements as to what's expected and needed from the music supervisor. Sometimes the show wants you to come up with a song, or a list of songs to choose from, or they have very defined ideas of what they want. You have to deliver what the producer wants; it's about his or her vision, not your vision. It's about making producers happy in terms of how they envision the music—that's the biggest challenge."

Time Keeps on Ticking

For a music-intensive show, clearances are an enormous endeavor according to Kaye. "It's a real balancing act of getting the requests out early enough so that the people at the labels and publishers—those on the other side—have time to clear the songs for your needs. It helps to have a good general knowledge of what songs are easy to clear and which are not when you're on a time crunch. You want to save the big favors for when you really need them. Another challenging aspect is the budget—you have to find songs the show can afford to do. With most shows I'm working on, you make an overall deal. For shows with huge quantities of music, there is no way the show can pay standard industry fees and make it happen—like game shows and other music-intensive productions."

The deals for quantities of songs have to fit strict budgets, according to Kaye. "You have to work out the deal ahead of time with the labels and publishers where you get the rights you really need—you might have to do a lot of options instead of getting every-thing up front. This makes sense for both sides: you can afford the deal and explain that you're talking quantity here—more uses, more exposure—so they have to come down on the price. You structure a 'favored nations' deal and get everyone happy ahead of time, and then get rolling on the show."

"Favored nations" refers to a clause giving the benefit of any better bargain reached with another party; it's a term from diplomacy, abbreviated from "most-favored nations." MFN clauses are commonly used when a company assembles a product, such as a compilation record album, in which rights are sought from various record labels. The company assembling the compilation record may reduce the time and trouble of negotiation by assuring all licensors that they will receive the same license fee, or royalty entitlement, or both. The same concept might apply to the acquisition of rights for footage in a documentary production where, perhaps, on a per-minute basis all fees will be the same.

Indie or Major Music

Robin Kaye says that often music-intensive shows may request recognizable songs, therefore necessitating conversations with major publishers and major labels. "These days, there are so many writers who have kept their publishing or it's reverted back to them, or they have formed boutique companies, so that you might have to go to 80 to 100 publishers during doing one series. When you have a show that needs a song or two and it doesn't have to be recognizable, then it is great to go to the inde-pendents. I love being able to place a great song in something; there are great master-quality releases and undiscovered songs out there that are wonderful. You can usually make a good deal—these folks want their music used and want the exposure and they're happy to get whatever the fees. It's a win-win situation. There are also a lot of artists who have re-recorded their hits when they've reverted back from the labels, so they can license their own masters now—they sound like the originals."

"It's a juggling process between working on songs you're trying to clear, songs for upcoming episodes, and sometimes dealing with different publishing issues. There are cue sheet issues, working with the editor, you're always juggling what you're working on and the new needs, and keeping it all flowing, and you have to work with people on the show—it's different all of the time."

Kaye recalls this episode with *Nashville Star*: "We were airing on Monday, and on Sunday there was a change and they needed a song cleared—there were nine songwriters and we were able to clear it. That happens all the time, and we're always trying to pull off little miracles. It's a service-oriented industry and it's all about relationships. When you have relationships, you can call most places and get help. I come from the other side, so I have a lot of relationships. If you don't, you can't do the job."

Breaking News

"I think it's clear to everyone that it's harder for labels to break new artists," Kaye notes. "There are stories about labels breaking artists through television shows. When Letters to Cleo had a song, 'Here and Now,' on *Melrose Place*, it became a big hit. In the big picture, maybe it doesn't happen all that often, but it's a great vehicle—these songs, promos, anything that gives an audience a chance to become familiar with a song, a big main title or a background use on TV, so it's good for catalogs. When I was at Polygram we licensed "Da Da Da" by Trio for a Volkswagen commercial. Radio stations were getting calls to play it. I called Mercury, and they got it out fast and it worked."

Dollars = Sense

The fees for a television usage, Kaye explains, can range from "$1,000 to $25,000 or higher. It's crazy because there are so many rights. It's gotten pretty complicated. When video came out, everyone had to look at their contracts to see if they'd gotten all rights, and if those covered video. They had to go back again—does DVD mean the same things? Does downloading? The networks don't want to keep going back, so they want all rights cleared. But it's so expensive that you can't afford to use much music or they have to come up with the big budget. It's a problem for newer shows, so one option is to clear minimal rights up front and get options for later, so if you need it you don't have to start over."

Levi Kreis: For Kreis' Sake

Singer/songwriter Levi Kreis is a joyful independent artist. "I'm a businessman, not just a musician. It's not a responsibility, it's a freedom, because we get to decide how far we go nowadays. The difference in the industry is fantastic. I don't have to sit around and wait for 20 record company suits to decide my fate anymore."

A series of indie releases have established Kreis as a recording artist while providing a bounty of material for film and television projects. Most recently, he wrote and performed three songs—two penned with co-writer Darci Monet—in the feature film *Kiss the Bride*, starring Tori Spelling. "I met [music supervisor] David Quan through a group of friends. We were drawn to each other because of our histories," recalls Kreis. "I didn't even consider what he did, but we got a call from him asking to hear some songs for a film. He knows people I worked with in Nashville. I love that we have a common past, not only in a business perspective but also from a personal standpoint. And now here we are in the present and he's got my back. I'm very grateful."

Born in East Tennessee, Kreis broke into the business as a Christian singer/songwriter in Nashville. Post–Music City, Kreis was groomed for a major label signing in New York City. "It was all looking so fantastic, but there was some shady sh*t that I was too naïve to navigate my way through," he confides. Stuck in New York, with no release imminent, Kreis snagged an appearance on the television series *The Apprentice*, on an episode where XM Satellite radio challenged the two teams to find an unsigned artist and deliver a produced song to be heard on XM Café. "I had about seven minutes on TV," says Kreis. "I had to make the most of this moment. I had all of these ballads the label didn't want, so I sat down at a piano and made the CD [*One of the Ones*] for $200. I went to a friend to do graphics, borrowed money to manufacture CDs and set up a website. The show aired and I couldn't keep up with thousands and thousands of requests for this album."

Joel Evans: Making the Screen Swing

Must you endure the rigors of L.A. life in order to be a successful songwriter and composer for film and television? Not if you're distinctive and resourceful: Meet Joel Evans, a musician and bandleader from the Bay Area whose extensive list of credits includes major Hollywood films, hip indie flicks, network shows, and daytime dramas. He has over 50 big-screen credits and 200 television episodes and counting—from *Wedding Crashers* to *Desperate Housewives*.

A self-professed "credits addict," Evans keeps close tabs on who is responsible for placing music in projects, but he's reticent to make the calls on his own behalf. "I think it's better if I could have a representative contact people for me. I feel awkward calling people and blowing my own horn. It feels untoward. I've gotten better about it, less shy; I can say I've got a few film and TV credits to lubricate the situation."

His sophisticated melodies are often used on screen to evoke sumptuous surroundings like hotel lobbies and upscale restaurants, so it's no coincidence that Evans spent many years performing in just these types of venues as a live player. Swing, big band, and jazz—he occupies a decided stylistic niche. "I can't do everything. I don't write stuff that's like what's on the radio. I decided early on to hell with it: I'm going to do stuff that I love."

Aaron Zigman Composes Himself

As a producer, songwriter, arranger, and musician, Aaron Zigman created a multiplatinum resumé that mirrored an annotated reputation as one of the West Coast's more prolific music makers. He walked away from it all to score films such as *Sex in the City*, *The Notebook*, *John Q*, *Alpha Dog*, *Akleelah and the Bee*, *Bridge to Terabithia*, and many others. Zigman's ability to create memorable scores in genres from drama and comedy to action films has, in just a few short years, moved him to the top rank of today's film composers. "You have to decide what you are in life," says Zigman. "Are you a composer? What are you a composer of?"

A native of San Diego, Zigman began his piano training at age six. In his early teens, he discovered classical music and jazz; he played in bands and after high school enrolled at UCLA. In his third year of college, he signed a songwriting deal with Almo-Irving Music. He produced demos, worked as a side musician, and began arranging and orchestrating. This led to his career as a producer, songwriter, and arranger. His formidable list of pop accomplishments includes projects with Christina Aguilera, Seal, Aretha Franklin, Natalie Cole, Phil Collins, Tina Turner, Chicago, and Carly Simon. Zigman's work has also been featured on film soundtracks for *Mulan*, *What's Love Got to Do with It?*, *The Birdcage*, *License to Kill*, and *Pocahontas*, among others.

Creating orchestral music for film, Zigman says, was always his destiny. "I produced all these pop records and worked with all these divas," offers Zigman. "Songwriting gave me the gift of writing melody—writing something memorable with harmonic aspects. Still, you can only go so far in pop writing. If you write a great tune—whether it's Ennio Morricone, or John Williams, or Mozart, who wrote 'Twinkle, Twinkle Little Star,' everything else is inside, intricate. Classical music is good melodies. And the listener will walk away with something evocative."

Zigman's cousin, George Bassman, a composer who scored classics including *The Postman Always Rings Twice* and a songwriter noted for the Tommy Dorsey Orchestra classic "Getting Sentimental Over You," offered a window into the wider musical world. "He turned me on to the litany of classical music," recalls Zigman, "I didn't formally go to music school. I've digested information over the years, but I'm self-taught. I'm musically educated but I didn't go to a formal institution; I got it all hands-on in the studio."

As his list of pop accomplishments grew, a larger musical picture evolved. "When I got a taste of being around orchestras, I began gravitating to classical music," Zigman recalls. "I started writing serious music and developing relationships with different groups of orchestral musicians, who were the best—hanging out with them, going to concerts, listening to classical music, getting educated." And he could draw a correlation between the concert hall and the recording studio. "Orchestrating is about writing other parts that fit the song. It's just a mini-form of orchestral writing. It's the same thing, just a different sonority."

Setting the Scoring Stage

Zigman also composes concert works. He penned a 35-minute tone poem tribute to Yitzhak Rabin performed by the Los Angeles Jewish Symphony and *Impressions*, a suite for wind ensemble rendered by the USC Symphony Orchestra.

Zigman's entrée into the world of studio pictures commenced when he invited film-maker Nick Cassavetes to a performance of a classical piece. "Nick put the opportunity to score his feature *John Q* in front of me. I went into the Capitol studios with 55 musicians and recorded my first opening." The composer himself footed the bill for this prodigious venture. But Zigman's music didn't make it into the temp score for the initial screening; instead, a version of "Ave Maria" was heard over the opening scene. "I couldn't sleep," Zigman recalls. "I thought this was a signal, since 'Ave Maria' was there I would have to write my own version of it. That was the second phase. I wrote a template and recorded with opera singers from the L.A. Chamber Orchestra. I wrote a six-minute cue and went into Capitol and did it again. Nick loved it, the editor loved it, and then it had to get past the studio, New Line. I walked into a meeting at New Line, but I still didn't have the job. I had to prove myself with the temp score. I was given a little budget for a full day of scoring at Todd-A-O. I jumped three hurdles and then the movie wailed in the previews. I was attached."

www.aaronzigman.com

Gustavo Santaolalla: Rocking the Oscars

"To affect people in a positive way is a spiritual task."

To date, composer Gustavo Santaolalla has scored only seven films. "I'm very picky," he concurs. "I'd rather do not so many movies, but really good ones." These credits include two Academy Award–winning scores: *Brokeback Mountain* and *Babel*, as well as *Amores Perros*, *21 Grams*, and *The Motorcycle Diaries*.

Defying convention, Santaolalla will often create the music before the film is shot. Director Ang Lee's *Brokeback Mountain* was the most extreme example of this approach. "I met Ang Lee only once before I did the music. I find it better to work from a more abstract side rather than scoring, 'When the guy comes out of the car and goes into the house and we're supposed to be scared.' I prefer to work from what the story makes me feel, or makes me think about, and obviously listening to how the director perceives the story."

The taciturn director offered few verbal clues. "Ang Lee is not a director who talks too much, and you can probably certify this with actors who have worked with him. When I met with him, I had already read the story, and we were talking about guitar and strings. We were in sync, and I added it should have dissonant elements. Then I went to the studio and did it. In an interview, he said he put together the narrative of the movie to the music, but it was his genius. When he did his first cut, it was magic to watch the film and see how he blended the music with the images and the story."

Santaolalla's signature cinema sound includes silence. "That's been one of my trademarks. I don't discount the possibility of doing a big symphonic piece or something more beefy because I like to explore everything. But so far, I've tried to develop a style using an approach that is similar: a minimalistic use of instruments, use of textures, and space and silence. I think you will find that in every score. *Brokeback Mountain* is not like *Babel*, but they have that in common."

Born in Argentina in 1952, while still a teenager Santaolalla co-founded Arco Iris, a group that pioneered the fusion of rock and Latin American folk. In the mid-seventies, his band Soluna, which included future hit maker Alejandro Lerner, recorded one album before Santaolalla departed for Los Angeles. In California, he played with Wet Picnic with his future partner in Surco Records, Anibal Kerpel, and briefly returned to Argentina, where he tracked his first solo record. Emerging as Latin alternative music's preeminent record producer, Santaolalla subsequently worked with Mexican acts Fobia, Molotov, Café Tacuba, and Julieta Venegas, with Colombian superstar Juanes, and with Argentine rock bands Divididos and Bersuit Vergarabat, among many others.

Accolades, Oscars, Grammy awards, and gold and platinum records notwithstanding, Santaolalla divines a deeper purpose to his creative endeavors. "As a kid, I was going to be a priest. I had my first spiritual crisis at 11—I came with questions that had to do with if God was almighty and infinitely kind, then how could eternal punishment exist? And if the devil and hell could exist, and God couldn't take care of it, then maybe the devil was on God's payroll. They wanted to send me to an exorcist! But my parents were very understanding."

"Then I started studying Eastern religion, and I joined a community and lived a monastic life between 18 and 24 years old. I was celibate; I fasted once a week, and I meditated. Then I split from that and regained all of the time that I had lost at full throttle!" His creative gifts, Santaolalla shares, come with deep responsibilities. "I've always been on that sort of quest, that search, and I have a powerful connection. It's a big part of who I am and why I do what I do. To affect people in a positive way is a spiritual task."

Randy Edelman: Images in Ivory

"You have to have your sh*t together, so if you're fortunate enough that if you get the opportunity, you can do it and not have it overwhelm you."

Individual ivory keys on the battered Steinway dominating Randy Edelman's tower-like writing room have been worn down to the wood. "If they don't like it here, they won't like it with a 100-piece orchestra," says Edelman. "They" are presumably the legion of producers and directors who have ventured up these stairs to hear the film scores Edelman has composed over the past few decades. Popular favorites such as *XXX* and *Dragon: The Bruce Lee Story*; comedies, including *My Cousin Vinnie, Kindergarten Cop*, and *Shanghai Knights*; historical epics such as *Gettysburg* and *Last of the Mohicans*. Blockbusters, cult hits, tele-pics, TV, symphonic pieces, Olympic and sports themes—Edelman has conceived them all on this piano.

As a student of the classics, Edelman commenced his career as a pianist in Teaneck, New Jersey. Continuing at the Cincinnati Music Conservatory, he orchestrated charts for the city's R&B label, King Records, and acts such as James Brown. Edelman wrote pop songs in New York, played in Broadway pit orchestras, and arranged and conducted on the road and in Las Vegas. He parlayed his songwriting artistry into a solo career, during which he attained cult status in England and toured with both the Carpenters and Frank Zappa and the Mothers of Invention. One song he included on his album *Fairwell Fairbanks* almost didn't make the cut. Performing at the London Palladium, he even omitted it from his set list. Later, that song "Weekend in New England" would become a definitive smash for Barry Manilow.

Although his opulent themes reflect his classical roots, Edelman's pop background helps him get to the heart of the musical matter. "To quickly come up with a track and the right mood is invaluable for me," he affirms. "Whatever is in my musical consciousness I draw upon. It could be the most sophisticated theme, *Firebird* by Stravinsky, or the best grassroots pop tune. That's what's a turn on. It's like making records, but you don't have the time—you have two or three days. If I'm doing a Southern Allman Brothers rock 'n' roll thing for *My Cousin Vinnie* or an Eddie Murphy film, or *Ed TV* or *Ghostbusters II*, or *The Whole Nine Yards*—a jazz thing—my background is invaluable."

After composing, orchestrating, and sequencing at home, Edelman will often take a small ensemble into the studio, sometimes with specialty or ethnic instruments, if the score warrants. He's equally at home conducting a 100-piece orchestra on a cavernous sound stage. "You're not just conducting a piece, you're conducting something that no one has ever heard in that time," he says. "My experience in Las Vegas is invaluable in terms of walking into an orchestra where people are screaming in your headset and making changes."

Edelman is possessed of a dynamic personality. "As a composer, I think you almost have to have one," he stresses, "you've got to take a stand sometimes. I go into these meetings and it's very easy for me to talk about music and creativity. I can't sit there and not be myself. Every scene and cue has exactly the same importance, and to the directors and producers as well. It's under the microscope."

For anyone who would like to break into scoring, Edelman offers this advice: "You have to have your theory and performing on your instrument, orchestrating, arranging, and conducting, and somehow get into a recording studio where they're doing anything. You have to have your sh*t together so if you're fortunate enough that if you get the opportunity, you can do it and not have it overwhelm you. And it's still overwhelming—to me too—but I'm a musician. That's what you have to be."

www.randyedelman.com

Carter Burwell: Sounds of Twilight

Twilight, a hit motion picture featuring lithesome teen vampires locked in eternal embrace, features a score by a composer known for his contributions to offbeat projects. Despite the differences in tone, Carter Burwell avows that it is his essential task "to make the film as a whole compelling, dramatic, emotional, and cinematic."

Burwell is probably best known for his scores to the films of Joel and Ethan Coen, including *Blood Simple, Raising Arizona, Miller's Crossing, Barton Fink, The Hudsucker Proxy, Fargo, The Big Lebowski*, and *The Man Who Wasn't There*. In addition to films by the Coens, Burwell has also scored *Gods and Monsters, Velvet Goldmine, Being John Malkovich*, and *Before Night Falls*. His approximate output is about five films annually. "Which in retrospect seems like too many," the composer says. "An important criterion is if the film offers me an opportunity to do something I haven't done before." Burwell professes that he doesn't pay attention to what other composers are doing in film scoring. "I'm generally not that moved by what passes for film music. But that's not being critical of anyone or style or instrumentation, so little is demanded by the people making films that there isn't that much interesting work going on. The people making the film want music to serve the film. There's no one demanding phenomenal music."

Burwell, a New York native, came up playing keyboards in bands. These days, his main live ax is the accordion. "At a certain point, I got tired of lugging things around and having to plug them in. I wanted something I play while I was walking in the woods." Among his non-screen credits are music for chamber operas and plays; he also wrote music to accompany the late author William Burroughs' reading of his novel *Junky* for Penguin Audiobooks. "He tended to use a monotone with precise rhythms," he recalls. "It was the last year of his life, he wasn't in great shape, so each day he'd be in various states of mind. It's pretty strange."

In films, Burwell's musical dialogue with the director is conveyed through sketches. "I make musical storyboards. I'm not trying to put a lot of expressive detail into my sketches. I'm using a lot of synthesizers and samplers, but I don't want to waste my time putting information in that will be replaced by live musicians. I'm not pretending they sound like the final recording. In *Fargo*, that solo fiddle—I wouldn't know how to synthesize that; it's easier to hire a real fiddle player."

www.carterburwell.com

Jeff Beal: Sounds of the Clean Slate

"I feel like I'm playing in a band. But this time, the band is the actors, the director, the photographer, and the editor."

In the farthest territories of North Los Angeles County, equestrians gallop on horseback down the street where Emmy Award–winning composer Jeff Beal lives and works. There also are saddles and stirrups aplenty in a film, *Appaloosa,* which he scored, but Beal clarifies that the saga with actor/director Ed Harris, Viggo Mortensen, Renée Zellweger, and Jeremy Irons is not a Western, but rather "a film that takes place in the West. It's the characters first. We found the right times to pay homage to the genre, but the music is motivated by these people you meet and follow through the story."

Pollack, a previous Harris-directed and acted film, marked a major career ascension for Beal, although not the way he envisioned. "I thought that film would launch me into a feature career. What it did even more was launch me into this TV world of really high-quality shows." Beal currently scores two popular series, *Monk* (USA) and *Ugly Betty* (ABC). He also scored *Rome* and *Carnivàle* (HBO) and *The Company* (TNT), for which he was honored with a 2008 Primetime Emmy Award for Outstanding Music Composition for a Miniseries, Movie, or Special (Original Dramatic Score). Beal notes that the increasing popularity of high-definition television makes the audio/visual experience more enthralling. "Acting talent and composers are rising to the occasion. And the projects are getting better and better."

Born in Hayward, California, Beal, an accomplished trumpet player, lived in New York City, where he was signed to a record deal. Returning to California, first to San

Francisco, and then to Los Angeles in 1992, he continued making solo CDs while composing for other mediums, including an orchestral jazz trumpet concerto for the Berkeley Symphony. His background in Latin jazz is advantageous for *Ugly Betty*. "It's refreshing to see a show that has this great Latin element to it," he explains. "I'm definitely a gringo, but being a trumpet player, I was playing with salsa bands every Saturday night in New York."

Beal recognizes that many composers have a signature sound, and although he avows that certain elements of his own work are equally identifiable, he prefers to change it up per project. "I like the 'ADD kinetic' form of reinventing. I get bored very easily. That's why I like to work alone. I move fast. I love the idea of wiping the slate clean and saying, "What are we going to do now?'"

Beal, who plays trumpet on many of his scores, including *Appaloosa*, says that his approach as a film composer extends to the freewheeling camaraderie of improvisational jazz. "I feel like I'm playing in a band. But this time, the band is the actors, the director, the photographer, and the editor. What I do as a film composer is only as good as how it fits in with everything else."

www.jeffbeal.com

Mike Knobloch: Sounds on the Lot

"Now you can cherry pick yours songs off iTunes. The landscape has changed. Film and TV are the new radio."

Mike Knobloch, senior vice president for film music at 20th Century Fox, says he "zigzagged" into his position. "I worked on my first movie in 1991 as a production assistant. I was on the set, in the cutting room, and when we got to the scoring stage, I saw the orchestra and realized the power of the underscore. I thought, 'That's where I've got to be.' I used any opportunity to get me to music or film. I've had a musical life personally and professionally. I was an assistant to filmmakers and then got a job working in the recording studio for composer/recording artist and producer Steve Tyrell. From there, I worked on a TV show, then to here. To do what we do, there's no kind of proper training or background. I was always pursuing or working as much around professional music as I could. Training is a good thing, but there's so much that can't be taught to be successful. Good people skills, attitude and intuition, and getting over a sense of entitlement. It's the 'nothing is beneath me' attitude that starts opening doors."

Curveballs

Knobloch confesses that although he might come to work thinking he knows the day's schedule, it will invariably change. "Somewhere between 9 to 11 a.m., someone will throw me a curve ball and hijack my entire day because we put out fires and 'emergencies.' My staff and myself oversee all of the music for all the films in production at 20th Century Fox, and Fox is split into different divisions. There are dozens of movies here in various stages of production. I have to make sure everything is on track and everything has been delegated properly. For example, in pre-production, we have to pre-record music or go to locations or sets. If there's a band playing in the movie, we make sure it all looks authentic. We might be anywhere along the timeline of putting these movies together, planning what needs to be done and checked off the list. It's a never ending 'to do' list."

Directorial Decisions

Working with film directors is a major part of the equation in Knobolch's creative universe. "I'll get as close as the director will allow. Everyone has an opinion about music and sometimes people don't want to be told anything. Some projects are intensely music-driven: *Titanic, Moulin Rouge, Walk the Line, Drumline, Juno, Alvin and the Chipmunks*. Sometimes we hire a supervisor and then I supervise the supervisor. We have to make sure the filmmaker is communicating with the composer and sometimes we act like a marriage counselor. You want to nurture a healthy relationship between collaborators. A lot of people say show me credits and give me a CD. That's not the right way to hire a composer. I don't think credits do it alone and I encourage directors to meet the composer. It's a process that is sometimes overlooked. You want to make sure people like each other and get along. We're a service organization. We're helping to build the foundation. Music is hugely important. Pick your favorite movie and listen to it without music."

"Sometimes the journey is complex, but when you intentionally or not arrive at your destination, you can't articulate how you got there—it just works. You don't want people to further complicate an already complicated process. A director shouldn't talk like a musician; if he does, you're in trouble, because it's not the director's job to speak like a musician. Guys like me exist because ego gets in the way of things. Artists are sensitive people. When things get off course, it's because of that reason. This is also why rock stars can't come in and score movies. Our deadlines are really deadlines."

Sync Sense

Fox employs an extensive licensing department and clearance personnel to handle film and TV. "It's a huge business. Since the traditional music business is imploding, the only thing still healthy is revenue from licensing and master recordings. There's huge frustration for me because people are unreasonable and it's usually major labels and major publishing companies. If I was at one of the majors, I would think it advantageous to bring in five $20,000 master licenses rather than hold out for one $100,000 license. It's annoying because as a supervisor, I'm spending way too much of my time simply swapping things out in movies because people won't be reasonable with their prices. I worked on an $8 million production where I could only afford around $5,000 for a license. But I'm straight with people, and I will do initial brokering, and I say up front what I can afford. I can't believe that after all of the years we've been licensing material, there's nothing scientific about it. There's no scale—you would think by now there would be a system, a way to dictate whether a song peaked on the chart or however you quantify how big a song is. This should dictate how much a song is worth to license."

Aspiring Hiring

For those who want to work in film or television music–related industries, Knobloch believes there are many opportunities to gain information and experience. "I lecture at USC and UCLA, and there is a NARAS [National Academy of Recording Arts and Sciences] summer Grammy Camp, where students score clips from Fox movies. Like any artist in any field where there is competition, you just have to be tenacious. Hook up with all your favorite peers who are aspiring filmmakers. Go where student films are made and say, 'I'll score your movie.' Generate material and approach people who are doing what you want to do."

But don't call Knobloch fishing for cues. "People will call up and ask what I'm working on. It's my least favorite question in life. Well, if I tell you, can I have half the commission? Read the trades. The resources are infinite and huge, and there's no excuse not to know what is happening. If you're starting out in your craft and want to get ahead, know the answer to these questions, and you're well ahead of the game. The other thing I would tell people is, in addition to learning the craft, understand that it is highly specialized. Someone who has a vague interest in what you want to do can't help you. Understand all of the facets of what you want to do and connect to these people."

8 The Lawyer

Some lawyers might think that they are God, and charge accordingly. But in this day and age of business, having legal expertise will be paramount. Throughout music history, there have been numerous stories of creative entities that did not have legal advice and signed contracts that were totally unfair. All labels will have someone who finalizes a recording or a production contract. A major record company will have in-house lawyers in their business affairs department. All artists, songwriters, and producers, for that matter, should have legal representation as well.

As you will read in this chapter, lawyers who represent artists are experts in their field and are involved in advising artists and negotiating contracts across the board; this could mean recording contracts, publishing agreements, branding deals, sync licensing, and many other possible opportunities.

Andy Tavel: Shifting Currents in the Revenue Streams

"The music business is more powerful than ever; it's the record business that's in trouble. And the long-term money is in songwriting—it makes money for you while you're sleeping."

Andy Tavel says he didn't choose the music business; "it fell into my lap. I always wanted to be an entertainment lawyer but, unlike many of my colleagues, I don't have any artistic talents. I can't sing, dance, or act but I'm a huge entertainment fan, whether it is movies, television, theater, or music. And a firm specializing in the music business was the first job opportunity that opened up for me. So music it was. Being an entertainment lawyer allows me to be involved with the industry, structuring deals, negotiating, and connecting people."

Tavel taught law school for a year in Miami. "I wasn't ready to enter the real world, which probably made me well suited for the music industry. While I was there, someone badly wanted to be in my class because he knew I, too, was interested in entertainment law: Fred Goldring [Goldring Hertz & Lichtenstein LLP]. He and I became close friends and took the bar together. I came to NY and worked for a large corporate law firm that promised me entertainment law but only did a minimal amount. Fred went to a small law firm doing largely music work." Goldring next got a job at Grubman, Indursky and Schindler and, when it was time for that firm to look for the next associate, he recommended Tavel. "Fred coached me what to say and I got a job at the Grubman firm (by the way, making half of what I had been making at the corporate law firm). I tell people all of the time: It's the paradigm of our industry—I gave Fred an 'A' and he got me a job in the music industry."

For over two-and-a-half decades, Tavel has practiced entertainment law in New York City. He served as vice president of business affairs at Def Jam Records prior to founding the entertainment law firm of Tavel, Thea, and Baker. In 1999, he joined Greenberg Traurig as a shareholder to launch the New York office's entertainment practice. Tavel's primary concentration is the music industry, and he serves as counsel to over 100 clients spanning the spectrum from emerging artists to established stars, from established labels to startup production companies, as well as industry executives, music publishers, songwriters, talent agencies, merchandisers, video directors, producers, and managers.

"There are certain projects we do for art and certain things we do for commerce," Tavel says. "I may greatly appreciate what an artist is doing and not get paid. Then there are those that pay the rent, but I'm really not that into what they are doing artistically. When you're more enthusiastic about the music you're representing, it's more enjoyable. And when art and commerce combine, fantastic."

"As a general rule, my loyalties are more on the artist side, looking out for the little guy. It can be rewarding to 'do good' and to make money at the same time, helping artists realize their vision by handling aspects of their career that they're not well equipped to handle. I help to put together the right team—manager, business manager, agent, and publicist—to surround the artist with all the right elements so that they can succeed. In all of my years, I've never been bored."

Deals for Real

"Fewer deals for fewer dollars" is how Tavel characterizes the current economic climate in the record business. "I recently did a deal with an advance of $400,000. A few years ago, it would have been a million dollar deal. Now that money is drying up, no one is doing as many signings and the nature of the deals have changed. Up-front dollars are being replaced by an opportunity for a greater back-end participation."

For artists to make the money comparable to what they earned a decade ago, Tavel says it is essential to tap additional income streams: "Endorsement deals, fan clubs, co-branded licensing, and sponsorships, to name a few. It's a big transition from when there were four primary income streams—publishing, touring, merchandising, and records. The artists that I especially gravitate toward are entertainers, accessible and multidimensional in areas other than the music business. Physical product is disappearing, and, unfortunately, we have a generation that now thinks music is free. Film and television projects can supplement this economic loss and afford the lawyers with more opportunities for creative thinking, as an artist's career is no longer as linear."

The 360 deals and the emergence of concert promoter Live Nation as an industry force in areas outside of the touring business signify the changes of which Tavel speaks. He negotiated that company's deals with Madonna, Jay-Z, Shakira, and U2. "Music is fast becoming the commercial that sells tours and merchandise. That's where the most money is being made—and that's why the record labels want to get into this. They now recognize that you don't have individual silos of income streams—records, touring, publishing, etc; they are all interconnected. In fact, the 360 concept that isn't sufficiently written about is the crucial and central role of the website. While there, the fan might want to buy tickets or merchandise, join the fan club, or download and purchase music directly from the website. It is one-stop shopping, 24/7, for the fan to acquire most anything they want related to an artist's career. And while the fans are happy, the artist is also making money."

The 360 or all-rights concept is important in another way. "Madonna didn't sign with Live Nation; she partnered with Live Nation. If a record company is a partner and works collaboratively with the artist and the artist's team, it makes for a better relationship and maximizes income streams as well as best advances an artist's career. It is doing what is in the artist's long-term interest. And it allows everyone the comfort and time to be more collaborative."

Establishing and exploiting a brand through a plethora of licensing opportunities is one of the primary means of replacing the artist's income stream that no longer comes from record sales. "This ensures that artists have commercially viable careers and are not momentary flashes in the pan. Madonna is a brand. When her name is utilized, you expect a certain type of and quality of products to be consistent with the Madonna persona, just as you do with other strong brands like Mercedes or Disney. Sean "Puffy" Combs created a clothing line and opened restaurants associated with his name/brand and has probably done better than most in this area. Songs in commercials for a product also help sell records. Shakira with Verizon, for example. Soon artists will have deals with advertising companies. Song exposure in return for helping to sell a product."

The Disney Dollars

Tavel thinks that, in general, there is far too much concern about percentages. "Artists get hung up on paying a manager 15 versus 20 percent. They should focus on what they are making, not on what someone else is making. If the manager is enabling you to pocket more money than you would on your own or with a lesser manager who may charge less, then don't begrudge their participation, especially if they helped to get you there in the first place."

A similar concept holds true when dealing with companies. "The Cheetah Girls on Disney, two of whom I represented, is a prime example of this concept as well a successful 360 project. With minimal fanfare and expectations, Disney produced a television movie and recorded seven songs. Nothing long-term was contemplated. The soundtrack was a surprise success and sold 1.3 million copies. Since then, five albums were recorded, and Disney's participation has included merchandise as well as touring. (In fact, the Cheetahs were the first tour that Disney had ever produced.) There wasn't any area of Cheetah Girls' revenues that Disney didn't partake and their percentage of the income was substantial; after all, it was a Disney property. But financially, the Cheetah Girls didn't do so badly either. As evidenced by *High School Musical* and Miley Cyrus, Disney has mastered this all-rights concept—but Miley is not suffering, despite the percentage of income that Disney retains."

The Glory of the Story

The DIY (do-it-yourself) method is what Tavel generally espouses for emerging artists, especially rock bands. "Use the Internet to generate enough exposure for people to take an interest in you. A lawyer shopping a demo? Those glory days are over. To get signed, you need to have a story, whether it's a song on *Grey's Anatomy* or selling 10,000 CDs on the road. Remember Lisa Loeb? She couldn't get signed; then she had a song in a movie ["Stay" in *Reality Bites*] that became a number-one hit. Everyone who initially passed on her now wanted to sign her. A great story. So develop your own story."

A corollary, the "do it without a record company" model, also can hold true for long-established, career artists who have both the advantage of leverage and a built-in fan base. "With superstars, a lot of what a record company offers can be outsourced by the artist, all to their economic advantage, as they are able to obtain far better deals than they would have with or through the record company, a middleman. Also, the artists' independence is far greater. I represent James Taylor, who decides when he wants to tour and when he wants to record a new album—as well as who the distributor will be for each product—without any record company constraints or dictates as to delivery schedules and recording commitments. And the Eagles' deal with Wal-Mart also showed how well financially an artist could do without a record label. The rules are being rewritten on a daily basis."

www.gtlaw.com/People/AndrewGTavel

Dina LaPolt: Legal Language

"I don't want to hear your songs. I don't want to go down to your show. I'm a business-person. I don't have any say of what's good and what's not good or what is going to sell."

As a Los Angeles–based entertainment lawyer, Dina LaPolt considers her role in the spectrum of the music business. "People who come to me say, 'This is something special,' and we'll build it together. I know my role in the industry. A big problem is that people overstep their boundaries a lot, and it's not appropriate. Some of my big rap clients will ask what I think, and I'm like, 'Why are you asking me? Please, do not make any decisions based on what I like. You have a responsibility to your fans. You don't want to take tips from a white 43-year-old lesbian lawyer.'"

Booking the Thrash

LaPolt informs that the legal profession was not her first entrée into the music business. "I never aspired to be a lawyer. I was in a band when I was 13. When I was 16, we started touring, got signed to a crappy record deal, and had a manager. I didn't understand any of the business. I was in the band as a creative person. I went to college and got my bachelor's degree in music. I was also doing concert promotion and was a talent buyer who brought concerts to the colleges. Then I started working for the drummer of KISS and booking heavy-metal female thrash bands."

She relocated to the West Coast from New York. "I ended up in the San Francisco Bay area doing concert promotion and I was also in a band again. I put myself through law school. I was approaching 30 and I thought, 'I don't want to do this anymore.' Health insurance became attractive. I was tired of living in a van and eating mac and cheese."

"When I graduated from law school and passed the bar in three days, I actually wanted to stay in San Francisco because I had a little bit of a name and I was managing punk bands. I started doing punk nights and that became a niche market for me. The music I was working with needed me to move to L.A. An ex-girlfriend's sister called me; she was living in L.A. and asked if I was an entertainment lawyer. She was Miss June in Playboy, and I was down in three days. I couldn't find a job; I didn't understand any of the business at all. So I got an internship for a lawyer in L.A. for 18 months in Century City and parked at the mall."

Bringing Up the Artist

Eventually, LaPolt understood the bigger picture of the artist/lawyer dynamic. "It's a business; once you know how it operates and understand the mechanics, you start manipulating the system to get what you want. As far as developing artists, it's not about who's good, but how you put it together to make audiences want them and then [use] other people's money to build your brand. It's contingent on how young they are, their star power, and the look. If they have the look, then everything is fine. I will take a group that is young and has star power, then start bringing in the experts—songwriters, producers, and radio promo—and start creating. Depending on that, they'll tell me what's good and what's not good. I bring together the people, huge producers and song-writers, and then I leave it up to them. What comes from those collaborations? Is it good? I don't know, but I give it to prominent radio programming people, or heavy-hitter A&R people that are my friends that wouldn't hold it against me if it's not good. So I give to those I have close relationships with. And I only go to a label when it's time to go to them."

Building the brand, LaPolt says, is imperative. "Now that the Internet has leveled the playing field, deal making is very creative. Indies are becoming a prominent force in A&R'ing the music. They have taken over what major labels used to do. The majors are a machine and you have to give them something. There is no difference from pitch-ing a TV show to a network and taking an artist to a major label. You have to be ready to go. You can't sit there with an idea and some executives and think you can create *Ugly Betty*. You have to come with everything attached—heavy-hitter producers on the record and the songs already complete. Find a great indie-rock label, make a great rec-ord for $50,000, and if the band is touring, then the ball is moving forward."

The Band with a Brand

"In order to get a company to want to put up millions of dollars, you have to create a brand, where the company says, 'If I invest, I'll get a return.' Whatever that demo-graphic is, if you're a rock band that appeals to mainstream, you can create a brand with Guitar Hero and similar media. Hip-hop or rap artists might get involved with an apparel or sneaker line. It's about who you're seen with; it's all about associations."

Spinning the 360 Deal

Indie labels, says LaPolt, have historically shared in multiple revenue streams with artists. "Indie budgets have gotten bigger. There are different types of 360 employer/employee deals where the label owns the entire brand, people are just employees, and they get a salary and expense account. Group members don't own any part of the brand—an example is Pussycat Dolls. Or the labels share in the income streams of merchan-dising and touring, but the artist controls everything. Or you have a deal, then also have an employment deal for TV and acting and branding, for example. So the deal-making process now is very creative. As a lawyer, that's most enjoyable. There's no 'No' any-more, it's more, 'What are you proposing and why?' Labels have to be open to other ways of business. By the time a major wants an act, there has to be something that's happening. They're no longer signing people because they're good, it's an antiquated part of the business. You have to tell them it's unique—everyone wants something different, but they don't know what's different until you tell them it's different."

"You're educating the labels. Another problem with big labels is they're demanding to be involved in building every aspect of the artist's career. They want input and approval rights with sponsorship things and touring and merchandise, and it's terrible. That's the atrocity of all this—they're sharing income streams, but they don't know what they're doing. You're sitting there educating these label lawyers, which is very difficult and time-consuming. I'm a firm believer that you need to be a deal maker and not a deal breaker. If you start killing deals and your artist is still working at Starbucks, there's a problem."

www.lapltlaw.com

Ben McLane: Law and Loyalty

"Nobody gave me anything—I had to go out and make it. It's the way artists have to treat their careers—they can't wait for anyone to do anything for them. You have to do it yourself and hope for the best."

In a city full of entertainment lawyers of all stripes and with all degrees of reputations, attorney Ben McLane sustains a sterling reputation as a champion of recording artists and songwriters. McLane, who contributes regularly to a wide range of industry publications, is the co-founder of the firm McLane and Wong (in conjunction with his wife, Venice Antoinette Wong, Esq.).

McLane has been awarded gold and platinum records for Big Bad Voodoo Daddy, the Dixie Chicks, Tracy Byrd, 311, Guns 'n' Roses, Cher, Mya, Eagles, Khia, Anita Baker, Alicia Keys, Mary J. Blige, 50 Cent, Nine Inch Nails, Keyshia Cole, Sean Kingston, and Jay-Z, plus soundtracks for *Above the Rim, Sparkle, Afroman, Swingers*, and *That's So Raven*. Additional projects have included such marquee names as Weezer, Black Eyed Peas, Katy Perry, and Santana.

"I'm a music attorney now, but I was always a fan of music," McLane begins. "I grew up in the Midwest, and I'm old enough that when I was kid, AM radio was still around and they would call it all pop music—pop, rock, country, middle of the road. I heard a wide variety and became a record collector who read the backs of the records; who wrote and produced the artists. I became a music fanatic. I played in the school band, but I was never good on a musician level; I figured a lawyer had respect. I moved to Los Angeles to go to law school so I could break in. It's who you know, so

I interned at Rhino and Priority Records and worked at a management company who had Bruce Hornsby, Rickie Lee Jones, the Posies, and Leon Russell."

McLane did artist management on the side, but avows that it was a tough road. "Unless you have a band on the road and they're making some money. If you're young, you can live off ramen noodles and sleep on a mattress. I focused on the law, but it was a tough time when we came out of law school in the nineties with not many job openings. I worked for firms and tried to develop a clientele on the side by going to clubs, meeting bands, and working cheap to get my foot in the door. It evolved to where we have our firm, although I never intended to have my own practice. You have to work hard, make yourself indispensable, and you have to love and understand music. There is no guarantee of rewards. You have to enjoy it. It's dealing with a lot of personalities. Be prepared—I don't want to dwell on it, but there are dishonest people, people who aren't loyal and will stab you in the back, so you've got to have a thick skin."

The Signing Buzz

"It's always been difficult to get a record deal with a legitimate label that's going to be excited about the artist, promote and stick with them, and give them a break," McLane acknowledges. "The slots have diminished at the major label level; but strangely enough, there are more independent labels popping up. Some are artist vanity labels that sign other acts, but Capitol, Warner Bros., Interscope, etc.—they don't sign acts unless they see a tremendous buzz, that there is something going on, so it's less of a risk."

A demand in the marketplace, McLane says, is a significant factor. "Artists need a fan base, to sell CDs, to play shows, to get in front of people, and get some kind of airplay, even if it is on the Internet, to prove there is some demand for the music that they're making. The A&R vision at labels that used to be there isn't there now, so they need realistic indicators they can hold in their hands. It's difficult when an artist is really good, but hasn't developed anything outside the music. It makes it hard for me to get anyone interested. If they can bring me great music—which they have to—there have to be other things going on to excite a label, because the labels just want to make money. It's a business. It's hard to get labels to take a shot on something that's new and unproven on any level."

That said, McLane avows that he does work with new artists "if they're great. Some aren't ready for a major deal, but they're ready for an indie. We go one step at a time. When we get involved, we want to be involved long term, hopefully. We try to do the big picture."

McLane notes that the independent labels have ceilings on sales. "With limited staff and resources, generally speaking, and there are some exceptions, but on an indie you're not going to sell more than 100,000 to 150,000 units. With the majors, the overheads are greater, they have to sell a lot more units to make it profitable. But if you want a giant career with all of the mass media, an independent usually can't provide that for you. They're good at starting things and dealing with niches—bluegrass, gospel, or jazz—that the majors wouldn't touch, so they're very important. I firmly believe that an act should have a record company backing them. This gives them more clout in the marketplace with that marketing and promotion machine."

What the Act Can Do

McLane sees artists making solid livings even without labels. "If they can create a fan base on their own, especially with the Internet, then fans can buy product: CDs, shirts, tickets to the shows, and the fans can invest money. You can create that on your own; it might not be as pervasive as if you're on the radio and people find out about you. I don't see why an artist can't connect with 50,000 fans worldwide if they're really good and they know how to work the Internet."

Deals These Daze

From McLane's perspective, modern deal making isn't overtly different. "As far as the contractual aspects, it hasn't changed. There's a piece of paper and key points: a record deal, a publishing deal, a management deal, a booking agreement—there is a checklist of things that go back 45 or 50 years and certain industry standards that haven't changed." That said, McLane is an avid reader of *Billboard* magazine so that he can stay current with issues relating to the Internet or to downloading. "There's no reason people can't keep up with it, but you have to do these things and get your hands dirty to really become an expert."

Labels are increasingly signing bands to 360 deals, allowing the label multiple income streams from music publishing, live shows, and merchandise. In exchange for getting a bigger cut from the artists they represent, the labels claim they will commit to promoting the artist for a longer period of time and will actively try to develop new opportunities. Although these deals are often viewed as a cynical money grab by labels that are facing dwindling sales and high overhead, the labels counter that these deals let them sign different kinds of artists, since they don't have to be so focused on recouping their investment purely from album sales. They can stop chasing the instant number one and work with the artist over the long haul because they don't need to rely on big sales figures alone to make signing the artist profitable.

McLane says these deals are not new. "Indie labels have always done these. It's only changed for the major label perspective. The indies, because they didn't have huge catalogs, had to commission multiple income streams like publishing and merchandising or they couldn't survive. And that goes back to the early days of rock 'n' roll; now they're forced to do this because sales are down—it's the reality of the new music business. If you're a new artist, and you want somebody to give you an opportunity and to invest in you and they're taking a big risk, you're just going to have to play that game. So the new entry-level artists are subjected to the 360 deal, which everyone says is so horrific—and it is to a certain extent. But if the artists didn't need a label, they wouldn't be talking to record companies anyway; they must need a record company to invest in them and promote them. It's just a trade-off."

Compiling fan databases of e-mail and cell phone addresses is of utmost interest to record labels, McLane emphasizes. "Because they can use those and sell everything—under a 360 deal, they can sell everything, but they have to have a database. I know they'll start selling records direct. You used to have the record clubs—those are dinosaurs, but in the contract, there's still language that says if things are sold directly, they can pay the artist 50 percent. Back in the day, you'd have a distributor, so they would pay half of the royalty. Now, many indies have a brand name and kids flock to them. I've had to debate the label: 'If you sell records direct and there's no middleman, there shouldn't be a 50 percent deduction.' But a lot of these labels don't want to move off of that. And packaging: In the old days, there were fold-outs, liner notes, and photos, and it's diminished, but the labels still want to deduct 25 percent of the CD price for packaging before they calculate the artist royalty. But a quarter of the CD cost? With the download, there is no packaging. You still have to battle with the labels because these are their profit centers. No one argued with them before because record sales were so great that everyone was happy."

Essential Alchemy

McLane explains that be believes it is imperative for artists to make their names and their trademarks—their brand—as pervasive as possible. "That's what will help them to maintain a career. If you establish yourself with the help of a label, then you can use a label as a tool to develop an audience. Eventually, you might not need the label anymore—you can interact with your audience one on one and take it from there, and grow your audience and sell direct. But in order to do that, you have to brand yourself so that people all over the world can know who you are and can connect the dots between your music, your image, and your name."

McLane prefers to work with artists intent on mainstream success since these will achieve more dynamic careers from a monetary standpoint. "Do you have hit songs for radio? If not, there's no sense in going any further. You have to have a singer with an amazing commercial voice. That's rare too; there are a lot of sound-alikes. The whole band should be dynamic. Touring long term is so important to an artist.

Video or airplay comes and goes, but if they have a live audience following, they can sustain themselves."

"You have to spend some time independently—doing it yourself, building a fan base, touring, Internet, film/TV placements, press, networking, and tying in with sponsorship and branding. Even if it's low level, these things add up and word of mouth kicks in. These are the tools I need to take an artist to a label."

www.benmclane.com

Owen Sloane: The Dotted Line

"Lil Wayne works 24/7 when he's not performing, writing, or recording, and he's talking to fans online and working them constantly. He puts out records periodically and builds word of mouth. That's what needs to be done today."

Owen J. Sloane, a principal in Berger Kahn's Los Angeles office and co-chair of the firm's Entertainment and Media Group, is one of the entertainment industry's most respected attorneys, with more than 35 years of experience representing some of the world's most successful talent in the music and entertainment industries. For the past four years, Owen has been selected by his peers as a Southern California Super Lawyer in the area of Entertainment.

Sloane handles a wide range of sophisticated and complex music industry transactions for recording and touring artists, songwriters, and record companies. He has negotiated all forms of talent contracts, recording agreements, songwriting and publishing agreements, distribution agreements, music licensing, sponsorship and song placement agreements, merchandising and touring agreements, and major live events.

His notable clients include Rob Thomas, Matchbox Twenty, Chris Daughtry, Chester French, Pink Spiders, Suzanne Vega, the Frank Zappa estate, Radio Free Virgin, Steve Winwood, and the Jay Livingston catalog, among others. Over the course of his career, Owen has also represented Jane's Addiction, Elton John, Lindsey Buckingham, Barry Manilow, Stevie Nicks, Bonnie Raitt, and Kenny Rogers.

Owen has been particularly successful at structuring and negotiating the licensing of digital media content. He is credited with negotiating some of the earliest agreements pertaining to the Internet, ring tones, video satellite delivery, mobile entertainment, broadband, and wireless, as well as some of the music industry's largest and most innovative recording contracts and the first artist-owned label in rock. A major focus of his practice is protecting the artist's copyright and intellectual property rights while providing for long-term revenue, career growth, and creative control.

Deals Go Down

Sloane cuts right to the chase with regard to signing acts to major labels. "I don't try anymore because I think it's a waste of time unless an artist has a proven track record, a big story and fan base, and objective criteria to show they're less than a risk. They would have to be as close to a slam dunk as possible, or they're not going to get any interest. Record companies will say, 'It's good, but just let me know what's happening.' You could have a great band with fantastic music and nothing's happening with it and no one at a major label will pay attention. It's not to say you don't get a deal once in awhile from a band without that kind of track record, but it's unusual. That's the extent of what's happened to the business. Five to 10 years ago, if a band was good with a fantastic demo but with little experience, you could get people interested, get bidding wars and the interest of a major label. I don't think that's possible today."

Indie deals, Sloane says, have their own drawbacks. "It's hard to deal with them because they have complicated contracts and there's no money to finance a lawyer to do a decent job. So it's hard to represent clients and making that kind of a deal. But I do it and sometimes we take a hit and have to make it up later."

Returning to the thoughts of the larger labels, Sloane says that deal making becomes easier when there is something to bid against. "It's easier when they know other people are interested. The basic change has been in the structure of the deals because they're now trying to go for some form of 360 deals. [The labels] want income from publishing, merchandise, and touring as opposed to just the record. When I first started, records companies tried to get publishing, but that went out in the seventies. Now it's come back with greater force. That's a major bone of contention and a serious area of nego-tiation. In terms of the money: I have noticed substantially less money. Those deals you heard about, million dollars up front, are probably not being made anymore. Normal deals haven't been affected that much."

iTunes Are Your Tunes

Artists receive payment from download companies such as Apple's iTunes, and Sloane says this leads to complexity and confusion. "Obviously it's expensive to audit those types of records, but we do if it's a significant number. There's a lot of creative account-ing, not just with reporting, but putting charges on it and not making it a fair payment. The other problem is that they get lump sums, including publishing, so they have to account for the publisher. The publishers have a tough time getting paid because they are not in direct relation with the distributor and are not connected to the record label. It doesn't say '9.1 cents for publishing,' and the record company has to break out those amounts from Apple and pay the publisher. They apply all sorts of reductions they're not supposed to because there's not supposed to be a cap for a digital publishing royalty. You should get paid for 16 tracks, but they try to cap it at 12."

Band with the Brand

Sloane believes that branding might well be the future of the music business. "We've always had some co-sponsors for tours, now we are talking about more extensive involvement of the advertiser with the artist. Anyone interested in marketing in conjunction with music is going to see that they can basically benefit more so than they did before, by actually being included in the whole recording process, joint-venturing a record or by pre-buying finished product and tying it into an advertising campaign. When people in the advertising business see what we spend on records, it is a spit in the ocean for them. One advantage for the master owner is that if they bring in an advertiser as a partner, the owner will recover some of the money that they've invested."

"The concept of branding and sponsorships are where money will come from in the future. If you have the right artist and product that fits with the right demographic, you could do without record companies if you had a relationship between an artist and a major advertiser."

In the Vein of Lil Wayne

Sloane advises artists to do the work themselves. "Don't rely on anyone else to build your fan base and get you to the next level. That doesn't mean having to spend a lot of money, but you need a lot of time and effort to build a fan base by going into social networking sites, by getting the attention of bloggers, and turning fans into salespeople that can turn on others. Lil Wayne works 24/7 when he's not performing, writing, or recording and he's talking to fans online and working them constantly. He puts out records periodically and builds word of mouth. That's what needs to be done today."

"The old-fashioned method of going to radio and approaching it from the top doesn't work, because consumers feel they're empowered and they have the ability to have a direct relationship with the artist and the Internet and they don't want 'the man' to tell them what to listen to. Basically, it now comes from the bottom up and not the top down."

Sloane doesn't believe that distribution is important. "Most important is demand. There's no point spending a lot of money in pressing CDs and putting them in the few stores that are left. If they take them, they'll just sit there because there's no demand. The only reason to make physical CDs is to sell at gigs for impulse buys. Real distribution is having direct online communication with people who can download."

Negotiation Communication

What doesn't change is the skill of an entertainment attorney to negotiate. "A lot of it is patience and arguing until you finally get your way. It sometimes takes six to nine months because you weren't satisfied with where it was. I was conducting a particularly difficult negotiation and the lawyer at the record company was training another lawyer. I would make a point and the lawyers would say, 'What he's really asking for is this.' I felt like my negotiation was being graded. It took twice as long."

"Also, during the days of drugs, I was negotiating with executives who were high as kites. That was always amusing; I always felt that I could get as much as I wanted in those negotiations because they were so mellow. The funniest response was from a band who complained that the deal I got them was too good and put too much pressure on them…that was the first time I ever heard that."

www.bergerkahn.com/attorneys/60

9 New Days, New Directions, New Ideas

Thined individual.

There are so many aspects and opportunities in our music business that do not fall within predetermined lines. We are unable to cover all of these in this book, but the following areas of expertise embody crucial involvement and distinctive, individual initiative.

Educationally, there are over 60 colleges and universities in the U.S. that offer music business curriculums. There are organizations, headlined by the industry's National Academy of Recording Arts and Sciences (NARAS), that are actively involved in various educational and artist advocacy endeavors.

Diverse areas of marketing in the music business include servicing the industry with information, catalog exploitation, and exposure of new artists to the marketplace via the digital domain. Many functions that used to be basically handled by the label might now be handled by independent entities.

The following interviews will cover many of these highly specialized areas.

Kevin Day: Rocket Science Lifts Off

"I deal with people at labels who are miserable and remind me of where I was four years ago. They know the end is near, and you can't fault them. Pressure is enormous in the majors. And I'm very fortunate."

"Maximizing the Artist Brand" is a phrase on the well-appointed website of Los Angeles–based marketing company Rocket Science. From retail to radio play, video production to publicity, the company coordinates all of the integrated details necessary to create a full-on music campaign for a new era for legendary artists, such as Dolly Parton, Motley Crue, and Jackson Browne and for relative newcomers, such as Cold War Kids, Elliot Yamin, and Brett Dennen.

"Most new artists—probably 80 percent—want to build a career, to self-sustain, and to make records on their own terms," says company founder Kevin Day. "It was once everyone's dream to be signed to a major label—it's exactly the opposite now. There are still artists that want to use the catalyst of their indie release to be signed to a major, but most artists want to have careers on their own outside of the mainstream music industry."

A "major label guy," Kevin Day spent 12 years working his way up in the Universal system. "I was fairly successful for a mid-level management person, and I was laid off, fairly unexpectedly. Thankfully, it happened before the real downsizing of major labels. I'd seen the front edge of lot of big-name artists who had been dropped by the majors who were still viable entities that toured and did well. I thought maybe there were opportunities to work with these artists in the indie world and help release records without labels or in a smaller context: Collective Soul, Jackson Browne, and Tommy Lee, who I worked with at MCA and were dropped at Geffen. They were the start of Rocket Science, as they were starting to work on their own independent releases."

Day recalls that each successive artist exceeded his wildest expectations. "At a major, I wouldn't know what 350,000 units really meant in terms of dollars and cents for an act like Collective Soul. Being independent, there was actually a lot of money for artists who owned their master recordings, and I began to realize there was a business there also. We began as a sales retail marketing entity, but over two years, we added a digital component, a full-time marketing direction, and a promotion staff, as we turned into a labels' services organization."

Online Alchemy

Kevin Day believes the Internet has deeply affected the industry in good and bad ways. "Music is more accessible now than it has ever been in history. Now is the best time to expose your music and connect to a fan or a potential buyer. The bad things are the condensed attention span with so much music everywhere, all the time. It is hard to focus. When you grow up and five channels [are] on your TV, the Internet is the opposite. It's hard to find a focus to a consumer and get them to actually purchase something because so much is available for free in the form of pirated content. What's done is done: YouTube, Facebook, MySpace, and so on, where you can watch any video you want in seconds, has affected the way music is shared and exchanged between kids and adults. What does it mean for the future? I have no idea!"

Retro Radio

Radio, Kevin Day says, "Tends to be the 800-pound gorilla that you can't ignore. It could take the record to the next level. Commercial radio as we know it is dying, much has to do with Internet and government regulation. Radio, in certain formats and genres, though, is irreplaceable. For pop and country, you must have radio airplay to sell CDs. In other genres, there are so many other ways to touch a consumer. Our philosophy is never to lead with radio. Do your best to go out of the box to build your story based on touring, previous sales, fan base—whatever you can do to get a record at 25,000 units; then we'll talk about a radio story. Radio is the most expensive part of a marketing plan and the least tangible as far as results."

Day doesn't think that CDs will completely disappear; rather, they might exist side by side with digital music. "I see it become a format like a cassette was to a CD, they complement each other. There are often times consumers buy both because they want portability on their iPod and one of a physical nature in their homes. This great synergy allows you to market physical goods to digital buyers and vice versa. They're crossing back and forth. Today, digital downloads are only 30 percent of SoundScan (a technology company that tracks sales of music), and it seems to be stabilizing. Seventy percent is still being sold in physical format as a CD. I see parity five years from now. I don't think the CD will go away. In country music, digital sales represent 10 percent of the market share. Their fans are not caught up with that technology [and the same is true for hip-hop fans]. Soundtracks tend to be 40 to 50 percent digital. There are fewer stores to buy catalog; therefore, consumers are forced to buy digitally. Would it be a smaller share if Tower Records was still around? It's hard to say. But it certainly hasn't overtaken the physical format yet."

Selling the Passion

Kevin Day relates that one of the elements of his company that he enjoys the most is locating outlets for unique artists who might not fit into pre-existing formats. "I found an artist that wasn't something I would typically like, this was a 'one-listen' artist, Oren Lavie, from Israel. I fell in love with his music; it was very stark. A DJ at KCRW Radio (a cutting-edge listener-supported public radio station in Santa Monica, California) found the artist and brought him here, but didn't know what to do with him, as they struggled to find him a label. I got Oren a TV commercial. In that case, I sold my passion to Whole Foods, I told them how I felt about this artist, and I talked about how his music could be used in commercials, plus how the KCRW connection would work in their world and could touch their consumers. I wanted to give them the CD for an exposure standpoint. We wanted to be on all counters of all Whole Foods nationally. I said, 'I'll give you the CD for what it cost to make it, just sell it for $4. That's all I ask. And they're doing it. They have a brand-new artist development series; it's about more marketing than sales, and it's about getting his name out there. I see Whole Foods customers as listeners that might go play this at a cocktail party and start spreading the word about Oren."

Executive Madness

Relating back to his major label tenure, Kevin Day recalls one story that makes him realize how fortunate he is to be on his own. "Early in my career, I was a new executive at a director level. There was a very powerful woman in our company in charge of soundtracks. And she was very much a queen bee, a total power player, and important to our company. I was new to the organization and not sure of myself. There was a situation where she called me and she insisted that one of her major soundtrack releases was not in Tower Records on Sunset Boulevard. And because it was not there, she was going to have me fired. She said she would meet me a Tower in 20 minutes and if the CD wasn't there, she would ask my boss to fire me on the spot. I climbed into the car with my boss, we took a long drive, and when we arrived, the executive was waiting for us. We walked into the store, and of course there was plenty of product 12 feet from where she was standing. I received no apology from her. I took a picture of my boss standing next to the display of the product and put in on my desk just to remind myself of how ridiculous this industry can be."

www.myrocketscience.com

Rob Light: Illuminated Agent

"It's not the same pictorial that it used to be: Everyone did it one way, and then everyone else did the same thing."

As managing partner and head of the music division of Creative Artists Agency (CAA), Rob Light works with a cross section of touring artists that includes Bruce Springsteen, Eric Clapton, Alan Jackson, Bob Dylan, Radiohead, James Taylor, Bette Midler, KISS, AC/DC, Bon Jovi, Depeche Mode, the Cure, *American Idol* artists, Tim McGraw, Faith Hill, and Green Day. "With touring, it's anything that sells a ticket, from family shows to the circus to theater—they all fall under that banner," notes Light. "Part of the great appeal with CAA is that we're a full-service agency. We are involved in sponsorships, licensing soundtracks, acting, song placement in video games and TV shows. We have our fingers in many different pies. Because of the reach we have in film and TV, this appeals to artists, because they want to know they can access those areas. Management uses their agency as an extension of their own business—to fill the void that labels used to occupy."

Managing Mavens

As an agent, much of Light's interaction is with artist managers. "Management has always been important," he notes. "The best acts always had great management; from the early days of Brian Epstein and The Beatles, or Journey's manager, Herbie Herbert, Bruce Allen with Loverboy and Bryan Adams, or Jon Landau with Bruce Springsteen, and Jim Guerinot with No Doubt and Nine Inch Nails. Smart management is a rare commodity and now more than ever it's critical because management takes on more responsibility: creating the marketing plan and setting the 24-month calendar. The sophistication level is critical—it's not just taking commission, you really have to be a CEO of a whole process."

"The beauty of being an agent is that the role never changes. It's finding the right venue, making the right deals, the right ticket price, and planning the campaign for the right time of year to take advantage of a record release. Skill sets to bring to the table haven't changed. I still do that day to day. I have the privilege to run a big business—from three agents initially, now 70 agents in Nashville, New York, and London, where I'm helping advise agents around the world who are marching to the same beat. It is administrating egos and interaction of such. Twenty agents are on senior staff and have all broken artists. It is like being an air traffic controller, trying to work it all together. I fly around the world a lot."

Light notes that China is emerging as a touring base. "Western artists are just breaking through. It's still a fairly closed environment with what you can promote and whom they accept from the outside world. Chinese artists can play 200 arenas just in China; this is tenfold to what America is. There will be a huge explosion in eight to 10 years."

Butts in the Seats

Light says that it is too early to declare an impact from the U.S. recession. We haven't put enough shows on sale since the economy turned. I think that must-see shows will still be must-see—AC/DC or Britney Spears, those shows will do well. The youth market will do fine as well, because young people are rarely affected by the economy. It will be the middle events that are perennial. Skip them one year because they will come back next year. The Harlem Globetrotters? They tour every year, so the family of four that will usually go to see them might skip it until next year. I think that is where you'll feel the impact. They're already feeling it in Las Vegas a little bit. We're going to feel it, and it will be impactful, but I think people still want to be entertained. The rich don't get taxed and the poor are already poor, so the middle class will get squeezed."

From Major to Minor

Light works with artists on both major and independent labels. "The relationship has changed in that it used to be the tour came at the end of all the marketing. Labels don't have financial resources or access to do that anymore. Touring has become a key marketing component of a record, and the balance has changed in regards to what comes first. A&R I respect, but there's a different energy they can bring now. They don't have the access or the ability. Radio is greatly diminished and people don't read newspapers the same way. Labels are trying to find new ways to market."

Light says CAA is very focused on artists on indie labels. "We are incredibly aggressive in that space—that's the next generation of artists. We can't afford to not be there. We signed Radiohead before their first record came out; we booked the first tour with Alanis Morissette. Kings of Leon, Katy Perry, we have been constantly signing young bands that may not have major support, because we believe in them. Now Kings of Leon are having a major hit after their touring base was solidified.

Signing Status

Light avows that in connecting with new artists there is not one magic button, rather a number of pertinent factors. "I'm always looking for a band that can play live and turn on an audience. And the next time they come through, the audience has grown. We signed an artist in Atlanta, Zac Brown. One year ago, he was playing for 400 people a night and selling out of t-shirts. It wasn't hard: You could watch the audience response and that put it over the top. The relationship with an audience in a live setting is key. At the end of the day, it takes a great song, chemistry, and charisma. Charisma is a tough thing to fake; either you have it or you don't. Zac will be the next Dave Matthews or Jimmy Buffett."

"For an artist, you need to be your own best manager. The catalyst is finding a local market and developing an audience and a fan base that wants access to what you do. It's the best statement for people who want to come in and exploit that for you. Have a clear sense of who you are and what you want to be, not so much emulating someone else. Have people around you that you trust who can tell you when you're good and when you're bad so you can continue to grow."

www.caa.com

Bob Mercer: Building the Brand

"It's perfectly possible for someone to form their own record label, never press a CD, and still make a living out of it."

Music executive Bob Mercer has heavy hitters in his résumé. As EMI's UK marketing director, he was responsible for guiding projects with Paul McCartney and Queen into the marketplace; as an A&R executive and then as a managing director for the company, he added artists Kate Bush and the Sex Pistols to a star-studded roster that included the Rolling Stones and Pink Floyd.

After a stint helming EMI Films, he managed Paul McCartney and Pink Floyd's Roger Waters before moving to Nashville to run Jimmy Buffett's record label, Margaritaville. Later, at Polygram Records, he initiated the label's TV marketing campaigns, and now, based at EMI in Los Angeles, continues in that role with the highly successful NOW That's What I Call Music brand. "We release three albums a year of the last four months of hits, coming largely from Universal/EMI and Jive Records, but with other third parties brought in—like the band Nickelback—and they share in the profits," he qualifies.

Mercer says that since consumers can now create their own compilations of hits with digital downloads, the game is harder. There is another monetary consideration. In the UK, where compilations are very successful, the mechanical rates (monies paid to songwriters and publishers) are based on the retail price of the CD—(no matter the number of tracks) approximately 15 £ UK. In the U.S., there is a fixed mechanical rate paid for each song, which can limit the number of tracks used. In the UK, compilations account for up to 27 percent of the total retail market. "Walk down Oxford Street in London, and it's all compilations," says Mercer.

So NOW releases other types of packages, such as country, Christmas, and classic rock collections. "We do it to make up for the lack of volume, and to derive more benefit from the brand than just three records a year," says Mercer. The sales of the compilations drive the individual artists as well, with a whopping 60 percent of buyers noting that after hearing a song on a compilation, they then bought music from an individual artist who was included in the collection.

Considered Opinions

Mercer notes that the meltdown of the modern record business is due to a variety of factors. "The record companies have been slow to act, slow to analyze, and slow to do anything. Then people came in and bought the operations with pretty inadequate due diligence and realized they'd paid too much. Then the money market started to crunch. They were paralyzed and had to raise money. They now have to figure out how the interest gets repaid. The people they hire are from outside the record business; that has proven to be a mistake. Illegal downloading is a significant part of the dilemma—but it's also a significant part of the opportunity. I maintain that the business is in dire straits because there are a lot of stupid people in it."

Online Exposure

Mercer observes how the Internet has affected the A&R process. "It has really provided a massive amount of exposure for new and young bands, and a potential filtering process, which is what A&R is. You probably don't need to go to a club, you need to live on a computer to see what's going on, to get a feel for and and see what's available. There is another feature: One of the consequences of the way we live our lives and the way the Internet has affected us, especially young people, is a short attention span. The way the business has transformed has led to instant gratification rather than building loyalty to an artist over a period of time. Over the last 10 years, we've seen a higher incidence of singles—and they're not driving the marketplace, because there is no f*cking marketplace. Singles are now driving the engine of the music business."

"If the business is about singles, and it is coming through the Internet, what use is A&R? It sorts itself out, it is a free market, someone puts the song out, it's picked up by Facebook or whatever, and all of a sudden you have a hit on your hands, and it's probably a 'one off.'"

When the Going Gets Tough

Mercer shines this light on the future. "Every major independent music business figure I've known over the past 30 years, from Chris Blackwell [founder of Island Records and the man who signed Bob Marley, U2, and Melissa Etheridge] to Mickie Most [classic producer of artists such as the Yardbirds, Donovan, and Jeff Beck] have all said, to a person, that when the record business gets into trouble, that's when they come into their own. It's very true. One of the ways the record companies save money is to sack half of their A&R and marketing departments. That doesn't mean half of them are useless; those people then go out and find bands to manage or form labels themselves. In these times, you're now seeing a whole marketplace out there that really doesn't need what the traditional record company can deliver, including distribution. Our roles as majors always stemmed from the fact that we controlled distribution. It didn't mean we were smarter or bigger. Distribution is becoming much different; it's perfectly possible for someone to form their own record label, never press a CD, and still make a living out of it."

Distinctive Directives

Mercer contends that the industry is enriched by career artists who perhaps have not produced astronomical sales figures, but whose paths have been illuminated by a purity of vision. He cites an artist that he signed, Kate Bush, as a sterling example: "Absolutely a unique artist. If you look back over her career, she's done what she wanted to do, how she wanted to do it, and when she wanted to do it. You can't say it's one of the most successful careers in the record business, definitely not, but you can say this is one of the most honest careers in the record business. Kate has all the success she's wanted and deserved. She didn't make it in the U.S., but that's not the beginning and end."

And Mercer, a veteran of many nights in the recording studio, recounts how he signed Bush back in the bad old days. "I was hanging out with Pink Floyd in the studio when they were making Animals. It was 2 or 3 in the morning, and we were all waiting for some blow [cocaine] to be delivered. And Dave Gilmour said, 'While we're waiting, there's a tape I'd like to play for you.' That's when I first heard Kate Bush. And I did a ton of blow and signed her the next day."

Hunter Scott: Inspired Entrepreneur

"The artist has to work with you. When you're not a label and don't have a lot of money, the artist has to make sacrifices: go on the road, sell albums out of their trunk."

As the jetliner in which he was seated taxied into LAX airport, Hunter Scott recalled the pilot saying, "Welcome to Los Angeles: land of opportunity, actors, musicians, models, and dancers." With two guitars and one a suitcase, he remembers thinking, "What now?"

Scott now heads La'Fa'Mos, a marketing and promotional company for new artists, with offices on Hollywood Boulevard. With a small staff and eager interns, he is making an impact in the modern world of independent music with aggressive, hands-on marketing and forceful energy.

As a student at Musicians Institute in Hollywood, Scott studied in the school's recording artist program and was rewarded with a scholarship into the school's music business program. An internship at Interscope Records introduced him to the inner workings of a label and also gave him a compass for his future direction. He remembers asking his boss, a former musician himself, why he was no longer a guitar player. "The boss said, 'At some point you have to realize that if you're not really good at something and you're really good at something else, maybe that's what you should be doing.' I was waiting for someone—other than my dad—to tell me that. Looking at the artists Interscope was promoting, I was blown away. I asked myself, 'How am I positioned with them?'" He realized that business would become his primary endeavor.

And Hunter excelled at the business. "Christmas came; Geffen Records [a division of Interscope] was closing down, and half the building was empty. There was no more artist development. I found myself looking around me at empty desks. I looked into the future: How did I view myself? As a future 40-year-old playing the guitar in cafes in front of 10 people? I had a vision, I had a goal, and I was looking at the best way to get to that place."

Over the Christmas break, Scott put together a business plan to create a marketing company. "I was a musician who'd spent a lot of money and it didn't work. I probably wasn't alone. I had a bunch of musician friends saying the same thing. I figured I could do something for musicians, cheaper and better." With a small group of investors, Scott launched La'Fa'Mos.

Investor Investigation

"Everyone I met I asked for a card. I contacted everyone I knew. My dad was involved with startup companies, so I contacted people he knew, anyone who had money and knew who I was could check up on me, see I was a good student, that I am intelligent, had good references, and was good for the money. I wasn't starting a record label. I had a plan. Month number one I would make $180, but by October I can pay my bills, and a few months later I could start paying money back. We were talking only thousands of dollars. I also had a backup plan of doing a sales gig and making money and paying it back if I needed to."

He also searched out other marketing companies working in similar pursuits to find out what they were doing right or wrong. He also asked his potential client base. "I put out a survey to find what kinds of services were important, how much people thought it would cost, and how much they'd be willing to spend. We're targeting the indie field, so we charge less."

Initially, Scott ran the business from a breakfast nook in his house "I needed to calculate the money I needed to go full force. I started with a partner, so we had two of the lowest salaries you could think of. The one thing I thought I figured out is that other companies offer marketing and publicity, but they didn't offer design service. I decided we would offer that as well. I had another guy at another office to do design. Then I started looking for clients."

Bridge to the Bands

Scott began by approaching local bands performing at showcases. He enlisted his first act, put in the requisite time promoting them, and continued looking for new clients. Gradually, the trickle of prospects became a steady stream of committed artists. Scott, who initially signs a service agreement and a name and likeness agreement with each artist on the La'Fa'Mos roster, keeps it all above board. "Everything has to be legal. I'm not going down any other route," he qualifies.

"I created another survey for the artists, their complete history, their image, how the band or artist wanted to be marketed, and also their goals. We could work on them for 10 hours a month and every time someone in my office punches in on the project, the client can have a time report that represents that, so they know we're working for them. The first month, we do the blog, CD reviews, and MySpace design."

The company adopted a slogan: "Letting do-it-yourself musicians be musicians, period." "The idea is taking everything I've learned and would want to do: college radio, promotion, putting together a press kit, writing a bio, getting a MySpace design, maybe a website, writing press releases, soliciting CD reviews, blogs and message boards—things that are do-it-yourself and would be normally free, I will do for the client and the client pays for my hours on a monthly retainer."

Many clients who are ascending in the business must, by necessity, hold down day jobs. "And they use that day job as an excuse to say they don't have time. It's an excuse; you can call people at lunch time and e-mail people at night. We do have the contacts. We can mail packages. It's hard for musicians to sell themselves. You have to do it every single day. Sometimes it's awkward or maybe the musicians say, 'Who am I?' They're now being represented by a company who calls on behalf of them."

La'Fa'Mos has a $50 reward referral program, and referrals from satisfied clients also bolster the company's roster. Scott still makes it a point to go out and meet bands and artists. And with the interlocked world of musicians, he soon established a strong network.

He created stronger, more intensive packages and began doing national radio campaigns with an emphasis on college radio. "You look online and people are charging thousands of dollars. These companies have been around and are great, but so are we. Interns start making phone calls. If the station doesn't pick up, I don't send a package. You have to look at the stations you are going to follow up on and qualify them. We do the homework—we don't just waste the band or artist's money. We know who we send the music to."

The very nature of rock bands is a reality as well. "Bands break up; bands run out of money. By the time I got 10 bands, four had left. I learned and made it more efficient, and began adding acts."

Ultimately, the artists or bands who can benefit most by the La'Fa'Mos connection—and Scott's kinetic energy, know-how, and charisma—are those who are willing to put in the effort. "The artist has to work with you. When you're not a label and don't have a lot of money, the artist has to make sacrifices: go on the road, sell albums out of their trunk. It is still a good way of getting there. Look at Maroon 5 or Fall Out Boy—both bands that did this. It's still about getting out there and reaching the fans. The bottom line is that I don't do anything someone can't do on his or her own."

"The traditional music industry is transforming. The big artists may not be making the money [they] used to, but the beauty is that people now have many more options."

www.lafamos.com.

Gary Stewart: Gospel of a Music Fanatic

"It was the way I was brought up. I worshiped in a different type of church."

As Gary Stewart tells it, his sanctuary was a record store, the hymn book was *Creem* magazine, the sermons were delivered by soul shouter Edwin Starr ("War"), and the choir was Creedence Clearwater Revival. As an unabashed disciple of music, Stewart discovered Rhino Records, a store in Los Angeles that became his house of the holy.

"I became hooked on AM radio and then FM radio, going to concerts and buying records. I was reading *Hit Parader* and *Rolling Stone* magazines and I knew there was a cool record store I heard about, Rhino Records. Like an alcoholic goes to a bar, I think [I visited Rhino Records] for about two-and-a-half years. I spent a minimum of three days a week there and soaked up all the info. They got tired of me hanging around and offered me a job."

When a nascent label—also named Rhino Records—evolved from the store, Stewart was enlisted as the sales director. "I had no experience in sales; certainly not the temperament for it. My primary qualification was that I was 'a nice guy.' Which shows how grassroots it was at the time. Instead of getting fired, I was hired to oversee business affairs, which I knew less about."

Stewart recalls that there were no A&R people per se, but that everyone at the label was expected to discover and sign talent. "We did that on the side or for love. I was asked to sign these great bands out of San Diego. When they reached a certain place, my position evolved into that job and Rhino found professionals to do the business stuff. I love to give people a sense of discovery with current music or non-current music. One of the things that happened for me back when I was reading *Creem* magazine was discovering bands from the British Invasion or the garage band movement. I was really only eight years old at the time. I got deeper and deeper in the sixties, and the *American Graffiti* soundtrack got me into the fifties era. That was all a revelation for me. The nineties are my weak spot but the 2000s have been a renaissance of good music, from White Stripes to Gnarls Barkley."

Rhino Records' reputation was hinged on their reissues of classic performances. "CDs had become the predominate form and major labels were looking at their catalogs. We weren't good at breaking new artists. A lot of majors realized they weren't good at working catalogs. You can't necessarily walk and chew gum at the same time. We already had a strong track record and were lucky to work with the legacies of Otis Redding, early Ray Charles, and Aretha Franklin. That was like our 'kid in the candy store' moment. We knew what to do."

The label also released records by the Beat Farmer and solo CDs by X principals John Doe and Exene Cervenka. "American roots music, which is normal now, was invisible then. It was like a club you wanted to be a part of. We didn't consciously create that image, we just did it. It came out in our marketing. A lot was inherited from the Rhino Store—a passion and sense of humor at all times. People who ended up working there were good at excelling at that. I did a box set version of [the Lenny Kaye collection of garage bands] *Nuggets,* and looking back, I see that record created a genre of garage rock. I probably didn't know what I was doing, and if I did, I wouldn't have gotten it right. That's how it was with Rhino, very organic. We put out records we liked, and it worked out. If you were in Los Angeles and worked for Rhino, people would say, 'I love that store.' In the rest of the country, people would say, 'They have a record store?' Late in the game, we realized how cool we were and that was a good thing. You want enough so you can maintain your self-esteem and motivation, but not so much that you need an ice pack to put on your head from all the swelling."

Online Music

"I grew up in the age of the records and mailing away for things. And the good thing about that experience is that when you have to work that hard, it deepens your relationship to the music. Today, with the Internet, when you hear about something, the odds are you can get it. There's a democracy about that."

"So much of what I discovered was revealed to me through writers and great record store clerks. I had no career development, just an urge to push things in front of me."

Stewart's experience is now utilized in his executive job at Online Music, where he oversees music content on Apple's iTunes Music Store.

Ted Cohen: Digital Dominion

"The definition of quality in the digital world is something that resonates and makes a connection."

In college, a mere two weeks after being put on academic probation, Ted Cohen recalls that he was running the college radio station. "I was music director and I met all of the promo guys in Cleveland. Then I became a music buyer there for retail record stores." Later he moved to Boston and began working for Columbia Records before taking a senior management position at Warner Bros. Records. "Warner Bros. decided to turn bad behavior into a new job: artist development. I worked with the Pretenders, the Ramones, the Beach Boys, George Benson, Prince, and a lot of the 'hair metal' bands."

Across the course of his career, Cohen has evolved into one of the music industry's most vocal proponents of new media. Integrating his widespread digital authority in music, mobile, Internet Protocol Television (IPTV), and product and service development, he is the managing partner of TAG Strategic. Known throughout the technology and music industries as being "part ambassador and part evangelist," Cohen was instrumental in crafting the licensing agreements upon which the Rhapsody subscription service and the iTunes Music Store were built.

In his previous role as senior vice president of digital development and distribution for EMI Music (home of artists such as The Beatles, Coldplay, and Bob Seger), Cohen led next-generation digital business development worldwide for this "big four" record company, which includes labels such as Capitol, Virgin, Angel/Blue Note, Parlophone, and Chrysalis. During that time, EMI led the industry by embracing and exploiting new technologies and business models such as digital downloads and online music subscriptions, custom compilations, wireless services, high-definition audio, and Internet radio.

In addition to seeking out, evaluating, and executing business opportunities for the company on a global basis, Cohen served as both a strategist and key decision maker for EMI's global new media and antipiracy efforts. He worked to establish companywide digital policies, which have provided EMI's artists and labels a substantial advantage in the digital music arena. He recalls his ascension to this position. "I was at a digital conference in Atlanta and somebody handed me the agenda for the conference. And on the pamphlet it said 'Ted Cohen VP of New Media at EMI.' It was so new that it hadn't sunk in yet."

Prior to his role at EMI, Cohen served as executive vice president of Digital Music Network, Inc., where he co-founded and served as chair of the groundbreaking Webnoize conferences.

Cohen also led two highly successful new media consulting operations, DMN Consulting and Consulting Adults, attracting clients such as Amazon.com, Microsoft, Universal Studios, DreamWorks Records, Liquid Audio, Wherehouse Records/Checkout.com, and various other entertainment, technology, and new media organizations.

Evil Powers and Clueless Kids

"Music as a service is going to replace music as a product," Cohen observes. "A song for 99 cents is still worthwhile. There are expectations now about the development of devices that can hold tens of thousands of songs and the only ones that are stopping them are evil people at record labels. No one has ten thousand dollars to fill their iPods. We went from wonderment to empowerment to a sense of entitlement. We have a whole generation of kids who think they're entitled to all the music they want. Artists need to be compensated—publishers, songwriters, labels—everyone deserves a return. This whole thing about, 'music should be free'—I don't buy it."

As one of the earliest and most visionary prophets of the digital/musical alliance, Cohen continues to recognize opportunities for artists on all platforms. "We're in an industry that really gets excited. If we sell a half million units, we're pleased. Sell a million and we have a party. If we sell 10 million, we give the artists their own record label. But music is not selling as a unit anymore, so it should be about getting people to experience it. Establish careers and a sustainable environment where an artist like Chrissie Hynde [the Pretenders] can still go out on tour and not have to worry about how many units she's sold."

The Connection

Cohen believes we now have the greatest tools ever to connect music to audiences. "Here we are in a time when someone in Dayton, Ohio, can go on Pandora and have artists recommended to him that he has never heard of. The old gatekeepers that lead to people's discovery of music don't matter anymore. There are so many technologies now to take their places, combined with passionate music and people that know how to use it. What you can do at home now with [programs such as] Logic, Reason, or Pro Tools can do what thousands of dollars of gear used to do. They're surveying music, not controlling it."

"Try everything," Cohen enthuses. "There are so many tools to experiment with. I did a panel in a few years back with [songwriter/artist and now Tony-winning Broadway composer] Duncan Sheik. He said, 'You can't protect your music; you have to share and let people experience your music. If you believe the song you wrote is your best-ever song, hold it near. But if you think it's just the beginning of what you're going to do, then you need to share. Let people experience it; the more they experience it, the bigger your audience will get.' He said a song from his album is like a trailer from a movie. I took that to heart. The definition of quality in the digital world is something that resonates and makes a connection."

"Prince left Warner Bros. over what he thought were restrictions. He wanted to release his music when he finished it. He didn't want to wait for a release cycle, he wanted it to be out there, fresh. You need to exploit that connection. There has never been a better time for innovative music and musicians."

www.tagstrategic.com

Kim Burse: Imagining the Image

"This business has its own lingo. If you can't talk it, it's harder to walk it."

Kim Burse should credit herself as an inspiration to all fledgling music business hopefuls. Even though she was attending the prestigious Berklee College of Music in Boston, she followed her own indomitable instincts and a belief that actually getting into the music business would ultimately depend on what she could accomplish outside of school.

When she returned home to Atlanta, she proceeded to work her way up in the music business. The only catch: She wasn't being paid. She toiled for free as an intern at Motown and MCA Records for years with only an unflagging hope that she might somehow, someday, get hired. One job in the record business involved Burse packing up records into shipping boxes to be sent to retail stores. "The room didn't even have a light in it. I had to open the door up, because it was next to my boss's office and it had light, so if I opened the door, I could see to pack." There was another advantage to this proximity: Burse could hear her boss on the telephone, cajoling program directors for airplay reports. When the boss had to go out of town, Kim was asked to make the calls. "I knew how to do it because I listened." Burse's abilities as a typist also helped her advance. "The boss of my boss didn't know how to type fast; she saw me typing once and asked me to type for her. She started handing me more and more stuff to type—and I then got my own cubicle with a light. I worked my way up to my own office."

She recalls having to console her concerned mother regularly with these words: "Mom, I can't even pay for the knowledge that they're giving me right now." This knowledge combined with determination and hard work eventually propelled her into the world of A&R for Sony Music. As an A&R rep, she would discover such artists as Dionne Farris of Arrested Development, and she was an integral part in the signing of a fledgling girl group from Houston, Destiny's Child.

Bouncing with Beyoncé

Burse subsequently launched Bcreative Productions while working predominately as Beyoncé's creative director. In that role, it is imperative to somehow channel the artist's vision into reality; for example, when Beyoncé announced the idea of creating an all-girl touring band to support her CD *B'Day*, Kim Burse understood, but she had only two weeks to put the band together. Burse knew that she and the rest of Beyoncé's creative team had a chance to make history. (Burse's counterpart was Beyoncé's musical director, Frank Gatson. Both are responsible for the look, feel, and sound of Beyoncé's stage performances.)

"As always, it's based around whatever music project that she has out," Burse says. "With the sound of the songs on *B'Day*, she wanted it to just be very empowering because that's how the lyrics came across, so she wanted that to be represented in the stage show. It was a big motivation for her to have an all-female band. Once she decided she called me and Frank and gave us two weeks to put the band together because they were going to perform with [her] on the BET Awards."

Burse and the team rose to the challenge setting up auditions in Los Angeles, Atlanta, Houston, Chicago, and New York City. Over a thousand women turned out in the cities for a chance to show their skills on keys, guitar, drums, bass, and percussion. "I was very amazed at the turnout, and the caliber of musicianship was great," Burse says. "It was great to be in a position where I had more than enough to choose from. It was a joy doing that for her. Beyoncé is very headstrong about what she wants, and I knew if I put the right people in front of her, she would know within herself that this person could hold it down. You don't have a show at all unless you get your music right."

Expanding Parameters

"When word got around that I wasn't exclusive, people just started to contact me," notes Burse. Since her emergence with Beyoncé, Burse has since lent her innovative talents to such artists as Nelly, Chris Brown, Ciara, and Jamie Foxx, meticulously directing and developing their live performances. When asked to describe the nuts and bolts of how she conceptualizes a live show, Burse explains, "It's like I'm a wedding planner for a live show, and I can create a music track for the performance. I don't play string instruments, but can understand how to read, how they sound, and the key I want them to be in. I can still speak to a musician even if I don't play his or her particular instrument." Other notable performances orchestrated by Burse include Jeezy on the BET Hip Hop Awards, as well as directing Beyoncé and Tina Turner's performance of "Proud Mary" for the 2008 Grammys. The sheer magnitude of that powerhouse duo onstage was overwhelmingly revered as the most indelible highlight of that year's ceremony, and it marked Turner's first concert performance in more than seven years. The performance was inducted into the 2008 Grammy Hall of Fame. "I was humbled to be a part of that show," says Burse.

When it comes to seeking talent, Burse is always open to hearing new artists and has never shied away from what might be regarded as uncharted or unconventional. "I'd listen to material sent to me, I'd go to showcases. Any way I could hear it, I would do it. When I would find something I liked a lot, I could always feel it in my gut. Even if the company would pass on it, it would show up somewhere else. Like Da Brat, Escape, the Fugees, or even Destiny's Child—it was always something that I hadn't seen before. That's been my track record, so I tend to stick to that."

Acknowledging that the music business comes with its share of hurdles and obstacles, Burse advises aspirants to stay positive, open-minded, and patient. "You may have to alter your dream because sometimes you have to figure out what it is that you're really supposed to do. If it's music, then do that. Playing golf? Then do that. Just figure out what it is, because there can be so many different variations of what it is. If it's meant to be, it's going to happen."

John Alexander: Facilitating the Muse

"We were on a promotional tour with Alanis Morissette when she was 16, in Canada doing promotion. The maids at the hotel were always very nice, but on this one day they were very cold. Alanis had gotten up in the middle of the night and put one of her bras on the doorknob of my hotel room. So when the maids came in the morning and saw this young girl's bra hanging there, their attitudes changed."

Like many kids, John Alexander began his career playing in local bands. A Canadian, Alexander graduated to his hometown's biggest band, which was signed to MCA

Records. When the band had run its course, he inaugurated a management company with some friends and achieved a number-one hit with the band Sheriff. At that juncture, he was invited to run the A&R department for MCA Canada and signed some local bands. Then he signed a 14-year-old girl named Alanis Morissette.

"After MCA Records Canada, Leeds Levy, then worldwide president at MCA Publishing, asked if I would move to New York and become head of talent acquisition East Coast, which I thought was a great opportunity. I did that, and while there was promoted to executive VP of MCA Music North America Creative, and eventually transferred to the Los Angeles office. When I moved from A&R to publishing, Zach Horowitz at MCA called me. He said, 'I don't care if you sign anything in your first year.' He ran down the heavyweights, and said, 'In your first year, connect yourself, the second year start making deals.' It was a great plus to have people take my calls and go to lunches."

"In 1997, I moved over to VP of Creative for ASCAP. I've now left ASCAP to pursue consultancy/artist development. I've been asked to work with a number of artists on projects. It's late in my career to make a change, but I'm going to do it."

North of the Border

Alexander recalls the evolution of Alanis. "I was in Ottawa, Canada, speaking to a producer/artist about a band called One to One. Before I left the studio, he said, 'Do you have 10 minutes to see a video of this young girl?' It was Alanis at 14—I was taken. I went back to Toronto and talked to my boss and said, 'I've got to go back and meet this girl.' The funny thing is, it tweaked something in my memory: A DJ friend from Ottawa had sent me a tape when I was head of A&R at MCA and it was an eight-year-old Alanis Morissette. I thought, 'My bosses aren't going to think much of my first signing if it is an eight-year-old girl.' From Ottawa, I sent her a 'pass letter' that she still has—damn it—but I went back and had dinner with her when she was 14. There was talent, commitment, a fire in her eyes—something that compelled me to meet with her parents the next morning at breakfast and to say, "I want to sign Alanis to MCA Records and MCA Music Publishing.' They agreed—they knew me from my band; I think I'd played at their high school. They said okay, but the stipulation was I had to personally take care of her, not in the economic way, but to make sure she was protected."

Initially, Alexander didn't get the full support that he needed from MCA Records Canada to sign Morissette, so he spoke to Leeds Levy and asked if MCA Publishing would sign Morissette to a publishing deal and also help finance her record deal. (This was possible because MCA Publishing had set up an independent label called Hot Mustard

Records, distributed by MCA to fund and develop promising new artists.) Levy too was a believer in Morissette's talent, and he personally approved and fully supported her signing. As a result, Morissette's album was recorded as a production venture financed by MCA Publishing (via Hot Mustard) and distributed by MCA Records Canada. Morissette's debut album, *Alanis*, was subsequently released in Canada, and featured the number-one chart single "Too Hot." The album eventually sold 150,000 units. She used only one name at this time to avoid possible confusion with fellow Canadian singer Alannah Myles. In 1992, Morissette was nominated for three Juno Awards, the Canadian equivalent to of the Grammy Awards: Single of the Year, Best Dance Record, and Most Promising Female Vocalist (which she won). In the same year, she released *Now Is the Time*, her follow-up. That album attempted to move Morissette away from her debut album's dance-pop sound and featured the single "An Emotion Away," but it was a futile cause; audiences identified her with bouncy dance tracks. Subsequently, *Now Is the Time* sold less than half the number of copies of her debut album, and with her two-album deal with MCA Canada completed, Morissette was without a major label recording contract.

"At 18, she was staying with me in New York. She said, 'John, I don't think I'm going to have a career doing what I'm doing now.' I said, 'What do you want to do?' She said, 'I really want to express what's on my mind and what's in my heart and what my experiences are rather than sing about what someone else wrote.' It made sense: You change a lot from 14 to 18. I put her together with writers in Toronto and Vancouver, and I called my staff in Los Angeles. I said, 'I have her now writing with people, and I want to put her together with some MCA writers.' One was Glen Ballard. She met with Glen and *Jagged Little Pill* came out of that very quickly. I said, 'Glen, is she bringing anything to the table?' He said, 'All the lyrics and melodies—yeah, she's bringing something to the table.' A lot of people don't know this, but the album was a series of demos that we tweaked. It was not a full-blown production album that we were doing. We made it for $70,000 in Glen's studio at home and a little studio on the lot." *Jagged Little Pill* ultimately became *Billboard* magazine's Album of the Decade, and has now sold nearly 30 million units worldwide.

In 2005, Morissette revisited *Jagged Little Pill*, re-recording an acoustic version of the record with Glen Ballard. Having emerged as one of music's enduring artists, she continues to redefine her artistry as her music influences successive generations of strong female singer/songwriters.

Morissette recalls, "It was a real collaboration, the ultimate collaboration, the connection that Glen and I had. From a production end of it, he was much more versed in so many more things than I was at the time. I think there were elements of who I am as a person, as well as an artist, that really stretched him and were both propelled to move forward, so that was a really good connection." Ballard is keenly attuned to vocals, he says: "The connection is always, to me, to someone's voice first, and through that instrument I'm able hopefully to nourish and enhance their real artistic self. I'm a good listener. I'm a better listener than I am a singer. When I hear someone's voice, it's a source of great inspiration to me, just the pure voice, and it seems to be that I've worked with a lot of female singers and writers in equal measure with males, and it's all about being a good listener first and being sensitive. Whether it's Michael Jackson or Alanis Morissette, the first step is to listen, and to listen sensitively."

And Glen Ballard listened intently to the sound of Alanis Morissette. "I heard her voice and it seemed to be rich and powerful and full of potential. I predicated everything on that voice, on that incredible instrument, and it didn't take long. We had a cup of tea when we first met, and I knew that she had a lot on her mind and a lot she wanted to express. I just instinctively felt there was some way we could collaborate, to give her the platform to say what she wanted to say. And I certainly tried to encourage the honesty everyone is familiar with now. But for a 19-year-old woman coming to Los Angeles from Canada, the kind of fearlessness with which she was able to express herself was, given that context, even more remarkable. We take it for granted now, her outspoken and fearless explorations of her own life and soul and relationships, but that's hard for a 19-year-old in the circumstances in which I've described, so if I did anything well, it was create a sanctuary in which she felt safe in saying what she wanted to say and to help her with the music and define the musical landscape she felt comfortable to run through."

Ballard, who has since worked with No Doubt, the Dave Matthews Band, and Christina Aguilera, among others, concludes, "I've been lucky enough to fall into it in other instances, but that one taught me just to go with what felt right. When you have someone who's only interest is to just express, not, 'Is this a hit or not,' it's liberating. Because I'm going to try and make it a hit anyway. I'll sabotage it. I'm kidding! I'm always trying to make sure people get it. I choose to be able to communicate rather than to have something be obscure. If you have to explain a song, you're in trouble, you know?"

Says John Alexander, "Good for me for recognizing talent in Alanis doing the early stuff, but better recognizing at 18 she wanted to be her own artist and songwriter, to speak her heart and mind. I've always allowed artists to be who they want to be. It works or it doesn't—it's a risk. I inducted her into the Canadian Music Hall of Fame last year. She could have had anyone induct her, but she said, 'No, I want John Alexander to induct me.' And when I brought her up on stage, rather than saying

'Here's the superstar or multiplatinum artist,' I said, 'After this number of years, here is my friend—Alanis Morissette.' That's one of the things that's so engaging to me—we're still friends."

Performing Rights and Artist Development

At ASCAP, one of Alexander's duties was as to be an ASCAP liaison contact. "I would have continuous lunches with top entertainment attorneys and ask them if their clients who were ASCAP members were happy, or did they have any BMI members who are unhappy? I did bring Alanis over to ASCAP, and obviously relationships had something to do with that, but it was a good business move. I brought over Ringo Starr, Taylor Hawkins from the Foo Fighters, I signed Avril Lavigne, Ashlee Simpson, and Ryan Cabrera—and other high-profile writers through my relations with managers, business managers, and attorneys."

Alexander is also working with 18-year-old singer/songwriter Sara Haze, introducing her at selected music events worldwide. Haze even performed for Microsoft at the Houston Astrodome and has signed with the powerful APA Agency. "I brought her to Canadian Music week, which led to *CMJ* [*College Media Journal*]; and she's off to PopKomm in Munich, Germany, where she's been invited to be a feature artist. We turned down one major label deal; the contract was more like we want her voice and image and we do everything else—that's not what Sara Haze is about."

Meet Sara Haze

In Hollywood, where fresh-faced young singers can be transformed into innocuous Barbie dolls suitable for consumption by the lucrative "tweener" audience, the superlative artistry of Sara Haze is even more remarkable. At 18, after developing her singing and songwriting for five years, Haze has arrived. "I had to challenge a lot of people who tried to dumb down my music and lyrics and make it more into a Disney thing," she recounts. "I'm a legit artist who wants a career, not to have one big single and disappear." While her list of co-writers and producers includes platinum and Grammy-winning collaborators, it is clearly Haze's vision that powers her debut CD, *The Ladder*.

Originally from Orange County, California, Haze, who began singing in church, grew up around the entertainment industry with a mother who was a vocalist, television performer, and vocal coach. Both of her parents encouraged her budding musicality. In her early teens, she met artist/songwriter/producer Dave Woeckener, who hired her to record a television track. "It ended up airing multiple times, and he was, 'who is this?' He kept inviting me back to do tracks and he decided to manage me."

Television placements have been a vital component in Haze's visibility. *The Young and the Restless, One Live to Live, One Ocean View*, and *Bad Girls Club* are among the shows that have featured her songs, and she sang the theme song for one season of *The Simple Life*. A licensing and administration deal with PEN Music Group, Inc., led to an introduction to Elicit Music, the writing and production team of Heather Holley and Rob Hoffman (Christina Aguilera, Quincy Jones, Sheryl Crow). Additionally, Pam Reswick and Nathan Meckel of Spin Box Club collaborated with Haze on songs for her debut. "This writing process is new to me," she says. "Pam Reswick influenced my style, direction, and the way I approach songs. But they all have so much to teach—they've been doing it a lot longer than I have."

The sound of *The Ladder* (available on iTunes) features stripped-down instrumentation that pinpoints the emotions of the songs while enhancing the sensitivity of Haze's voice, surrounding it with subtle percussion flourishes, austere piano, and shimmering acoustic guitars. "We wanted to showcase the songs and vocals—not to have some huge productions," she explains. "We experimented with styles throughout my development, and this is the production style we feel is the best for me."

Haze won the 2007 Pump Audio Song Submission Contest and also performed her song "Dust from the Stars" at the ASCAP "I Create Music" EXPO. John Alexander, who quite famously made the historic connection between Alanis Morissette and producer Glen Ballard, made a similar introduction of Haze and Ballard. Now, Haze is also writing songs with the pop patriarch. "I was really nervous before I went in to write with him. 'What if I'm not good enough?' When I got there, it was so calm. He's very humble and didn't intimidate me in any way. It was very surreal, all of a sudden, it was, 'I'm working with Glen Ballard,' and there are all of these Grammys on his windowsill."

An assured live performer and a facile pianist, Haze is equally effective solo or with a full band in clubs, conventions, festivals, and concerts, from small venues to large halls. A recent L.A. show took place at the El Rey Theatre. "My voice sounded like it was 100 feet tall; I absolutely loved it," she enthuses.

For a rising artist, the title *The Ladder* forms an apt metaphor. "We came up with it after all of the songs were written," Haze explains. "The album for me was a lyrical ascension above all of the issues I was having with myself and in relationships. Everyone says music is therapy, and music as the ladder—to be able to write and perform is a ladder out of my life."

At this career juncture, Haze contemplates the course of her development period philosophically. "When I was younger, I obviously wanted things to move faster. 'I want a record deal.' That's the first thing you want. Looking back on the entire process, I know we did everything right."

ASCAP and BMI

"ASCAP and BMI are more the A&R source these days than they were before," notes Alexander. When I talk to the major labels, it's interesting how it's changed—they're looking for an artist with a platform. 'Has she been a finalist on *American Idol?*' I said 'What? Now you guys are waiting for *America's Got Talent* or *American Idol* to sign your acts?' It's kind of scary."

www.glenballard.com

Neil Portnow: Grammy Gold

"Having been a musician and never getting anywhere, I have an empathy towards others' objectives."

The View from Behind the Desk

Arriving at the president's chair at NARAS and being given the responsibility of helming the world's most influential music organization afforded Neil Portnow a comprehensive overview of a powerful organization. "Not being an employee, you can see with a different perspective. There was a great platform to build on, but there were some goodwill issues—with respect to my predecessor, who built this organization and gave us a good platform—and there were cultural/personality issues that provided a little bit of a challenge. The Academy should be the 'happiest place on earth' because it brings so many good elements and programs to the industry. It lost a little luster and I wanted to rebuild that trust and good will. It took a lot of time and energy, but we did that. The mission of restoring good will is something I don't take for granted. It's part of my agenda every day—neutrality and fairness—so I have an advantage because people know that I'm a fair guy and an advocate for the artist community."

"I was on the outside but not a complete outsider," Portnow recalls of his ascension to the head of NARAS. "When I moved to Los Angeles in 1979, I got one recommendation from Eddie Lambert. He said, 'You should get involved since you're new in town.' It wasn't long thereafter that I got elected to the local board of governors, ran for trustee for a number of terms, then became the national secretary/ treasurer for the Academy. So I had more insight into the organization than other candidates for the position had. NARAS is a corporate industry responsibility and a member organization. We have 12 boards in 12 cities across the country, and a huge infrastructure of elected and volunteer leaders."

They call it "Music's Biggest Night," and the annual Grammy Awards, presented by the National Academy of Recording Arts and Sciences is without question the preeminent honor bestowed upon any recording artist. As an organization, NARAS does much more than produce an annual telecast, notes Portnow. "The Academy is a not-for-profit organization. We have two supporting charities: MusicCares helps music people in time of need or crisis. Almost 20 years ago, it was a glaring omission, whereas the Motion Picture Academy has a fantastic infrastructure. We fund-raised and distributed $2 million to victims of Hurricane Katrina and we're proud of having donated $4 million to over 3,500 music people. We were there before FEMA to give assistance to the folks there in New Orleans."

The second of the two divisions of the organization is the Grammy Foundation for music education and promotion of the arts. "With a primary focus on young people and the importance of the arts for our citizens and archiving and preservation of our history. We administer a $650,000 grant writing and music-related research on hearing health and understanding the importance of music in early childhood development. We also promote advocacy in protecting copyrights for members of the community. It's had tremendous impact on services we provide and fund-raising that we do and general awareness of what these foundations do. We have a chapter in Washington, D.C., for a full-time effort, a lobbyist, and numerous programs for leadership in advocacy."

Jive Talking

Interested in music as a kid, and demanding guitar lessons at age six, Portnow played in bands through high school and college, then switched instruments to become a bass player. "I came up with an idea with my buddies that we could be producers, so we started a publishing company and signed some acts. Then I was hired at Screen Gems, a major music publisher. I began song plugging and signing artists that might be good songwriters, but were also feasible as recording talents as well, so we did production deals which were revolutionary for those days. So I produced those things and was then hired as an A&R person at RCA in New York. Later, I worked in the corporate world with 20th Century Fox, Arista, and EMI America, and as an independent music supervisor. Eventually, I was hired to work at Zomba. I was there in 1989 prior to the boy band era. At the time, it was more renowned for indie rock acts out of the UK. Jive Records (a label under the Zomba umbrella) got into rap with KRS-One and artists of that nature."

As a premier label in the world of hip-hop, Jive promoted the talents of Whodini, DJ Jazzy Jeff and the Fresh Prince, E-40, and a Tribe Called Quest, and R&B acts such as Aaliyah, Kim Fields, and R. Kelly. "It was kind of a cutting-edge company," recalls Portnow. "And then we got into the pop market and we saw a niche in the U.S. market and it paid off." A classic understatement: Jive signed pop acts Backstreet Boys, *NSYNC, and Britney Spears—all of whom achieved massive success, and would become the three best-selling acts in the label's history, with Spears selling over

85 million albums worldwide, the Backstreet Boys moving 120 million, and *NSYNC adding 50 million copies to the total.

Young Blood

The Grammy Foundation maintains a website (www.grammyintheschools.com) dedicated to educating future music business luminaries. The site features information and programming of interest to young people interested in music business careers, and not only musicians, Portnow stresses. "It is equally about people who have an interest in being a part of the support system for talent: lighting directors, managers, publicists, music business attorneys—all of those courses are things that we help to facilitate. We also offer career-day programs, and 'Grammy Soundchecks' all around the country. If artists are on tour, we bring in classes of high school and college students who can observe the soundcheck process and then have the technicians spend 15 minutes talking to these students."

Now in its third year, the Grammy Camp is an expanding NARAS endeavor. "One hundred kids for two weeks attend to meet the movers and shakers in the industry for a one-on-one hands-on experience. At the end of camp, a live show is produced— 100 percent by the Grammy campers. The Grammy U network presents programs on college campuses. Individual chapters do programs every year for financial health for musicians, dental plans, available wellness programs, and safe-harbor rooms at events for people with addiction problems. We also have seminars with producers and engineers talking about their craft, or advocacy briefings to panels of A&R people in addition to the independent music world. So there are many points of entry for people who are interested in advancing their careers and learning more about the business."

Music's Biggest Night

Education and advocacy nothwithstanding, it is the annual Grammy Awards presentation that projects the Academy's name worldwide. It is an endeavor that Portnow professes requires a great deal of patience. "One of the things that helps me navigate is coming from that world myself. I also realize I can't make everybody happy, it's impossible. The politics are me trying to be as honest as I can. I respect every artist, manager, publicist, or promoter who gets on the phone or who sends an e-mail or delivers packages—anyone who creates awareness for their artist in our eyes. Because that's what they should do, that's their job. I'm never reluctant to talk to someone and hear them out. But at the end of the day, we only have so many slots. We have the public, and we have to remember it is a TV show, so there are elements that have to be appealing over three-and-a-half hours, to make it visually compelling to have people stay with us for the duration of the show. We need to be mindful of who and how many people are watching, for ratings. As good partners, we want to deliver good ratings, so that's a big factor as well."

That said, Portnow emphasizes that the program carves out time for those who are not big stars. "We try not to look at record sales. We'll try to balance it by having performers and genres that aren't in the obvious mainstream areas. It could be classical, jazz, or an indie band or artist. We have a group of people that make these decisions—a TV committee with trustees who have various expertise. We always desire to platform as many genres as we possibly can during the show."

Given the tempestuous nature of recording artists, something the music business veteran has dealt with for years, Portnow takes a philosophical view of the drama behind the proceedings. "That we have to be pretty important to get people to be silly, obstinate, or angry. That's a barometer to tell us that this is really important and it's nice to get that reaffirmation. People are passionate and it comes out in different ways. It's a once in a lifetime opportunity and certainly we know the power of a Grammy performance or nomination. And it stays with the artists for their whole lifetime."

www.grammy.com

Rich Esra: A&R Insider

"Over the next three to five years, we'll see a different type of artist emerge. Given what it takes for an artist to have a career, it will take a different type of person to make it happen."

Working at Arista Records, a company helmed by a man of legendary status in the music business—Clive Davis—provided an unparalleled education for Rich Esra. "I started my record business career as an intern in the radio promotional department at A&M Records for nine months before I moved into a part-time job in the promotion department for Arista Records, then assisting the director of A&R, getting his office in order, listening to music, writing up evaluations, and helping with the volume of submissions. Then I moved into the A&R department full time. I spent six years at the company. I worked A&R directly with Clive Davis. There was never a head of A&R because all of A&R answered to him."

Today, Esra is the publisher of a series of industry guidebooks that includes *The A&R Registry*, a *Music Publishing Registry*, and a *Film & TV Music Guide*. Forthcoming is an *Artist Management Directory*. His views on the shifting world of A&R are direct. "It's about a shrinking market. We've seen change at majors with the shrinkage of personnel. A perspective that doesn't get talked about is that there are many new indie companies that have come out that can put their hat in the ring to say, 'We are here and we are an alternative.' Now there are small companies where people don't need huge amounts of money to make and market records anymore. It will all result in even more downsizing in personnel at the major labels. But I think there's an entire new landscape coming up in terms of small but expanding companies—hybrid companies with multiple disciplines. Some are smaller record labels formed by management companies who don't need the label system. Middle-class artists who have successful tours and fan followings but don't sell many records have left the label system. Some have strong touring bases and can afford to pay companies to market the music. The artists own their masters, so they can make more money per unit. Then there are big major artists abandoning the label system altogether: Radiohead, Nine Inch Nails, Paul McCartney and Madonna, etc. They don't think the old system can enhance their careers."

Artists in pure pop music, Esra notes, continue to require the marketing muscle that a major label can provide. "That is always the genre that is very expensive and needs money for radio play for marketing."

Slipping on Pink Slips

Fear of termination and gratitude for a job are two of the trends that Esra notes among the current music business workforce. "A lot of them don't know what's going to happen. You talk to people who've seen their brethren go by the wayside. Universal Music Group let 5,000 people go. If they're still in the system, they show up and work as hard as they can. A lot of people in the business have to do twice the amount of work than before. They work what they're working and try to just get though it, as opposed to thinking outside the box and being creative. Once, there were diverse rosters on majors, from Sade to Metallica. What we see on major labels now is very limited artistically. They just cut out what doesn't sell. I don't see them being able to make their numbers with that mentality anymore. All the money that they invest in these artists, and they still can't sell large quantities. Major labels can't survive on singles."

Conventional Thinking

Esra believes that one of the most effective ways for bands and artists to connect with the industry is by attending music industry conferences, and he offers this assessment: "If you're a young urban hip-hop artist or producer, go to the Atlantis Music Conference in Atlanta in the fall. If you're in the rock-pop arena, Musexpo takes place in California every spring and in the fall in Europe. If you're a rock band, there's the Oklahoma Music Conference in Oklahoma City. But the granddaddy is SXSW, but although I recommend it, it might be too much: 1,800 acts. You're just another act that's performing somewhere. Unless you have a strong buzz with a lot of press, I wouldn't really recommend it."

Continuing with the litany of possible conventions to visit, Esra includes the following: "The Winter Music Conference in Florida is excellent for pop/electronica music. PopKomm in Germany has a large amount of public attendees. For roots music, there is the Americana Conference in Nashville. Also valuable are the Nemo Conference in Boston, NXNW in Vancouver. For songwriters, the ASCAP "I Create Music" is all about song-writing, and the Taxi Road Rally alone is worth their annual membership fee."

For acts whose music might appeal to college-age audiences, Esra notes that the National Association of College Activities (NACA) offers exceptional showcase opportunities for artists to perform for college bookers. "With one performance, you can book yourself a 20 to 30 city tour. NACA showcases every kind of entertainment, from singer/songwriters to comedians to bands."

Casting the Internet

As a way of communicating with fans, Esra believes the Internet—although a medium where it is now harder to be noticed—is essential for communicating with dedicated listeners. "If you have your own site, you should have an active relationship with fans and give them a reason to come back. Give them something different: a new song or podcast to keep. You have to provide something each and every week. Artists should treat this communication as consistent, organic, and interactive. Although the Internet allows you to sell your music and to be exposed, you can't hope and wait for the world to find you. You have to actively go out into the blogs, where people are going to talk about you. The hardest thing is to get people to care and pay attention to you as an artist. You have to be creative and diligent and this has to become your life."

If the Shoe Fits

One truth that will never change is that artists will have to re-imagine their creativity and their sales techniques. Esra recalls this classic example of ingenuity: "One artist who never could get a meeting with A&R people sent a box with a baby shoe and a note that said, 'Now that I have my foot in the door, how about lending me an ear?' He got his meeting and the company eventually produced a single."

www.musicregistry.com

Jason Bentley: Eclectic Airwaves

"If you're doing the right things out there, I will find you."

Here's the paradox: A small radio station that operates from the dark recesses of the base-ment at a college in Santa Monica, California, and emits a terrestrial signal that barely stretches across Los Angeles is acknowledged as one of the most influential radio stations in the world. KCRW is supported largely through the donations of subscribers, but what subscribers they are: a retinue of media tastemakers and cultural champions.

As a public radio station, KCRW offers programming that includes news, politics, and culture. Via Internet radio, the station has expanded its listenership exponentially, and in the musical realm, the station sponsors concerts and events across the U.S. Very famously, Coldplay, Norah Jones, Radiohead, and Dido received their first radio play courtesy of KCRW's forward-thinking DJs, and the station features live performances from artists and bands who make a musical stop at the station de rigueur on their promotional visits to Los Angeles.

Jason Bentley is KCRW's music director and he holds down the 9:00 a.m.-to-noon slot with the influential show *Morning Becomes Eclectic*. He began his KCRW radio career as a telephone volunteer, answering calls during music shows, and working in the station's record library, before heading off to college on the East Coast. He returned to California to attend Loyola Marymount University and DJ at their college station KXLU. Former KCRW music director Chris Douridas recruited him after a softball game between the two stations in 1991 and he took to the airwaves starting in the summer of 1992. He became the station's music director in late 2008.

"As a kid, I had a mock radio station and recorded songs off the radio. I was that guy that read the daily bulletins at the high school. I was fascinated in the theater of imagination of radio, the music and the culture. When I came across KCRW, that's when it hit me like bolt of lightning," says Bentley.

As the host of the station's most popular show, Bentley takes his cues from his predecessors: Nic Harcourt, Chris Dourides, and Tom Schnabel, the station's previous music directors. "I was friendly with and a listener to all of them. I have to now stir in my own influence. I steer away from dance/pop stuff and I needed to assure the station that I would play world music, soundtrack composers, and singer/songwriters. I have dropped the electronic stuff a little bit, but I bring in stuff that people aren't accustomed to hearing in the morning, like urban. We don't want to dismiss any genre outright. We are challenging people to broaden their horizons and we hit on popular music that is infectious and new, and will become tomorrow's big sensation."

Air Checks and Laptops

Bentley says his continued enthusiasm is reminiscent of the passion he experienced in his teenage years. "It's similar to approaching music as a 16-year-old with your ears and mind open. It is being immersed in that world; you're just tuned in, approaching it as a collector, sensitive to what's around you. I use technology. I audition music through my laptop for any songs I want to put into rotation. I'll upload these to my computer and I have them in a folder on iTunes for the ones that will become active rotations. On Sunday evenings, I'll go through the playlist to toss stuff out and throw things in. I am also sensitive to artists that are coming to town or have new releases. Much of what I do is connecting points to the bigger music world. We're lucky to be in Los Angeles because people are so interested in what's happening here. Act locally but think globally: We make what's around us available to the rest of the world."

KCRW's considerable influence is attributable to its listeners, among them film and television directors, music supervisors, and record company executives who can hear new music and potentially pass it on to millions of fans. "We have an elite listenership," Bentley agrees. "They carry an influence outward to various projects and that can make a difference. It is the 'long tail theory' of offering more of less. You don't hear one song 30 times, but on KCRW, the listener is hearing more artists less often."

Influential Potential

Although he acknowledges the potency of the Internet as a method of promoting music, Bentley believes that it ultimately requires an experienced collective of creative thinkers to launch an artist or a band with impact worldwide. "The expertise of record labels won't be duplicated by MySpace. Online digital distribution certainly empowers artists. But I still have a lot of respect for the expertise of record labels in creating timeless artists. You need so much input at so many different levels, to put the right producers and songwriters together is so important. Even if you hire freelancers to work with artists, you still need to put a team together."

Because of their non-commercial status, open-door policy, and an influential positioning in the business, KCRW receives massive amounts of music submissions. While anyone can theoretically mail in a CD for on-air consideration, Bentley says that building a real story is more essential. "Build communities: You can just do one thing really well, so now create a group or team of people who are on the same page and do something really significant. People will send me a CD-R with one song—that doesn't speak to me. I want to see the story and feel that it's real. People who are doing this the best will naturally rise to the top. Don't expect to be an overnight sensation, but be confident. If you focus on creating a genuine story, people will respond to that. If you're doing the right things out there, I will find you."

www.kcrw.com

Kenny Kerner: Straight Shots

"You can't go around life being stupid and expect to be successful. The more you know, the less likely you are to get screwed."

A recent article in the *Los Angeles Times* described Kenny Kerner thusly: "This beefy, no nonsense industry veteran with an old school New York accent...." It's an apt portrait of a man who, after 40 years in the line of fire, still possesses an unquenchable fire for the music business. As a vice president at Musicians Institute (MI) in Hollywood, California, and head of the school's Music Business Program (MBP), Kerner now heads up administration of the West Coast's largest and most active music industry educational curriculum. As the author of two highly regarded industry books, *Going Pro* and *Get Smart*, Kerner continues to wield influence over a business that he has been a part of for four decades.

"I do everything until I get tired of it," says Kerner. "I started at *Cashbox* magazine in New York, then I began producing records. I went to a management company; I did public relations for seven years, then I became the senior editor at *Music Connection* magazine. I taught at UCLA Extension. When stuff stops being creative for me, I go on to something else. I've had this job at MI for 11 years because it's different every single day: new fires to put out, new lies the students tell, new instructor problems, schedules, I don't know what's going to happen from one day to the next."

The Big KISS

While Kerner was working at *Cashbox*, he began managing and writing songs for a band called Dust. When the group signed to a label headed by industry legend Neil Bogart, Kerner and his partner at the time, Richie Wise, produced the record. "Because Neil liked the production, he allowed me to come to his office every Friday to pick up boxes of tapes that he left outside his door. I was supposed to take them home over the weekend, listen to them, and if I heard anything interesting, to bring it back and tell him. I did this for weeks until one day I took the box home and there was a reel-to-reel demo tape—I put it on, and it had stuff like 'Cold Gin' and 'Firehouse' and 'Black Diamond' and 'Strutter.' I said, 'This is really good, raw street rock 'n' roll.' I took out their picture—they were wearing $5.99 t-shirts. I got the idea from their makeup. I brought it back on Monday, showed it to Neil, and said, 'You should sign these guys to Casablanca.' Neil was looking for a major rock act that was credible and could get radio play. So my partner and I produced their first two albums."

Although the makeup wasn't as refined and the outfits weren't as extravagant as they would become, Kerner said he instantly realized the power of KISS. "I knew in a second. I have that kind of vision. When you produce, you have to have that. I could hear songs finished when I listened to the demo. I could see dolls, merchandise, and presented it that way to Neil."

These days, Kerner notes, it's a much different topography. "The days of sitting on your ass waiting to be discovered are over—all you'll get are calluses. Ideally, what the labels want is an incredible songwriter with a great voice and a great image—not much! When I used to manage, I would look for people who looked incredible [because] my philosophy is that if someone had a great voice but was an okay writer, you could always find great songs. You could call publishers and find hits. But if you look like sh*t, the only thing you can do is have surgery. I wanted that extra edge of marketing. Look at Justin Timberlake: He's incredibly talented, but that image certainly didn't hurt him. Britney Spears, if she looked like Phyllis Diller, would she have sold as many records?"

Manager as Dictator

Kerner's style as a manager, he testifies, was decidedly hands-on. "When I managed, I woke the artists up in the morning, then told them their schedule and what to wear. I sat down with them if they were doing an interview, got them to networking places, produced a lot of their records, picked the songs, took care of the savings and checking accounts, and helped get the rest of the team together. The manager is the quarterback who does everything. There are managers who are, 'You're an adult. Ask me a question, and I'll give you answers.' I never liked that—it's not hands-on. If the artist fails, the manager should be responsible. If the manager and artist are both successful, they should share in that. I did everything, and it was a full-time job."

"I never managed more than one artist at a time. I was a dictator. I never subscribed to the theory of letting the artist fail and he'd come back. I thought it was easier if I explained to him what could work, rather than to let him fall on his face."

Very few artists make it without an effective manager, Kerner observes. "And those who do, wind up getting ripped off or have to go to a manager eventually. If you are a successful artist, so many things are happening. If you take the time to manage yourself, you're not going to be writing songs or doing interviews, you're going to be doing business."

Education Situation

Over 60 colleges in the U.S. currently offer music industry programs. Kerner, as head of the highest profile among them, is adamant that an education is a key component in the music business, even for aspiring artists and musicians. "You can't go around life being stupid and expect to be successful. The more you know, the less likely you are to get screwed. The more organized you are, the more you can put together a plan of attack. And the more you know about people, the easier it is to put together a band, to know who is going to be a friend. I get to my desk every morning at 6 a.m. to read every trade, every press release. Learning is never ending."

And there are always changes and challenges. "In one of my books, *Get Smart*, I have a segment called "Phone Calls from the Road"—true stories, and these happen to artists all over the world. At 3 a.m., I get a call: 'Kenny, I'm in jail.' 'The truck blew up.' 'Are we supposed to be in Arkansas or Arizona tonight?' 'Did you see the equipment truck anywhere?' You're 3,000 miles away and you look to the sky and say, 'Why me?' But it always changes—it's funny and exciting, and no matter how old I am, I'm 18."

www.mi.edu/majors/music-business

10 The Publisher

Publishing might be a more stable business environment these days than a traditional record company, but both have much in common: They are copyright owners. There is more music usage in various media than ever before. Music publishing refers to all business done on behalf of the songwriter and his or her creations. There can be an enormous amount of income for the owner of a copyright. While a songwriter can be his or her own publisher, being connected to a full-service publishing company can have definite advantages. Those companies are basically set up to exploit copyrights in all of the media that are available in this day and age, including master recordings, film/TV placement, commercials, Internet, iTunes, ring tones, and so on. They also are in place to do all of the administrative paperwork that is necessary when a usage is created.

Danny Strick: Strictly Speaking

"The most important thing? A total knowledge of what's happening in music."

Danny Strick knows about artist development. After all, he was behind the executive desk at BMG Music when an associate brought in some grungy kid she'd heard playing at a street fair in the gritty Silver Lake neighborhood of Los Angeles. Over time, this bohemian vagrant—Beck—became one of modern rock's preeminent innovators. The company also funded Cypress Hill and advised them on the demos that became their inaugural CD. Other artists introduced under his tenure at BMG included Erykah Badu, Duncan Sheik, and Nelly.

Later at Maverick Records, the label co-owned by Madonna, Strick was an A&R executive. "A fantastic change," he rhapsodizes. He made two successful albums with Michelle Branch before moving back to the publishing world, this time to industry giant Sony Music Entertainment. Today, as co-president of Sony/ATV Music Publishing, Strick oversees the firm's East Coast, Latin, and Nashville divisions. Songwriters and artists signed to the company under his auspices include new country star Taylor Swift, hit writer/producer J. R. Rotem, rock sensation Fall Out Boy, teen-pop superstars the Jonas Brothers, singer/songwriter Sara Bareilles, "Apologize" hit-makers One Republic, and writer/artist Sean Kingston.

In his current position at Sony/ATV, Strick combines diverse dimensions of his expertise. "I can combine my people skills and blend that with creative sensibilities. It's been good for me because I enjoy both sides of the business," he says. And since the publishing company is affiliated with the Sony record labels, there are opportunities for Strick to nurture and steer talent in that direction

And pop goes the music. "I'd rather keep it that way for now. It hits our sweet spot. If I have a good artist/songwriter, I can put him or her with our producers and writers. Jason Nevins does dance remixes for Pink and Kelly Clarkson, so we're doing dance versions of a lot of our catalogs. We're going to go to radio or onto dance compilations."

The Signability Signature

In order for an artist to be considered signable, according to Strick, it is imperative that there is already a framework in place, "where we're not starting from complete scratch. We try to sign talent that's far enough along where we can jump in with a lot of energy and input and see results within six months to a year; if there's talent and potential to create hits, and if they fit our roster, then we can make things happen for them."

Since Sony/ATV is an international corporation, writers and producers can work on projects in other music capitols, including London, Germany, and Paris. "We have writers that go back and forth between the UK and the U.S., says Strick. "More so with songwriter/producers, where we can cross-pollinate. In synchronization, our commercial guys do well with obscure bands from Finland, Denmark, and France, placing their music in all kinds of cool projects."

And songs for commercials, Strick says, have to fit the listener's "lifestyle thing," as he clarifies. "Like iTunes—the ultimate example is the certain feel in the songs they use for their commercials, left-of-center types of things. A lot of companies emulate what Apple does, that cool, commercial poppy female type of sound."

Rarely does Strick sign a songwriter who is not an artist, but it does happen. "We will sign a 'top-line' writer [one who writes both the lyric and melody] and add someone on the track side, particularly in urban. We signed Frankie Storm out of Philadelphia and put her with Stargate. They then wrote a number-one hit, 'Don't Stop the Music' by Rihanna."

Ultimately, for a pop artist, Strick says a striking image doesn't hurt either. "An alt.rock band shouldn't look like Clay Aiken. It's genre-specific, trying to look the part, so to speak. Chameleons like Katy Perry and Gwen Stefani can look a million different ways. Pink, Madonna, they never look the same; it's amazing."

Ring Tone Revolution and the Guitar Hero

Immense transformations in the music business are mirrored in music publishing. Strick needs only to look at his own family to chart these changes. "My kids don't care about albums, even old albums. It's always song by song. With [video games] Guitar Hero and Rock Band, they can learn classic rock songs and they can download them. They don't think of a Supertramp album as amazing from start to finish. They don't want to look at the artwork. They just want to hear 'Bloody Well Right.' It's interesting to watch. They appreciate it because it's great, but it's different. And it is song by song, totally."

In his professional role, Strick relates that these types of changes now have a definitive economic impact. "You can make a lot of money as a publisher without calculating huge mechanicals from album sales. We never used to look at deals that way, and it's all because of the Internet and downloads. You have to aim for singles and single down-loads, ring tones, and sync uses. The artist Flo Rida only sold 300,000 albums, but he had 4 million downloads of the single. The ring tone was number one for weeks, and it became a huge copyright.

And other than what Strick deems "intense alternative stuff or music from the metal world, there doesn't seem to be a lot of brand loyalty to an artist. It's rare, but Lil Wayne has it. And AC/DC hit 800,000 units in their first week with their most recent release. They've sold well over 2 million worldwide."

But the deemphasis on longevity and catalog is a reality that Strick recognizes. "There is nothing created today that is emotionally evocative enough that it will have that same effect in 20 to 25 years. The Eagles, AC/DC, Metallica—I don't see things today that are going to have the same impact with touring so that the band will revive and do it again when they're in their sixties. And I think that's a huge difference."

Final Coda

That said, Strick advises young and emerging artists to network, to get themselves out there, and know that conventional radio continues to wield considerable influence. "Associate yourself with people that are more connected and involved than you are so they can help pull you up. And it takes a little stroke of luck…and timing too."

www.sonyatv.com

Kenny McPherson: Sounds from the Cocoon

"You can use the Internet as a research tool. And you can definitely get an impression and check some stuff out, as opposed to the old days when you had to get on a plane and fly across the country. But you still have to look in the eyes to see, see them perform and believe their commitment. It still comes down to human contact, thankfully."

He avows that he was in a band in Scotland, but he "wasn't very good." As a music publisher, however, Kenny McPherson is very good. Currently president of Chrysalis Music, McPherson, based in Los Angeles, has worked on the management and record company sides of the business as well.

"I sang and I wasn't really into being a singer but into organizing the shows," McPherson qualifies. "From early on, I wanted to be on that side of the fence. Then I studied communication in Glasgow and booked shows at college. I went to work at a rock venue called Apollo. Everyone played there, including Led Zeppelin and The Who. After that, I became a tour manager for [English comedian/actor] Billy Connolly, traveling the world, then I worked for Harvey Goldsmith in London, who was a big entertainment promoter in Europe and the UK. Then I started booking American acts. I always wanted to live in America, so I worked for Manhattan Transfer, then went to work for the manager of Supertramp. While I was with them, we started a publishing company and that's how I got into publishing. I was told that if I wanted to be in the music business, I should be on the publishing side because it's the 'gentleman side' of the business. I managed bands, but then eventually went back into publishing for Warner/ Chappell and moved to New York. Five years later, I moved back to Los Angeles, then went to Chrysalis."

McPherson describes Chrysalis as a public company with an independent spirit. "The perception is that we are an indie, so who am I to shatter everyone's illusion? I'm the president of the North American company. We have offices in L.A., Nashville, and New York, and we have a management company based in New York also. Because of the size of our company, I have hands-on, day-to-day interaction with departments of the company. And you can have a certain agenda in the morning, then the first phone call blows the agenda out for the whole day. I deal with contract negotiations to royalties, copyright, business affairs, A&R, songwriting trips, making records—whatever the day calls for."

McPherson says that publishers in the past were the most important people in an artist's career because they had songwriters. "The whole Brill Building thing [the legendary New York City songwriting center, where scores of songwriters were employed to write hits for the artists of the day]. There are many very successful artists that never wrote their own songs—Tony Bennett, Frank Sinatra, Ella Fitzgerald. Even if an artist did write a song, a lot of people collaborated, so the publisher has always been important. Like anything else, they got a little old-fashioned and didn't keep up with some of the contemporary moves of the business. But everything seems to come full circle."

The Light of Ray

Singer/songwriter Ray LaMontagne was signed to Chrysalis by the company's Jamie Ceretta. "Ray didn't have management, an agent—nothing. He had immense talent. It's one of those stories that seems like a cliché. He came in and played three songs, and it was like, 'Let's go have lunch, and you can't leave until we sign you.' It was jaw-dropping. Goes to show there's no rulebook in how it comes to you. It starts with the songs and the voice. So we helped Ray develop and got him a manager and then a record label. We continue to do that with some other artists. Some work, some don't—that's the nature of the beast."

Among the new projects is an album of Cy Coleman songs recorded by contemporary artists. "These songs have lives of their own and are reinterpreted generation through generation. 'Best Is Yet to Come,' 'Witchcraft,' 'Sweet Charity'—a legendary catalog of songs. We started working with his estate two years ago to make a record. I wanted to do it with left-of-center artists: Fiona Apple, Nikka Costa, and Patty Griffin. I have high hopes because this introduces that era of songs to a new generation."

Image Confab

Using the history of culture as a microscope, McPherson relates that image is key. "Image is an important aspect and it has always been there. So again, I think it changes for each generation. I think anything that leads people to music is a good thing. People can dismiss it as a blatant pop situation, like *American Idol*. However, I think it's great because it's a talent show. And some of these kids can really sing. This is their chance and opportunity in our society to get their shot, and to do so by singing other people's songs—great songs by great songwriters. I think you can't turn your nose up at that. Some kid could be watching the show and that could be their first moment when music affected them. My belief is, if you are attracted to music that way, you will discover The Beatles, Miles Davis, the Police, Led Zeppelin, or U2. I think if it brings you to music—and life would be so boring without music—it's a good thing. Image and all forms of pop culture, if it spurs a spark in a human being to want to do that and create something, I encourage it."

Balance of the Biz

McPherson believes the effort that goes into developing musical songwriting talent should also go into the executive side of things. "You can have a very successful career on this side of the fence, and people need to be mentored and helped along the way. People should be aware of that. They have to know it's not just all about musical talent—there's a combination of why things work. To have this business talent as well, is almost as important in some ways. Artists have to pay attention to their businesses, and songwriters need to pay attention to their performing rights organizations [PROs]. I think in America, I meet a lot of songwriters who don't know what a PRO can do for you. They are like your union. It's very worthwhile for artists to find out about these organizations. They are very artist-friendly, and they can help protect your rights. Without PROs who stand up and fight for composer's rights in a big way, composers and songwriters wouldn't have the money that they have."

www.us.chrysalismusic.co.uk/index.cfm

Gary Overton: Country Follows Pop

"It's the music that gets you in the door—not who you are."

As an executive with industry giant EMI Music since 1995, Gary Overton, executive vice president/general manager Nashville, oversees day-to-day operations, including exploitation of copyrights, catalog acquisition, signing writers and artists, and securing record deals. He formerly managed Alan Jackson, served as vice president of Warner/Chappell, and was head of A&R for BNA Entertainment.

"Twenty-five years ago, I worked for a small firm that did everything for everybody," Gary Overton begins, "from management to publishing. I was a song plugger and Keith Stegall was our top writer." As the producer and/or songwriter of over 40 number-one hits, the producer of 21 platinum and multiplatinum albums, plus eight gold albums, and with over 70 million records sold, Stegall is one of Nashville's most valuable resources. "I got involved with everything from pitching songs or driving his tour bus, plus managing during the week, whatever he needed. I loved that; it was a great experience. Then I started my own company, song plugging and picking up individual writers or small publishers for three years. It's hard when you don't have a big corporation behind you, but it keeps you motivated because if you don't do it, it doesn't get done."

Eventually, Overton worked at Warner/Chappell Music and RCA before taking over the management responsibilities for superstar Alan Jackson. "We had a great run and a lot of fun," Overton recalls.

Ears and Eyes for EMI

Overton has responsibilities on both the creative side and the administrative side at EMI. "I'm involved with everything from assessing new writers and aspiring artists to signing a superstar looking for a new home. On the business side, I do negotiations and contract work, and then I love to get involved in pitching new artists to labels. We are at the front end of when they're forming their sound and getting a team together, such as the producer and manager. I love that part of the process; to help them accomplish their dream. We've been successful helping people get record deals in Nashville. When I talk to a brand new artist or even a mid-level artist, there's not a lot they can talk about that I haven't experienced myself. We then work on entrepreneurial ways of exploiting songs."

Country music is one of the genres where the outside song—that is, one created by a professional songwriter rather than a performing artist—is still a valuable commodity. "Conway Twitty once told me. 'I wrote "Hello Darlin," and then I got so busy I just wasn't writing the great songs anymore. I knew I needed to cut outside songs.' Alabama recorded outside songs; Kenny Chesney and all these artists now look outside because they have to have hits. If they don't continue to deliver great music to their fans, that's when fans get tired and say, 'I'm not going to buy that record; I'm going to buy from this new band because they cut a great new song.' I'm still amazed when one of my writers comes in with a new song with a brand new idea that I've never heard before or a familiar idea twisted into a different perspective. I would advise a songwriter to write something different or write it differently."

Dotted Lines Songwriters Sign

"Are songwriters inclined to write commercial songs or artistic songs?" is a question that Overton believes is integral to sign a new songwriter to a deal. "Don't outthink me—show me what makes you special. What are your strengths? I want to hear it in the music, but I want to hear your drive and focus and motivation. You could be a great songwriter, but it's a hard way to make a living and there's a lot of rejection. A song-writer must pound away at this every day, or it's not worth it."

"This is a partnership, and I may have questions—for example, about the second verse, when you switched from first to second person, why did you do that? Was it an inad-vertent mistake or is this intentional? If I didn't pick up on it, maybe you need to rethink it because maybe the audience won't pick up on it either. Two criteria we have with signings are that at least one person on the A&R staff is in love with this person's writ-ing. Second, do they have time to focus on this writer? The more these companies have grown, including EMI, they have also gained a tremendous amount of songwriters. If we don't have time, then we don't have a deal."

Two songwriters who Overton would have liked to sign represent divergent genres: country legend Merle Haggard and pop/rock singer/songwriter Sting. "I've always been a Merle fan. His music spoke to me. It was applicable to my life, whether a happy fun song or 'Momma Tried.' Alan Jackson writes the same way. They have deep songs, but the common man can still understand the message. That's why they are icons. With Sting, I think he's one of the ultimates in the current age of rock and pop music. He's so literary, he uses words you don't hear in songs, and yet people understand them."

For an aspiring songwriter, Overton believes the best method to learn the craft is to be mentored. "Just be around other songwriters and study the songs, to know that there is a reason the words are put here or there."

Biz Builds Buzz Online

Country music, according to Overton, has been less affected by illegal file sharing than pop or rock. "But it has shown us ways to help promote our new artists and songs through websites and webcasts and different avenues. We're now finding new ways to bring more of our music to the people, and fans will hopefully get to know our artists and become involved, whether it's purchasing a concert ticket or a t-shirt."

"When Napster arrived, the record companies didn't even know what the Internet was; everyone said it was ruining the business. But my son had an account. I said to him, 'Go ahead and show me how to do it.' There were amazing things about it. The incredibly good news was that, in his library, my 12-year-old son had Snoop Dogg and Ludacris but also Dean Martin, Ben E. King's 'Stand by Me,' Queen's 'We Will Rock You,' and Louis Armstrong. He saw no boundaries between rock, pop, soul, or country. He downloaded what he loved, and he had it right there. So how do we serve the people's needs and ask them what they want? Is it per download price or subscription? The market will tell them what they want."

"This was a way to interact directly with the music user; to get accurate free demographic research and promote and market to these people with a free way of distributing music. Forces in the industry said, 'This is bad, let's sue them and shut them down.' They got millions of dollars in settlement money out of it, but at the time it was like weeds in your backyard, and the record companies missed these opportunities. It's a damn shame."

Pop Goes the Country

Overton notes that trendwise, country often follows in the footsteps of pop music. "I think image is important if you're a new act trying to get a record deal. There has to be an image conjured up when audiences hear their music—a musical identity. Dwight Yoakam is a character, and Shania Twain was the first to show her navel; but she has accessible pop music and that's why people like her—not for her navel. Image does matter because of the mentality of the record label, and they access by what's happening now. You have to find true artistry and marry this with a song. You have to have an image already established when you go to a label so they can figure out who you are. People are bombarded by visual stuff: When you hear Alan Jackson, you have an image of George Custer. It's too bad for the female side because the business is run by men who always seek pretty girls like Shania or Faith Hill, especially in country music. Mary Chapin Carpenter or Wynonna—you wouldn't think, 'she's hot,' but they have distinctive voices and hit songs. Zac Brown is on the charts, and he is a big burley guy from Georgia. He's the antithesis of what labels are signing, but he has a hit because it's great music, and he has a great voice."

Reviled in the Roadhouse

Overton recalls being hypnotized by hype when a notable Music Row producer extolled the artistry of an upcoming act. "He said, 'Could you set it up? We have a roadhouse south of Nashville in the boonies, can you get some labels to come out?' I was trusting he knew what he was talking about, so I called Mike Duncan at Capitol. We drove down there, and it looked like a horror movie; some dilapidated old building with sheriff's deputies standing outside waiting for fights to break out, and an interesting cast of characters in that bar. Then the artist started to play, and it wasn't very good at all. He dismissed the band from the stage, started to play solo, and then forgot the words two or three times. The evening went downhill from there; this guy was obviously not ready. One of the lessons I learned: When you go to see an artist play, don't trust even a known producer."

www.eminashville.com

Paul Morgan: Publishing Powers

"Who you know is as important as what you're writing."

Paul Morgan began his professional journey at age 19, scouting part-time for Atlantic Records in the UK. From there, he bounced from EMI and then to Polydor Records. With a reputation as a song-based A&R person, he was offered a job at EMI Music Publishing after it had absorbed Virgin Music Publishing. In his words, "There was a lot of work to be done." The transition from artist to songs was fluid as he went from "A&R'ing artists to A&R'ing writers." Among Morgan's formidable credits is introducing a band of schoolboys who named themselves, after their rehearsal date, On a Friday. (They would do much better after they changed their name to Radiohead.)

Cherry Picking

Morgan was recently named vice president of Creative Services and Marketing at Cherry Lane Music Publishing Company, one of the world's leading independent music publishers, with an array of notable artists, including Black Eyed Peas, Mariah Carey, Kanye West, Usher, John Legend, and Wolfmother, among other luminaries. In addition to these current artists, the company has an impressive collection of valuable catalogs, such as those of Elvis Presley, Motley Crue, the Sex Pistols, and Quincy Jones.

Morgan puts his A&R chops to use when it comes to seeking out additional songwriters and artists to plug and shop and he tailors his search to those with a keen eye and a "hustler attitude." He suggests to prospective clients that, "if artists had aspirations to be a writer for other artists as well, then there's far more shots at creating income with that writer."

That said, the bulk of a typical day at the office is spent working aggressively for the artists presently on Cherry Lane's roster. "My duty as publisher is to take every opportunity to leverage that success with collaborations with big artists. For example, I had to nurture a relationship with Shakira's manager for 18 months in order to have a song recorded for one of her projects and to bring that reality to fruition. There was always a little life there, and it implied to me that it could happen at any moment. If I feel there's a chance, I will continue to broach that until it finally becomes a 'yes' or a 'no.' I believe we owe it to our writers to work that hard."

As a publisher, Morgan has worked with some of the most successful songwriters and lyricists, including Steve Kipner, who wrote such prized teen-pop anthems as "Genie in a Bottle" by Christina Aguilera and "The Hardest Thing" by 98 Degrees. He notes that Kipner is an inspiring lyricist and a masterful songwriter. "Seeing how he observed his children on that level and listened to what kind of language was being used by them and then inspiring some songs out of that—it's amazing."

Good Gad

Furthermore, Morgan also gives kudos to Toby Gad as an exemplary example of a proactive songwriter who retains the steadfast "go get 'em" ideology. Thanks to "If I Were A Boy," a hit for Beyoncé, and "Big Girls Don't Cry," a number-one worldwide smash recorded by Fergie on her multiplatinum album *The Duchess*, these are prolific times, as the German-born songwriter/producer adds to his collection of cuts that includes hits by the Veronicas, Enrique Iglesias, Ricky Martin, and Disney star Hannah Montana (Miley Cyrus).

It was a lengthy journey to this destination: He began in his teen years and even wrote songs for the dubious duo Milli Vanilli. Although he had a Sony publishing deal, when he came to the U.S., over 100 collaborations yielded merely one cut.

"Rejection is what you have to go through to learn," qualifies Gad. "The first few hundred songs were a learning experience. Last year, more than half of the songs I wrote made it onto records. Before, it was 10 percent or less. You need to get good at A&R

meetings; when they say, 'This song sucks,' learn why and try to make it better. Sometimes a bridge or a chorus works, but to write songs that work all the way through is a challenge. Every word has to amaze."

Co-writing, Gad says, offers perspective. "You have an audience; every line, every word, you discuss it. I have to fight over every word of the lyric, and we go line by line and eventually we have a lyric that makes sense all of the way through the song, which can be hard to do by yourself."

Although he makes countless trips to the West Coast, owing to the fact that his wife is a simultaneous interpreter at the United Nations, Gad maintains his home and studio base in New York. He notes differences between the songwriting capitals. "New York is more ethnically mixed, and the music is way more urban. California feels more on the rock and songwriter side, while the east coast seems more beat-driven when it comes to pop. That probably shows up in the productions as well."

In Los Angeles, Gad, who records on his laptop, often sets up shop in Venice Beach, where a venerable Art Deco hotel provides a choice view of the boardwalk. "It's so noisy, but we sit there and record our songs. On weekends, it's madness." The proximity to the ocean also affords Gad a rare respite from work when he hits the waves for early morning surfing. "I'm on New York time, three hours ahead of the artist."

Gad avows that developing new talent is a passion, and shares what attracts him to working with unproven artists. "It's in the vocal, a voice that is recognizable throughout the range. Also, that the voice is authentic, and when the singer sings, you believe every word. That the image is marketable and that the artist is driven and will make the necessary sacrifices to be a star."

"If I Were A Boy" and "Big Girls Don't Cry" are both songs with auras of timelessness—perfect vehicles for the pure star power of Beyoncé and Fergie. Gad shares what he believes makes these songs memorable: "When a song functions with just the guitar, and it can live by itself—a good song can work in any genre."

Gad says that he threw away his old songs when he left Europe, and since his arrival on these shores, he estimates he's written over 600 songs. He offers this advice for songwriters: "Write a hundred songs a year for a few years. You will eventually write songs that people understand."

The Perfect Song

Morgan is cognizant of the role of an A&R man and understands that his writers will either value his input or not. Working with Siouxsie and the Banshees, he was of the firm belief that their career needed a signature song that would allow them to cross over in the U.S. market and further sustain their momentum in Europe. He eventually persuaded the band to work with noted synth-pop producer Stephen Hague (Pet Shop Boys, New Order, Erasure) on their 10th studio release, *Superstition*. That ingenious pairing resulted resoundingly in their first hit single, "Kiss Them for Me." This collaboration was fused with a foundation of complete trust and consideration for the band's integrity. "I enjoyed working with them because they knew where they fit in the marketplace but were at the same time looking to somehow expand their fan base without being perceived as sellouts. So one of my prouder moments was convincing them in the studio that that's the route they should go. We wanted to regain their presence in the U.S., and I felt my instinct was right."

So how do budding songwriters cut through the immeasurably thriving competition and get their songs noticed? Morgan assesses, "Well, it all starts with a great song, but connections in the industry will get you to the next level. But the song has to be stunning. That will ultimately get you noticed."

www.cherrylane.com

11 The Performing Rights Organization

From the days of piano rolls and sheet music to satellites and digital transmission today, the mission of PROs (performing rights organizations)—including ASCAP, BMI, and SESAC in the U.S. (equivalent organizations exist around the world)— is to ensure that songwriters receive fair compensation for public performances of their works. For example, whenever music is played on the radio or performed on television, these societies calculate, collect, and distribute negotiated performance fees to the writers and the publishers they represent. In a history built on verses and choruses, PROs are a monetary bridge that connects the most beloved and distinguished songwriters and composers to the world.

Del Bryant: View from Nashville

To be paid for a performance—whether it is on radio, television, or Internet new media or in concert—it is imperative that a songwriter is a writer member of one of the three performing rights organizations: ASCAP, BMI, or SESAC. The PROs are formidable allies, as they utilize their resources and deep relationships to connect writers to the industry at large.

Del Bryant is president and chief executive officer of BMI (Broadcast Music Incorporated). "I went to work at BMI on Monday, October 2, 1972. Do the math, as they say, and you'll see I've been there a while."

BMI represents more than 375,000 songwriters, composers, and music publishers in all genres of music and more than 6.5 million works. As a performing right organization, BMI issues licenses to various users of music, including television and radio stations and networks; new media, including the Internet; and mobile technologies such as ring tones and ringbacks; satellite audio services such as XM/Sirius; nightclubs, discos, hotels, bars, restaurants, and other venues; digital jukeboxes; and live concerts. It then tracks public performances of its members' music and collects and distributes licensing revenues for those performances as royalties to the songwriters, composers, and music publishers it represents, as well to the thousands of creators from around the world who have chosen BMI for representation in the U.S.

BMI offers an array of services and programs, including showcases, workshops, and podcasts, to help members develop their skills and gain industry exposure. In addition, BMI offers broad-spectrum musical instrument, health, and life insurance programs, along with discounts on professional tools, subscriptions, computer hardware and software, and more.

Noting the current trends in the business, Bryant offers this observation: "It's clear that we are moving from a product-based to a service-based world in the music business. The industry is trending towards digital. We believe that there will be a mix between digital downloads of entertainment and digital services that provide access to entertainment. One thing is clear: Today there is more music being played in more places than ever before. Just last quarter, we tracked more than 2.5 billion performances of music from our digital licensees alone. While the physical world of CD sales has not yet seen digital make up for losses in physical product sales, the growth rates are encouraging. We are also seeing new business models emerge that seek to create value for music through means other than selling physical copies—these means include advertising, sponsorships, creative bundling of services, and subscription models. In the future, we see digital contributing significantly to our revenue growth as the more traditional entertainment media mature."

Genius Genealogy

Del Bryant's parents, husband and wife team Felice and Boudleaux, are legendary songwriters, creators of over 1,500 songs, and best known for hits such as "Rocky Top" and their Everly Brothers smashes "All I Have to Do Is Dream" and "Bye Bye Love." Bryant explains, "My father passed in 1987 and my mother in 2004, but during their career, they were both inducted into the Georgia Music Hall of Fame (although my mother was from Milwaukee, she married a Georgia boy and they wrote a lot of their songs in Georgia early on), the Country Music Hall of Fame, the National Songwriters Hall of Fame here in New York, and the Nashville Songwriters Hall of Fame. Their songs have been cut by everyone from Jimmy Dickens, the Everlys, Elvis, Buddy Holly, Rick Nelson, the Beach Boys, Ray Charles, the Grateful Dead to The Beatles to just about anybody you can think of. Songs such as 'Love Hurts,' done by Orbison, the Everlys, Cher, Rod Stewart, Emmylou Harris, and Elvis Costello, Nazareth, only scratch the list of the artists who have cut their material. 'Rocky Top,' the State Song of Tennessee and the most-recorded bluegrass song of the last 50 years, has been cut or performed by virtually every country act in existence."

Music City Origins

"My parents were the first, professional, full-time songwriters in Nashville, Tennessee," says Bryant. "This is an amazing feat, as Nashville is synonymous with songwriters and it's hard to imagine a time when there weren't songwriters in Nashville who made a living solely by writing material for the artists that flock to that community. But there was a time when there were no professional songwriters, and my parents were the first to fill that void. So, that in itself is a pretty incredible overview."

"They wrote songs for what my father used to call 'vehicles.' He looked upon the artists as a vehicle for his and my mother's material, and a vehicle was someone who did more than one song. Jimmy Dickens was their first major vehicle—a very popular country act in the late forties and early fifties who did a dozen to two dozen of their songs: 'Country Boy,' 'Out Behind the Barn,' 'Take Me As I Am or Let Me Go,' 'We Could,' 'I'm Little But I'm Loud' [recently done by Martina McBride], just a tremendous amount of songs."

"Their second vehicle was Carl Smith, who did their first really big pop song, which was covered by Frankie Lane but first done by Carl. Carl Smith was a huge country act who is in the Country Music Hall of Fame. He did 'Hey Joe,' 'Back Up Buddy,' 'It's a Lovely, Lovely World'… a lot of big songs. He was later married to June Carter, and the song that was in the Johnny Cash movie, the duet by Johnny [Joaquin Phoenix] and June Carter [Reese Witherspoon], that title called 'Time's a Wastin','' was a song that dad had written for Carl and June when they were married. That was their second vehicle. Eddie Arnold was the third. This famous Country Music Hall of Famer did a number of their hits."

"And then, of course, they really were instrumental in the early development of rock 'n' roll with the ultimate vehicle, the Everly Brothers, who cut 'Bye Bye Love,' 'Wake Up Little Susie,' 'All I Have to Do Is Dream,' 'Bird Dog, 'Love Hurts,' and scads of others. They had quite a few of those one-off top-10 records from the fifties through the eighties."

Career Directions

During summer school as a high school student, Bryant worked at Monument Records, a label his parents helped move from Baltimore to Nashville in the early sixties. Bryant worked in the mailroom. "I later went to work for my family's publishing company right out of college before I joined BMI in 1972. And I guess you would have to say even as a young child, before my voice changed, I was doing little kiddie demos for my folks when they had songs that were for children, or had children parts. And then as my voice matured, I sang demos until I worked at BMI. But it was publishing, the song business one way or the other, or shucking records at Monument as a teenager."

"When my brother and I were working for my folks in the early seventies (my brother just out of the Army and Vietnam, myself out of college and the Air Force), we worked with my family and our office was close to our home where I was raised. So at lunch my brother and I would go over to the house and have lunch quite often. One day, Frances Preston called my parents on the phone, I happened to be there with my brother at lunch. My father yelled to my mother to pick up another receiver; she went upstairs, got on the phone, they were on the phone about maybe a minute. They hung up. I saw my mother then walk downstairs crying, my brother said, 'What's wrong?' My mother said, 'It was Frances Preston and she wants to hire one of my boys, and she doesn't care which one.' Well, my mother was so proud that Frances, who was very famous in Nashville as the head of the BMI office, beloved by most of the songwriters, my parents included, was really was honoring my folks by not caring which of their boys she hired. My father said, 'Yes, it was Frances and she wants to hire one of you, anybody interested?' My brother, who had just gotten home from Vietnam, said, 'Well, not me, I'm pitching songs.' And I, who had a two-year-old and one [kid] in the oven, who was just about ready to land, said, 'Well I might be interested.'"

"The truth being told, my parents—sometimes working for your parents is not the best way to get rich—believed in working hard and paying little or having me work hard and them paying little. I was taking home less than $100 a week. I thought that working for BMI might be a good way to work up my phone book.' That was my dad's way of growing the business, to have a good phone book. My brother and I had been pitching various songs and we were known as 'little Boudleaux and Felice,' and it was hard to really get a toehold in early Nashville even with the pedigree and the information and the training that we had."

"So dad said, 'Well, you know, that might be right, you might work there for a year or two and it might really get you connected and you could come back and we could really get some songs cut.' Well, he called Frances back; not even three minutes had transpired. He said, 'My youngest son, Del, is interested.' He put me on the phone; I was hired in less than 30 seconds. I was told I had to wear a suit to work, what my salary would be—which was three times what my parents were paying me—and that I had an expense account. She said, 'When can you go to work?' I put my hand on the phone and said, 'When can I go to work, Dad?' He said, 'Monday would be fine.' So I said, 'Monday.'"

"I got off the phone, told my father I had to have a suit and tie—I didn't own one. He sent me to his favorite men's store, gave me a budget of $1,000, called the store up, told them to get me a bunch of clothes—sports coats, suits, ties, shoes, belts, everything— you could buy a lot in 1972 for $1,000. And the next Monday I went to work at BMI. I started working with songwriters, introducing them to what BMI did for them, listening to their songs, making, hopefully, useful comments."

"Having been raised in my household, not only had I written songs, but I'd been raised understanding, I must say completely, what the hook was, what a good verse was, what a good chorus was, and the concept that rhyming was important. I mean, I'd been raised totally in the bowels of songwriting with songwriters who wrote at home every day and I got it. And so I started working with the writers and slowly developed working with bigger and better writers, helping them do anything that would lead them a step closer to getting a performance—which, of course, is what we at BMI do."

"And then in 1985, I was asked to come to New York and work on the distribution system because I knew well how writers liked to be paid and how they valued their creations and the performances of them. And that started me backing my rear end, I guess you'd say, into the business end of the machinery and I slowly kept on backing my rear end into the business, more and more, never forgetting that all gifts come from creativity, the writers, and publishers."

Coming Up in the Biz

For aspiring and new songwriters and artists, Bryant delivers this message: "I would suggest that people hone their craft continuously. Never give up, if indeed you want to be a writer or a publisher. That you listen to the hits, you learn what components seem to make up the hits that you best understand, and make sure when you're writing that you try to infuse your work with some of those components. It is a very, very tough business to break into. There are so many opportunities to be rejected. You have to be one who grows stronger from rejection and not weaker, and that is more easily said than done. But I know for a fact that if you look upon yourself as one who will succeed and you don't allow other people to rain on your parade, you have a far better chance."

"I would certainly hang around people that are in the industry and know what they're doing. That quite often means being in a community where entertainment is key. Much like New York, Nashville, Atlanta, Los Angeles, London, Austin, there are just a number of communities and most everybody knows where they're at and I would say that it's important to be with people that do something similar to what you aspire to do. It's certainly important to be around musicians, and if you're a band player looking for a band, you're more likely to find them in these types of communities."

"So I would say go to where it's happening and then seek out professional people who can help you polish your presentations. Whether it is just the way you present yourself in a meeting or present your demos and your music. Believe in yourself and work hard and, as I said, let rejection fuel you in a positive way."

www.bmi.com

The ASCAP "I Create Music" EXPO: Empowering Songwriters and Composers

The ASCAP "I Create Music" EXPO elevates the conference experience to an unparalleled magnitude. Since its inaugural year, the EXPO, open to all regardless of performing rights affiliation, has attracted more than 4,000 music creators, industry professionals, and exhibitors.

The star power is extraordinary: The EXPO's headliner interviews have featured Tom Petty and Randy Newman. Other panelists and performers have included Clarence Avant, Johnta Austin, Glenn Ballard, Alan and Marilyn Bergman, Stephen Bray, Darrell Brown, Chris Brubeck, Bun B, Kandi Burruss, Regina Carter, Chamillionaire, Tom Chapin, Desmond Child, Alf Clausen, Ted Cohen, John Corigliano, Marshall Crenshaw, Hal David, Patrick Doyle, Dre and Vidal, Jermaine Dupri, Barry Eastmond, Mike Elizondo, Michael Giacchino, Lukasz "Dr. Luke" Gottwald, Jerry Harrison, Mark Hudson, Brett James, Jimmy Jam and Terry Lewis, John King (Dust Brothers), Holly Knight, Russ Landau, Jerry Leiber and Mike Stoller, Tania León, Alejandro Lerner, Seth MacFarlane, Kenny MacPherson, Johnny Mandel, Tom Maxwell, MC Lyte, Rhett Miller, Rick Nowels, Martin Page, Rudy Perez, Linda Perry, David Renzer, John Rich, Matt Scannell, Stephen Schwartz, Jill Scott, Matt Serletic, Jeff Silbar, Marc Shaiman, Michelle Shocked, Jill Sobule, J. D. Souther, Don Was, Jimmy Webb, Paul Williams, Ann and Nancy Wilson (Heart), Bill Withers, and Dan Zanes, to name just some of the stellar participants representing a wide range of genres.

"The EXPO took off like a rocket," marvels ASCAP president and Academy Award–winning lyricist Marilyn Bergman, as she offers this overview: "For someone who wants to know what is the business is like today—who are the players and where help might come from—attending this event is a very wise thing to do."

EXPO Evolves

For decades, ASCAP has been presenting workshops and career development programs. Each year, the Society holds general membership meetings in Los Angeles, Nashville, and New York. When ASCAP began offering pre-meeting seminars, the response was immediate, says Phil Crosland, executive vice president and chief marketing officer for ASCAP. "Virtually everyone—about 1,000 people at each location—would show up an hour early to sit in. We would have panels of successful writers interviewed by ASCAP staffers, and we had tremendously positive feedback."

Clearly, as ASCAP members were surveying the landscape for networking and educational opportunities, the Society surmised that having one huge event under a single umbrella—100 percent dedicated to the needs of songwriters and musicians across all genres—could empower artistic creators. Crosland notes that a working group that included a key EXPO architect, Lauren Iossa, senior vice president of marketing, said, "We need to do our own music conference where we can be focused and make it more significant than an afternoon, a day, or even two days."

Beyond Songwriting 101

New Jersey songwriter/producer Deb Ferrara, founder and producer of the popular ASCAP showcase series NJ Songwriters in the Round, has featured hundreds of up-and-coming artists and helped the music community connect. Most recently Ferrara partnered with Askold Buk to form 901 Music Productions.

Ferrara was skeptical about the EXPO. "I was a big SXSW person. I wondered, 'Is this Songwriting 101?' Everyone I spoke to said that aside from the seminars being terrific, it is a great networking opportunity—and that's what it's all about." At the EXPO, Ferrara met a representative from Ricola, an EXPO sponsor, who was conducting onsite interviews, and she connected with Chris Devito, from Devito/Fitterman, the company's ad agency. "I asked if they were accepting CDs. He said, 'Sure.' Six weeks later, I got a call and Chris said, 'We love your song—we want to use it for the ASCAP/Ricola video.' The ad agency wants to work with us again. ASCAP put us in *Playback* magazine. We subsequently signed with an entertainment attorney in New York who is shopping our material. Askold Buk and I signed the artist, April Start, who sang the Ricola commercial, to a production agreement. Is it a coincidence that it all happened after? I don't think so."

Compose Yourself

Ernest Adzentoivich composes music for film, television, video games, and advertising in rock, jazz, orchestral, and electronic music. Originally a bassist, he observed an economic disparity. "I noticed the guys writing the music were making more that the guys playing the music," he laughs.

A key opportunity at the EXPO propelled his career forward. "ASCAP had a panel called 'Film Your Issue,' where they had a couple of shorts on their website and you were able to score them. Shawn LeMone [Assistant Vice President of Film and Television/New Media and Technology for ASCAP's Membership Group] picked two of mine to be shown. I got a great response, and immediately afterward Edwina Travis-Chin approached me from Associated Production Music [APM], who gave me her card and told me to call her when I got back home. Since then, I've made enough to pay for the trip to Los Angeles maybe 12 times."

"All of the ASCAP film and TV people were at the screening. I met Nancy Knutson, Shawn, and Sue Devine, who sent me to an IFP [Independent Feature Project] Film Market here in New York, where I met a director from L.A. who I had lunch with the last time I was there, and I'm talking to him about scoring some promos. Without going to the EXPO, I wouldn't have gotten all of this attention."

Adzentoivich notes that if you are self-motivated, professional, and visible, you can magnify the EXPO into a phenomenal resource, "especially for someone in my position. It depends on the person: If you're starting out, the panels are great; if you're a little further along, it's important who you're standing next to, who you get to talk to, and who you get to meet. You have to put as much into it as you can."

Fast Tracks and Individual Attention

To take writers to the next level, ASCAP devised a system of "tracks," suggestions for how to maximize the conference experience with the events and opportunities specific to individual careers. While there is plenty of basic information, the tracks are a way to address the needs of songwriters and composers who, like Ferrara and Adzentoivich, are at higher levels. As always, participants will pick and choose, but with so much programming available, ASCAP believes it will be advantageous to provide this measure of guidance.

Phil Crosland explains the expansion of the EXPO's one-on-one sessions. "We put attendees across a table from someone who can really help them with a particular career issue. It might be a successful ASCAP songwriter or a successful publisher or an industry influential of some kind. For the first two EXPOs, we said the first 500 people would be entitled to one of these sessions. We did it to market the EXPO—to add to the early registration numbers and build excitement. What we found was that we don't need the one-on-ones as an incentive any longer."

"We oversold it. Some people were cut out because they didn't hear about it until later. We said, for an additional administration fee of $25, we will guarantee a one-on-one session. It democratized the availability of these sessions. Eighty-five to ninety percent [of registrants] have said they want this. We know they're valuable, so there will be an opportunity regardless of when they register, as long as we don't reach capacity."

Jimmy Landry, an A&R rep and in-house producer for Capitol Music Group in New York, has his own label, Audiostrike (www.audiostrike.com), but he considers himself "a songwriter at heart." He has been one of the mentors who meets with writers, offers advice, and listens to music. He notes that he has heard some signable talent with whom he has stayed in touch. "Out of all the conferences I've attended, this one gives participants opportunities to sink their hooks into the industry. Everyone is approachable. I think you get more bang from your buck. Some conferences are overwhelming, not focused. This is very focused. It's not like you come, give someone a demo, and get signed. At this conference, you come and roll your sleeves up and learn how to possibly make some money by getting your music licensed, or you're going to have a mentor session with someone who can give you some guidance. There is camaraderie—everyone is there for the right reasons."

Biz Realities

Empowering the songwriter with tools to understand business adds another dimension. ASCAP board member Leeds Levy is president of his own independent music publishing company, Leeds Music. Levy was formerly the president of Chrysalis Music Group, Inc. From 1981 until 1991, he was the president of MCA Music Publishing, the world's third-largest music publisher. Levy also established Elton John and Bernie Taupin's American music publishing operations. "A songwriter is an inventor; a song is an invention; now, they have to create commerce from it," he remarks. "You cannot just come to the market with a great song—you have to have a plan of execution. The more that writers are at EXPO to glean that information, [the more] they can move their careers forward."

Levy, who has helmed high-profile publisher panels at the EXPO, notes that the terrain of music publishing is far different in this era than that of his father, Lou Levy, who quite famously signed Bob Dylan to his first publishing deal. He says his EXPO panels have been reality-based. "There was reluctance on the part of the publishers to give anyone false hope in terms of a deal. I think one thing that writers today realize is that in the early stages of their careers, they are going to be their own publishers, record labels, and artists. The burden, if you will, is on the back of the creator to, as they say in Hollywood, be a 'hyphenate.' Still, if the publisher could write the hit songs, he wouldn't be looking for the writer."

Crosland notes the heavyweight panelists and performers from the ASCAP community. "Our Membership Group does an absolutely heroic job in reaching out to those ASCAP members who can not only draw a crowd, but say something meaningful and relevant to aspiring music creators. The other point I would make is that a lot of our well-known writers contact us and say they want an opportunity to give back. It is not all that difficult to recruit panelists and keynotes. Sure, schedules are always a problem; if you're successful, you have no time. That's what we find about business in general—you keep giving the work to the people who get it done. The people who are making things happen are first in line if they can shake their calendars loose."

Final Thoughts

Marilyn Bergman avows that the ASCAP "I Create Music" EXPO, despite its inspiring glow, offers a sobering reality check on the business today. "I think writers are learning that they not only have to be their own publishers, but they have to been their own outlet of music. The funnel is narrower than it has ever been. They either have to find a way to widen the bottom of the funnel or find a way to go around it. It's not just about coming together and networking. Hopefully, people learn something from all of the wonderfully talented people who have paid dues over the years. Everyone they hear—panels, discussion groups, performers—all of these people have skills and crafts that they've honed."

"Talk to anyone who's been to an ASCAP "I Create Music" EXPO, and you will hear it's the best money they've ever invested in the music business," says Phil Crosland. "We keep the price low so it can appeal to the kinds of numbers it does draw in. You get three days that are totally focused." Deb Ferrara agrees. "If you're a songwriter, you have to be there. It's about being at the right place at the right time, and this is the right place."

www.ascap.com/expo

SESAC: Foreseeing the Future of Performing Rights

Founded in 1930, SESAC is the second-oldest performing rights organization in the United States. SESAC's repertoire, once limited to European and gospel music, has diversified to include today's most popular music, including R&B/hip-hop, dance, rock classics, country hits, Latina music, contemporary Christian, jazz, and television and film music created by the cream of Hollywood's hottest composers.

Over the years, many thousands of artists have performed SESAC-affiliated songs, including Usher, Mary J. Blige, Justin Timberlake, Pink, Nelly Furtado, Beyoncé, Garth Brooks, Ludacris, Kenny Chesney, Eric Clapton, U2, Luciano Pavarotti, LeAnn Rimes, Mariah Carey, Alan Jackson, Christina Aguilera, and UB40. SESAC has signed artists such as Bob Dylan and Neil Diamond, representing their deep, income-generating catalogs of songs for public performances. SESAC's influence in the nu metal scene is especially significant and includes such genre leaders as Shadows Fall and Killswitch Engage.

Unlike its sister organizations, ASCAP and BMI, SESAC is privately owned. While SESAC may be the smallest of the three U.S. performing rights organizations, size seems to be its largest advantage. SESAC prides itself on developing individual relationships with both songwriters and publishers. And because SESAC concerns itself only with quality copyrights, the music user isn't required to sift through the millions of infrequently used titles to access the usable ones.

SESAC's corporate headquarters in Nashville, under the direction of president/chief operating officer Pat Collins, houses all of the company's divisions, from creative to licensing to administration. The company also has offices in New York, Los Angeles, Atlanta, Miami, and London.

New technology illuminates SESAC's path, states Hunter Williams, vice president of Royalty Distribution and Research Services. SESAC has recently created an alliance with DigSound, a new watermarking technology that dramatically improves the way that music is tracked and credited. With an indelible and inaudible code permanently embedded in the music, this watermarking survives compression and duplication, enabling it to be tracked across a broad range of media. This signifies more efficient methods of tracking performances, especially for music libraries and their composers. "If the watermark is there, even if the producer forgets to update the cue sheet, there's still a way to track it. Technology is key for a number of reasons; there's the accuracy and transparency factor—not all this 'voodoo.'"

SESAC pays its writer and publisher affiliates for live performances at all sizes of venues across America through SESAC's Live Performance Notification System. Live concerts are weighted according to venue size or seating capacity and the songs performed must be registered with SESAC.

The West Coast SESAC division is active in television and current and syndicated shows such as *Ugly Betty, Monk, Two and a Half Men, House, Grey's Anatomy, Dr. Phil, Deal or No Deal, Entertainment Tonight, Boston Legal, Extreme Makeover, How I Met Your Mother, The Insider, Rachael Ray, My Name Is Earl, Access Hollywood, That '70s Show, The Late Show with David Letterman*—all feature music created by SESAC composers.

States Hunter Williams, "We're always looking for quality composers, but we approach it as a partnership. If the relationship doesn't make sense for both sides, we don't do it. But when the determination is made that we have something the other needs, both sides can flourish. Once the bond is made, it holds."

www.sesac.com

12 The *American Idol*

Since the advent of television, there have been talent contests: from *Ted Mack and the Original Amateur Hour* and *Arthur Godfrey* in the fifties to *Star Search* in the eighties. *American Idol*, and its counterparts in many other countries, however, has dwarfed all of its predecessors to become a cultural juggernaut of epic proportions and a worldwide phenomenon. Artists now have an unprecedented opportunity to showcase their talents in front of millions of potential fans. For those in our business who might view themselves as cool and trendy, a televised vocal competition might not be their thing; but it must be respected for what it is, as it has spun off a roster of current stars, including Elliot Yamin and Kellie Pickler, who you will hear from in this chapter.

One crucial element of *American Idol* is this: It showcases "pop" stars. "Pop" is short for popular, and there is a world out there that embraces this. Ultimately, this audience crowns the winner.

Debra Byrd: Flying with *American Idol*

"When I look at Chris Daughtry, Jennifer Hudson, Carrie Underwood, Kelly Clarkson, Ruben Studdard, Fantasia, Elliot Yamin—these people who go all across the board, period. And I am so grateful to have had some inkling of information I can give them to propel them into stardom."

Broadway, records, tours, and concerts—Cleveland, Ohio–born Debra Byrd has an extensive career within an extraordinarily wide panorama of the entertainment business. But she harbors deeper ambitions. "My goal is to become the Martha Stewart of all things with vocal products to make you a better singer," laughs Byrd. Instructional DVDs, songbooks, and a digital pitch pipe are products she's developed so far to fulfill that mercantile destiny.

Byrd has enjoyed an enduring tenure as a charter member of Barry Manilow's extended musical family, as she says, "from 'Mandy' until now." But it is her role as the vocal coach and an arranger on *American Idol* that has brought her into living rooms coast to coast. She relates that in conducting seminars across the country, she encounters a certain mindset in future hopefuls. "I run into many young people who are talented, and I ask them what they want to do and they say, 'I want to be a star.' And I say, 'Wait a minute—that's not a goal. How about being a great musician?' This generation looks at it a lot differently than our generation did, who viewed music as becoming your passion, enjoying what you do, honing a talent. It's disturbing to me. So I try to reroute them into having a sustaining career by giving seminars and providing them with information."

"My theory is that our generation grew up listening to music, but the eighties babies— that's what I call them—grew up looking at music. They were baby sat by the television, and they learned from VH-1, MTV, and BET. And they sit in their homes and say, 'I can do this.' Consequently they think it's easy."

"That's why you see those people who show up on the early shows on *American Idol*, these kids who really think they're talented and they aren't. And we're amazed, 'They can't really think they're talented.' But they really do. It's a bit unnerving. That's because they grew up thinking they could do this, and the people around them bought into it."

"I studied voice from when I was 12 years old until I went to university. I had my own band, an independent church choir, and at the age of 15, I had the nerve to have people audition for me. I wanted great singers for these arrangements I heard in my head. I was performing in singing competitions at the same time. In another place and time, I would have been that contestant you see standing in the line to audition."

Season Sensations

Byrd has been on each of the seasons of *American Idol*. The first time that television audiences see her is during the tempestuous Hollywood week, where the hopefuls are whittled down. Byrd recalls her introduction to the show. She had just been offered a role in the Tony Award–winning musical *Bring in Da Noise, Bring in Da Funk* on the exact same day she was recording a demo for a Diane Schuur project that Manilow was producing. "I was driving on the 101 freeway saying, 'Thank you, God, it's so wonderful to have a job, but I wish I had a job that kept me at home.' I'd been touring my entire life. Then I heard a message from the music director from *American Idol*, who said, 'It's a new show, we need a vocal coach. I need one that can help up and coming singers— you are not the singer or the performer, but I love working with you in the recording studio. I like the information you give, you're fast, they get it, and we move on.' So I said, 'I don't know what *American Idol* is, but count me in.' I had no idea. The executive producer, Nigel Lythgoe, told me in season one what a great impact that television show would be on the music industry. I was very glad to be a part of that on the ground floor. Here we are—the artists are household names."

Byrd relates that prior to her *American Idol* gig, she'd had five record deal offers—one that happened and four that did not. "I remember trying to get a record deal. And an A&R guy saying, 'You sing too many styles; we have to pigeonhole you.' But I said, 'I do so many things.' And that was my frustration many years ago. However, I didn't know a gazillion years down the line there would be a television show where I could use all of my faculties: my rock, country, and pop sensibilities. I said on Oprah Winfrey's show: 'I get it, this is my destiny gig.' It is about me giving back and guiding all of these other people. I have the happiest heart you can imagine because of this."

Cooking with David

Season seven *Idol* champ David Cook is an artist that Byrd believed in early on. Audiences and the press didn't share her enthusiasm. "David Archuleta, Carly Smithson, and Michael Johns—the media was picking up on them and ignoring Cook, which I thought was fascinating. [Associate Music Director] Matt Rohde and I were in the room and David was singing, and I was hearing a magnificent voice and musical sensibility and everyone was overlooking him. I said, 'I need people to pay attention to you.'"

Byrd asked a close friend to offer her estimation of David Cook. "And she said, 'Oh, I don't like him.' I asked why. She said, 'The way he comes off on camera isn't good.' I knew I had to work on media training with him. He was very receptive to everything I said. You can see him at the beginning and at the end, and people say you can see him visibly change. I was just with him at the Hard Rock Café in New York, and he introduced me to his band by saying, 'This is the woman who made me work for the camera.' I taught him to be camera-friendly and to appeal to the masses through that lens."

"He was so disciplined and determined, he had the courage, not to mention that talent. I can say that about him and others who have gone through that machine. It takes a lot to become a successful recording artist and to sustain it."

From the Stage to the Studio

Jennifer Hudson is an artist who Byrd explains can bridge the transition from theater to recording. "On *American Idol*, everything she did was way too big. I said, 'Every song you sing doesn't have to hit the last row.' That's the theater mindset. The goal of this show is to make records. I said, "Pull it all back so that when you get big in your performance, it has an impact as opposed to starting big and staying big.' I was working with her on musical dynamics. That will span from theater, which is huge, to television, which is very small, to recording, which becomes a little bigger. And you can see the big payoff. I have to brag at this moment: I was the one that pointed DreamWorks casting to Jennifer Hudson for *Dreamgirls*. They asked me about Frenchie Davis or Fantasia, and I said those girls would be wonderful, but they had to see Jennifer Hudson is the Effie White character."

"You have to show your heart and the emotion of the heart. That's the connective tissue. No matter what area you thrust yourself in, you have to let people hear the emotion of the song. That's what takes you from being a good singer to being an artist. That's the journey of *American Idol*. I don't want people thinking these are flakes who got a quick ride to stardom. I wanted to make sure these young talented people didn't become a joke."

Beyond the Voice

When Carrie Underwood was a contestant, the *American Idol* team brought in a world-class fiddle player to accompany her on the show. "I said, 'I would like for you to go up and say hello.' She said, 'I can't do that.' I said, 'You're going to have to speak to your band.' I went with her, and she said hello. It was a huge obstacle for her to overcome. She doesn't have that problem anymore."

"I make it my thing to get them beyond the singing, to help them to understand the business, and that they have to know how to deal with their production team, producer, and a manager, to know how to do the artist's job within all of this. It's not an easy ride."

Byrd has been recently involved with developing an artist named Marisabel, a young singer who had not passed the *American Idol* audition, but still impressed Byrd with her tenacity. "This girl tracked me down like a bloodhound. She had such a commitment. I finally said all right, and then I said, 'Eeeek—so many bad habits and obstacles.' But with her determination and courage, she got over every obstacle. It took a year. Could she have done it within the *American Idol* machine time frame? No way. This is artist development. In the old days, they would take the time to develop an artist. Her CD is for sale on CD Baby. She had to jump through so many hoops, but she's made it happen. When she called me, she said she couldn't sing in tune—but she was singing with guitars that were never in tune. We started from there, and now she's got a band and a producer; she bought studio time, and did everything she could do to make her music come alive. It can happen. You can make it if you are determined. There were so many who made it before *American Idol*. But it is not an easy nor a free ride."

"I've had singers tell me, 'You're not just a singing coach, you're a life coach.' Singing isn't just in your head. My mother used to say to me, 'Your entire body is your musical instrument. You're going to perform with a band. The guys can put their instruments in a case and lock them away. You carry your instrument with you, so you must take care of it. As a teenager, that was my head space. There's a discipline that's part of the information I pass onto these singers who are on this rapid journey to being the *American Idol* to having a recording career."

"You have to be where it's happening, New York, Los Angeles, Atlanta, or Nashville. You can't be a star in the bedroom. That's why *American Idol* works. Figure it out, and see what it takes to get to this next step."

www.debrabyrd.com

Kellie Pickler: *American Idol*'s Small-Town Sweetheart
"You don't see what's behind the scenes. All you see are the red carpet pictures."

With her Southern charm and disarmingly naïve sweetness, Kellie Pickler became one of the show's most beloved stars in season five of *American Idol*. It didn't hurt that she had a riveting back story: a daddy in prison, an absent mother, and a loving pair of grandparents who raised her in rural North Carolina.

"I had heard of *American Idol*. People would say, 'Why don't you go try out?' I was originally supposed to audition in Tennessee, but the arena was canceled because of Hurricane Katrina. My grandpa's sister lives in Nashville, so we could drive to Memphis. Then, auditions were rescheduled to Chicago, and my grandpa couldn't afford to do that. I asked God, 'If it is Your will for me to do this show, You're going to have to bring it to me because I can't afford to go.' The next day I had the TV on, and they said they would hold auditions in Greensboro, North Carolina. God did bring it to me."

Her stint on *American Idol* introduced her to millions of viewers. "My life did a 180. I went to bed one night as a roller-skating waitress at the Sonic Drive In. The next day there were cameras on my doorstep. Back home, our breaking news was when we got a new dollar store. After *American Idol*, there were cameras all around. People would drive from Ohio to come see us. It was insane! You have to be ready for the ride, 'cause it doesn't end. After *American Idol*, you might have every opportunity in the world, but you have to be sure to make good decisions along the way."

Time Travel

Picker says that for her, being essentially on her own, it is easier to devote the necessary time required in building her burgeoning career. "I was never the type to settle down. I have no strings attached anywhere, so when I left, I left, and I didn't leave anything behind. I'm not married, I'm young. I have no responsibilities but my pets and myself. I have a Chihuahua, a cat named Tickles, and a snake. I take them with me in the road—the snake, too. Nobody better just walk into my bus anymore; they know better!"

The notable Nashville-based management firm Fitzgerald-Hartley directs Pickler's career. "The hardest part is finding the right team of people because you have so many coming after you, wanting to be a part of you and your career. I didn't know anything about the music business. I only knew how to sing and that was it. I was igno-rant. I was signed to another manager and that didn't work out; then I had meetings with a couple others. I just clicked with Larry Fitzgerald and Mark Hartley, and we've been together ever since."

"There will be opportunities that I won't be aware of, and I have to trust that the man-ager will make the right decision for me. You have to figure out what you want. Fox offered me my own sitcom. I sat down with my managers and said that the most impor-tant thing for me was my music: I want to be on country radio and in the Country Music Hall of Fame. I have to figure out my priorities. TV and film will always be there. One wrong choice, and it could be damaging for the rest of my life. There's no way I'd be the star of a sitcom until I had a lot of acting classes and trained for it. You have to ask yourself, 'Why do you want to do this?' I heard they did a survey in public schools. 'What do you want to be when you grow up?' Eighty-five percent of the kids said they wanted to be famous. You have to ask yourself, do you want to be famous or a credible artist? There's a big difference."

Behind the Glass

As a result of her affiliation with *American Idol*, Pickler's record deal was through the show's recording division, 19 Entertainment, in conjunction with Sony Music Nashville. The duration of this arrangement is for her first three albums, after which she will be signed to Sony. Pickler, in the direct language that is her calling card, said that the recording of her first album was "hell! *American Idol* had just finished, and the label was really persistent that I get my album out as soon as possible. In six months, there would be a whole new *American Idol* and I would be old. We had to strike while the iron's hot. I was in the studio after the tour and made the record in two and a half weeks on whatever days I had off. Sometimes it was right after I got off stage with the *Idol* tour." That expansive trek included 60 cities in 90 days. "I would record until 2:00 a.m., then get up and do a show. It was very rushed."

Pickler says she didn't foresee those constant demands on her time once she became a valuable recording and touring commodity. "I remember once going to a Kenny Ches-ney concert and thinking, 'Wow! He has it made.' That's not even the case. You don't see what's behind the scenes. All you see are the red carpet pictures."

Just Rewards

Pickler was named Fan Favorite in Nashville at the CMT Awards. "It's the only fan-voted awards in country music. This means so much to me because those are the people that buy our records and go to our shows. So to be picked as Fan Favorite is incredible—it means more to me than any award. In this case, there are no politics involved.

Everything's political—it's not just those that are in politics, but everything in the world is politics. You get your job at the Sonic Drive In because your cousin works there. You get this because of that, and [it is] very much that way in this business. Be thankful that you're in the loop."

Notably, Pickler is an emerging songwriter who works with collaborators such as Taylor Swift, Aimee Mayo, and Chris Lindsay. "I have so much to say. I'm young, but I feel that I've seen a lot as far as life experiences. I write about my life and the things that I've been through, and it's very personal. That's the great thing about country music; it's very personal. People relate to it. When you write about your life, you are writing about somebody else's life, too. On *Idol*, my personal life was public, but it really helped my career because people got to know me and know who they were investing their money in. I wrote about my relationship with my mother that I don't have—it's kind of my signature song. My favorite artist in the world is Dolly Parton. As a kid, I always wanted to be the next Dolly. I'm a fan of her writing; I can sit down and read the lyrics to her songs and it can make me laugh and cry. That's what I want to do. I want people to discover things about themselves that they may have forgotten. The power of music can change people's lives."

And the power of determination, Pickler says, is the directive. "You just have to do it. When I made my mind up, I was going to make it happen. You have to figure out what your priorities are. I knew I wanted to do this; if *American Idol* worked out, or if I had to go to Nashville and play in the bars for 10 years, I was going to do it. If I can do this, anyone can. I came from nothing, and I didn't have anyone. If you want something bad enough, you'll figure out how to make it happen. And be prepared to be told, 'No.' No is good because when you do get that 'Yes,' you appreciate it more."

www.kelliepickler.com

Jon Peter Lewis: Singing for the Stars

"You have to put yourself in a position to become lucky. It's like going to a bar every night and asking the hottest girl out. If you're not a bad-looking guy, you might get one to come home with you sometime."

Season three of *American Idol* may be as notable for those contestants who did not win the crown, notably Academy Award–winning actress and singer Jennifer Hudson. With his three-octave range and incandescent performing prowess, Jon Peter Lewis became a finalist and a crowd-pleasing contestant in that competition, praised by no less an authority than Elton John for his "excellent pitch and phrasing."

After the requisite *American Idol* tour traveled to 50 cities, Lewis returned to Hollywood to write and record his debut, the first-ever independent album released by an *Idol* contestant. His second full length, *Break the Silence*, released through Cockaroo Entertainment in conjunction with Adrenaline Music Group, was praised as "one of the best pop/rock CDs of the year" by Monica Rizzo of *People* magazine.

"Before *American Idol*, I hadn't taken music seriously." Says Lewis. "I had been a student, and I started working in a semi-professional musical theater group. But I always wanted to be a musician, and I always imagined I would." Although he was in Montana at the time, Lewis secured a student loan to fly to Hawaii to audition. "That audition was probably the most discouraging part of the process. It was financially risky, to spend a couple of thousand dollars to go to Hawaii on the off chance that I might make it onto some TV show. And I was surrounded by all of these people singing who were pretty good. It's not like the TV show, where everyone is pretty horrible."

He didn't have anything to wear other than his church clothes—a clean white shirt and a dark tie. "That gimmick, and my singing, ended up getting me a spot on the show. I sang a Van Morrison song, 'Crazy Love.' Simon Cowell said I looked like a pen salesman! I remember coming out as a finalist, walking out and seeing someone with my name on a sign and the words, 'I bought the pen.' Being able to sing with Elton John was a highlight for me. He's the guy that John Lennon said was the best rock pianist around. A huge, international character, and I got a chance to sing with him."

Post-*Idol* Possibilities

"*Idol* is a special animal in the music business," Lewis observes. "People who are on it are in a unique position. When you are on, you are the biggest TV and music star in the country. No one is as big as you are. But at the same time, you are nothing. It only lasts as long as your face appears on television; it doesn't belong to you. The real stars of the show are the judges and the machine itself. It's the Cinderella 'rags-to-riches' story that is the star of the show. And that will be substituted the moment the show starts up again. There will always be someone brand new."

"The trick is becoming your own brand when you leave the show, and it has to make sense in terms of what you were on the show. It's a very backwards way of working the music business. It's not like you hone your craft for years and then write a great song and go tour the country. As an Idol, you can tour the country, but only if you have other Idols with you and tour under their brand. The Jon Peter Lewis brand doesn't have that loyalty, power, or credibility. That's why they spend millions of dollars on the winners. They each then have to establish their own brands. It is like starting fresh or even, in some ways, changing people's ideas of what you are as an artist. It's something to consider for anyone thinking of trying out. You have to be on top of the game, and eventually you will be competing with your favorite artists that you hear on the radio."

Lewis notes that he learned valuable lessons with his first record, so his second release was targeted to the millions of listeners who had embraced him on television. "The record could be dynamite, but people in America like to bet on a winning horse. It's not like Europe, where the underdog is king. People want to feel like they're part of the winner. Because of *Idol*, I've come through mainstream channels, and anything less than that might be perceived as a failure in the eyes of the fans. It's important for that perception to exist, that they feel like there is success here."

Office Hours

With the release, Lewis embarked on major promotional tour. In addition to the expected concerts and radio appearances, he often performed in offices for intimate audiences. "It's very strange, because all of the lights are on, you can see everything. When you can see everybody, it gets hard to figure out what to look at. People feel awkward if you're looking at them. You have to stare into the distance like you're on a big stage and talk to them like normal people. Thankfully, because of the summer stock theater that I did, I feel confident and can ham it up."

"It's very intimidating. The hardest place was *Billboard* magazine with a bunch of jaded industry folks in the room when I was playing my songs and they were folding their arms like, 'Entertain me.' It started with four people and ended as a full room, but it was the weirdest. Artists have to do this to get people to listen, to be able to turn it up a notch when you're in a crowded room. You have to control the room, especially in that environment. You have to take listeners on a journey when you're there in front of them."

Three Words

"Talent, persistence, and luck," Jon Peter Lewis says, are essential to success in the music business. "You have to put yourself in a position to become lucky. It is like going to a bar every night and asking the hottest girl out. If you're not a bad-looking guy, you might get one to come home with you sometime."

"I have always been baffled by people who get bogged down by what they're afraid of. Most people in this world, because they're afraid of something, don't do it. I can't relate to that. If I don't try, I've already failed. In order to get anywhere, you have to take big risks sometimes. That's what it's all about, taking a chance on the possibility of making something happen for yourself. I didn't want to be 40 or 50 years old working in a nine-to-five job and thinking, 'What if I had done this? What if I had done that?' I didn't have any reason to believe that I couldn't do it."

www.jonpeterlewis.com

Elliot Yamin: The "Anything's Possible" Poster Child

When Elliot Yamin was named second runner-up on *American Idol* on May 17, 2006, it was not an ending, but rather the beginning of a stratospheric career. Yamin is an underdog: A history of ear infections as a child and eardrum replacement surgery at 13 left him with a 90 percent hearing loss in his right ear, and he was diagnosed at age 16 with Type I diabetes. Born in Los Angeles, he relocated with his family to Richmond, Virginia, when he was 14. It was there that Yamin developed his vocal talent while singing karaoke. Although he had not been musically trained, he sang in a local jazz band and in amateur performance forums. A high school drop out, Yamin attained his GED while working at shoe retailer Foot Locker, and he also played music as an on-air DJ at the local R&B radio station.

Everything changed, Yamin says, when he decided to audition for *American Idol*. "What did I have to lose, really? That was my whole motto. I actually went to audition a couple of days after Hurricane Katrina hit. I was working a dead-end job, and my life wasn't going in a good direction. I didn't have much ambition at that time or a well-devised plan, and I certainly didn't have a career going. Boston was the closest audition. Initially, I was going to drive to Memphis, but that was a longer drive, and they canceled the audition because they were taking hurricane evacuees. I drove from Richmond to Boston. It was a typical cliché: My girlfriend and I spent the last dimes in our checking account to rent this car to make it to Boston. We only rented for a couple days, and we didn't know what to expect or what the audition process would be. I made it a couple of rounds and we had to extend our time and the car rental, but we couldn't afford the extension on the car so we had to wait at the rental car place for her brother to bail us out. It was pretty embarrassing."

Idolization

Yamin says he didn't audition or perform on *American Idol* with the idea of winning. "I just wanted to get enough exposure to become a professional singer and get a record deal and establish a career in this industry. I have never done anything like that—never tried out for anything in my life. *Idol* is a well-oiled machine; they know what they're doing, and it was an amazing experience but a really hectic schedule. After you make it through, you sign your life away through August of that year. They throw so many things on your plate. You don't see all of what we do behind the scenes. We're in the studio recording background vocals, doing video packages for our songs, working with the mentor, and shooting commercials every Sunday and always doing press. It's 14 to 15 hours daily. I learned a lot about myself and what I'm capable of and how to handle myself in front of a camera. It was a great learning experience for me. It was a blast. The schedule didn't really bother me. But with TV, it's a lot of 'hurry up and wait.' It was always a lot of sitting around and waiting for our turn to go rehearse. But it was great; I made so many great friends. There's an amazing group of behind-the-scenes people who make the show what it is."

At the conclusion of the televised season, the contestants and winners take a brief break before the summer tour commences: three months and 60 cities in all. "I spent the summer traveling with *Idol*. That was the first time I traveled around the country, and I always wanted to do that. It was a dream come true. I felt like a rock star, with people waiting at the hotel and playing on huge stages in an enormous production in front of 30,000 people a night every night. It was great. I couldn't wait to get back out on the road when we got back. Back in L.A., I felt like I was home, and back where I came from originally. In the back of my mind, I always wanted to return to L.A. to be a singer; I wanted to chase that dream, and *Idol* brought me back home."

From the conclusion of the show through the end of August, the *Idol* juggernaut retains the right to pick up options on either management or recording for the participants. "I caught wind early on during rehearsal that they weren't going to pick me on a record deal. I certainly didn't want them managing me, because they did during the show. I was a small fish in a big pond, and I probably wasn't going to make the record I wanted to make. I called [producer] Simon Fuller and we spoke. I said I wanted to put my record out on my own. He said he would do anything he could do to help out in the future, but he asked to not put out a record before Katherine McPhee or Taylor Hicks. During the time I went to the Firm and established a relationship with Jeff Rahban. I knew I was in good hands."

Rahban was aware of Yamin since they had both attended the same school in Richmond, Virginia. "We knew each other's families," Rahban recalls. "As Elliot climbed the ladder at *American Idol*, I was introduced to him and we talked about his future. I felt strongly after working with Clay Aiken and Kelly Clarkson and having a good understanding of the *Idol* system that Elliot could create his own business and his own label with the springboard from the show. When a major label didn't pick him up, we were free to go our own route."

Grassroots Revelations

Yamin's cousin, Josh Abraham, a major record producer who has worked with luminaries such as Velvet Revolver, Staind, Linkin Park, and Limp Bizkit, formally introduced Yamin to Rahban. Abrahams was also an integral link in the recording process, as Yamin explains. "I recorded 70 percent of my record in his studio. He helped by bringing writers in and introducing me to people that would later on become a part of my band. But we had no well-devised plan for the sound of the record, we just played it by ear. We wanted to get the record out at the right time and go to radio. We found a hit song with Stargate, and I went to New York to record it. I wasn't sold on the song—it took convincing from Jeff for me to go to New York and put vocals down on the song. But as soon as I heard playback, I had a feeling we had something special on our hands; it sounded amazing. But you never know how it's going to be perceived by the audience."

With the single in place, Yamin embarked on a radio tour. "I went city to city with my guitar player. We were like country music stars! And we played on every station. We did tons of radio appearances and meet and greets, and it worked. We'd do three different cities or states in one day."

International concerts are now on Yamin's itinerary. "The song did well in the Philippines, and we did a 10-day tour and also opened for Whitney Houston in Malaysia. In Japan, it's still kind of new, but I've been there five times in six months." His second album is titled *Fight for Love*.

Manager Jeff Rabhan says that downloads and ring tones were both key to exposure, as was radio. "The digital world allowed the song to go platinum. Typically, with new artists they like to release a single six weeks before the full-length record comes out. We released it two weeks before. Nevertheless, it was great; the stars were just aligned and everything just worked out. The tie-in with *American Idol* got us on [Los Angeles radio station] KISS-FM, and a lot of stations mimic their playlist and format. [*American Idol* host] Ryan Seacrest does the morning show there, too. They were instrumental in introducing me to radio. We went on air with Ryan Seacrest and debuted the song and just started taking off from there."

A Single Sees the Light of Day

The success of this equation hinged on relationships between Rabhan and Kevin Day at the music services firm Rocket Science. "There was a lot of support from the fans, and since he was signed to a publishing deal through Sony/ATV, they really believed on some level that this kid was a star," Day recalls. "Physically, he was far from being a star, but he used the internal assets of Sony Publishing to bring great writers and songs to make a fantastic record. And the head of the company, Danny Strick, called Clive Davis, who passed without even hearing it. Danny cut more tracks and made a better record and called Clive again and said, 'Please listen.' Clive finally listened as a favor and said he wasn't interested."

Danny Strick put the company's formidable resources to full use to create songs for Yamin's debut on the company's revitalized virtual record label, Hickory Records. "We wanted to find projects where we could control the process and put out a few records a year. Other publishers have talked about doing this—we did it," Strick says. "We signed Elliot from his base on *American Idol*. We utilized our resources, our writers, and had a huge hit single 'Wait for You,' that Stargate had written."

Kevin Day shared Strick's enthusiasm for Yamin. "Danny called me and said, 'Is it true we could put out a record without a label?' So we rushed. It was almost Christmas, and we got the record out before *American Idol*'s next season. We put one song up on iTunes to see consumer reaction. Within first week, we had 29,000 downloads, and it wasn't even advertised. Then, without even going to radio, he went on *The Larry King Show*. In a market that was downsizing, he had the highest debut of an indie pop artist in *Billboard* history, debuting at number two on their charts. There were over 600,000 units sold—a gargantuan number in the indie world with a team of just 15 people. There have been very few releases that have had that magic. It was a self-perpetuating machine, and it was exciting for our company and for Elliot. The neatest part of story is that Danny Strick at Sony made a partner deal with Elliot, entitling Elliot to own half of the masters. He wouldn't have been able to make that deal on a major label."

Notes Rabhan, "The best thing about it is that a bunch of friends got together to make this happen, which was spectacular, and we didn't have to wait for next Thursday's marketing meeting to get our answers. We just ran with it. We made mistakes, but the mistakes were squashed by our ability to move quickly. It led me to shy away from major label deals as much as possible. It boils down to this: The companies are weakened by the state of our business, and they're very corporate. And I'd rather bet on me than somebody else. And with these 360 deals, my philosophy is I'd easily agree to do a 360 if they had the people to service it. If they had tour, marketing, or a publisher or merchandise person, I'd be happy to give them a part of merchandise."

Tenacity and Triumph

For emerging artists, Yamin acknowledges that having a belief system is a fundamental value. "Everyone has their own talent, so expose that talent as much as possible and work diligently on your craft. If you're a singer, go to open mics. There isn't a day that's gone by that I haven't sung, in the shower or in the car, whatever. I was always working on my craft. It's important for any aspiring artist. Work on it in every way possible. Never give up. I'm kind of a late bloomer, but I didn't give up. There can be all kinds of forks in the road, and there will be plenty more in the future, but you have to stay focused and believe in yourself and your talent. I'm a poster child for 'anything's possible.'"

www.elliot-yamin.org

13 Music as the International Language

While the influence of American roots music and the power of American pop overseas are well documented, there are numerous success stories of artists from other countries, most notably the UK, who have given the world magnificent and life-changing music, from The Beatles to Bob Marley. Music is truly international and great artistry can come from any corner of the earth. As the world has become smaller, the beat has become bigger.

Sat Bisla: Mapping the Muse

"With an MP3 player, you can be the president of your own radio station and discover music from anywhere in the world without any barriers. That's how we are hearing so many great artists."

As president and founder of the marketing and information powerhouse A&R Worldwide, Sat Bisla's mission is creating advanced discovery, consulting, and marketing systems that can potentially transport an act from regional recognition to a global audience. Bisla is universally respected for A&R Worldwide's executive networking and consultation services, which encompass creative endeavors that are emerging with an ingenious international marketplace for music.

"The appetite for music hasn't waned, it's still very strong," Bisla says, "but paying for music is a different matter altogether. We, as an industry, did a very good job of devaluing music and allowing those not involved in the artist development process to come along and dictate the rules. For this current generation of listeners, most feel that music is like water: They should get it for free. When you start bottling water, they see the value. I think the key is to start implementing this value proposition in the minds of the consumers—that there is a value to the music that people create, and they need to be paid. For centuries, we drank water without paying for it, but when we realized it was running out, we didn't mind paying more for a bottle of water than a gallon of gas. If people thought that artists—especially new artists—would quit creating music, this might stop. This is a simple solution. The public is more complex, but there needs to be a uniform policy worldwide, a mandate of people working together for a global solution."

Globally Challenged Visions

Early in his career, Bisla bounced between his native UK and the U.S., programming music as a DJ on radio and in clubs, booking bands, becoming a club promoter and eventually a music journalist. In Los Angeles, writing about international music for a trade publication, he was approached with the possibility of consulting for Interscope Records. Concerned about his journalistic credibility, he was skeptical until it was explained to him that he didn't have to write about music he discovered, only to alert the company to its potential. As the record company topography shifted, he worked with a variety of labels and formed a working alliance with Dave Holmes, then at Nettwerk Records, who became the manager of the band Coldplay.

"A&R Worldwide began in 1999 out of my bedroom. It was called Globally Challenged. The music industry was going through this huge vacuum—Napster was on board and technology was playing a bigger role in music. I felt like the industry hadn't grasped what was going to happen. I had information on breaking emerging artists, what producers were working on and the tastemaker radio stations around the globe; A&R-related news that became a directory of sorts."

Media giant Clear Channel took an interest in the venture and offered to pay Bisla for what he had put into the project (whose name was changed to A&R Network). "Until I proved it worked. At the time, I was helping an artist named Bonnie McKee, advising her management on re-recording her demos and getting her music out to attorneys. They got the music to president/CEO Tom Whalley, and she became his first new signing at Warner Bros. Records."

Next, Bisla met Missy Higgins, an Australian artist with immense potential. "I played the music for a few A&R people and it was across that board that this girl was amazing. John Watson came on as her manager, and I told him to bring Missy to the states. He said she wanted to go backpacking, but they eventually came over. And out of that visit, they were offered major label deals and also signed with Warner Bros. A couple of months later, I talked to this band from the UK called Keane. Through A&R Network, I was able to get interest at Capitol, but because EMI Records in the UK [which owns Capitol] had passed, they wouldn't sign them. I told their manager that I'd send demos to radio stations to see what they thought. The stations included Radio 1 [BBC], l-FM, and KCRW. In that same week, all three stations played the demo and I wrote about that in the A&R Network newsletter. Within 24 hours, their lawyer was bombarded by phone calls from labels that wanted to talk about signing them."

Beyond Clear Channel

"Clear Channel saw there was something there. Label execs, publishers, managers, booking agents, technology companies, and labels liked what I was doing. It naturally evolved into a consulting style where I was giving these people common-sense advice. It ended up becoming a pretty good business and it was quite easy to introduce them to great music. The CEO of Clear Channel asked me to come up with a plan to turn this into a consumer portal. I said it needed to remain industry-focused, but maybe we could do something more consumer-oriented. We came up with the New Music Network, which was Clear Channel's first social networking platform, in 2002. They were going to leverage all of their unused airtime on this site by having bands submit music to be played on air. I put together a game plan and they believed in it, but they didn't have patience for the time it would take for the revenue to kick in. After a year, they pulled the plug. It could have been MySpace, but everything happens for a reason. It wasn't meant to be, so I stayed focused on the A&R Network."

All Around the World

At home, thinking of new names for his venture, Bisla, in conversation with his wife, came up with A&R Worldwide as a name that best epitomized his approach. "We have passion, vision, and a great team on board. We're able to focus on the music and building around the music, connecting it to every platform that the consumer and the industry connects to. We've made amazing progress—it's all things music."

Among these endeavors are a film and television music placement division and the annual MUSEXPO, originated in Los Angeles, with a similar event in Europe and plans for a Pacific Rim version in Australia. The idea was born from a series of dinners that Bisla hosted to connect the disparate factions of the business in a social environment, which the MUSEXPO now does on a grander scale. "It brings together all aspects of the industry with a vested interest: technology, mobile platforms, live music, the traditional labels, and publishers, managers, video game companies, and film and television studios —everyone with a need for music and sound. Often, these areas are fragmented. This brings everyone together with collective minds in a comfortable environment—decision-making people, people who love music and the artists."

International Appeal

Bisla maintains his connection to the airwaves by hosting on Indie 103.1 FM a weekly radio show that is syndicated in numerous other markets. He notes that in the current music climate, when literally anyone can record and release music, there is a lack of filters. His radio show, *Passport Approved*, is a method of hearing the best new music selected from around the world. Artists such as Lily Allen, Wolfmother, the

Claxons, Adele, and Duffy have been among the successful artists first championed stateside on this show. "If a band gets signed out of the show, that's fine, but my focus is to make sure the show sounds great," says Bisla.

"Fans don't care where music is from. Politics have sometimes overwhelmed common sense. Bad decisions have been made. People say there are many in our industry with egos, and egos show insecurity. If you're confident about what you do, you're not going to have an ego, because you believe in yourself and others believe in you. People who are timid have egos, they're insecure about themselves and what others think about them. If you're confident, you move forward, follow you're your instincts, and do what's right."

"Music is more diverse than it has ever been. There are more outlets to discover new bands and there are no rules. With an MP3 player, you can be the president of your own radio station and discover music from anywhere in the world without any barriers. That's how we are hearing so many great artists. There are so many areas, not just television, radio or print—it's a multifaceted kaleidoscope of music."

"Ultimately, it is about a great song; without it, you have nothing. Second, make sure you have a live performance to back it up. And third, make sure to have a great business team. It starts with creativity, but in order to move forward, it must be a sustainable business."

www.anrworldwide.com

David Stark: International Connections

"There are basically no rules; if you're an unknown songwriter but have got something really special, there's no reason at all why it shouldn't happen."

As widely noted in this book, since the music business is increasingly international, it is imperative for songwriters, artists, and executives to reach for potential opportunities in overseas markets. London-based David Stark publishes *SongLink International*, an insider industry tip sheet.

"Each month we find out which artists and labels around the world are looking for hit songs or co-writers, and publish this information as 'leads' sent by e-mail to our many subscribers, who are mainly music publishers or songwriters around the world. There are also regular interim updates during the month, while the hard copy *SongLink* magazine is published quarterly and includes other industry articles, news, photos, and features which supplement the 'who's looking' tips and leads," Stark explains.

SongLink has approximately 1,500 members worldwide. Stark qualifies who can subscribe: "Established publishers and songwriters with some track record are welcome to subscribe, but we always ask all new or unpublished writers, or new one-man publishing companies, to submit a couple of songs first, so we can make sure their material is suitable for pitching to our leads placed by industry professionals. I've always done this in order to maintain some quality control, unlike various other tip sheets and song-plugging services on the market who will happily accept songwriters' cash without question. I think it's very important to do some basic vetting, as there's nothing worse than advertisers telling me they're receiving garbage. Also, many of the songwriters I've had to reject initially have thanked me for my honesty, with some even coming back to me later with upgraded tracks which have then passed the test. All I'm listening for are well-structured songs with some commercial potential and reasonably produced demos, written by someone who seems to know what they're doing. New writers just have to remember that this is the music business: When pitching songs for covers, you're trying to sell a product—and yourself—in a highly competitive market unlike any other. You just have to be as professional as possible to make an impact."

Northern Lights

Stark began his career at Dick James Music in London in the mid-seventies, working for the man who was lucky and shrewd enough to publish The Beatles (via Northern Songs) in the sixties and Elton John in the seventies. "Even though I was just a runner [go-fer], it was a great introduction to the industry. I was on the bottom rung of the ladder, but I made a few contacts who are still friends today. However, after a couple of months, I landed a job as international press officer at Decca Records, the original home of the Rolling Stones, the Moody Blues, and many other British household names, as well as U.S. acts like Al Green and the Chi-lites on the London Records label. My boss there was another iconic figure, Marcel Stellman, who as well as being a great record man was also a lyricist and songwriter who wrote English lyrics to some big hits like 'Tulips In Amsterdam,' had cuts with names like Les Paul and Gilbert Becaud, and also produced novelty acts like the Goons, the Smurfs, and other artists."

"I was with him for a few years until I joined the MAM Organisation, who managed such names as Tom Jones, Engelbert Humperdinck, Gilbert O'Sullivan, and others, and also had a small label. However, I got a bit fed up there pushing records I didn't much like, so I gradually moved into the print and publishing side of the industry, working at a couple of pro-audio magazines before joining *Billboard*'s European office in Amsterdam in 1988, which I enjoyed for a couple of years. I eventually returned to London in 1990 to work for a company which published specialist music industry titles, including a fascinating tipsheet named *Songplugger* that I'd previously been aware of as an occasional songwriter myself, and which I ended up developing and running until that firm was sold off in July 1993."

The concept for *SongLink* evolved from there. "I had built up *Songplugger* from what was a six-page tipsheet, originally started by London-based American publisher Tim Whitsett a few years earlier, into a little magazine with leads for music publishers and songwriters, which was getting quite popular. When the company I worked for was sold, as I had no contractual restrictions; I just wrote to all the subscribers and told them I would be relaunching independently under the new name of *SongLink* and sent them all a subscription form! Luckily for me, the orders started to come in more or less straight away, which meant I never had to take out any bank loan, and *SongLink International* was launched in September 1993, with an exclusive cover story about Paul McCartney's MPL publishing operation.

Transatlantic Ties

"Many independent publishers and writers rely on us as their main source of information, and I've also become involved with various industry events, showcases, and workshops over the years which are 'supported by *SongLink*.' One of the most important shows I put on in London each year features students of LIPA—the Liverpool Institute for Perfoming Arts—at which in 2005 I was proud to be inducted as a 'Companion' by Sir Paul McCartney himself. I've also been invited to judge or attend many song contests and festivals around the world, as well some interesting songwriter retreats. For the last 10 years, I've also compiled the *SongLink* CD of new songs by subscribers, which are distributed at trade shows like Midem [France] and Popkomm [Germany] as well as sent to labels, managers, and producers around the world. And I also now publish *Cuesheet*, which is a similar service as *SongLink* but for the film/TV music market."

Genie Genius

"One of our biggest successes was with Christina Aguilera, who we had a song request lead from A&R man Ron Fair at RCA before she was famous. UK-based songwriter Pam Sheyne read it in *SongLink*, and her co-writers in L.A., David Frank and Steve Kipner, pitched Ron a new song the three of them had written titled 'Genie in a Bottle.' The rest, as they say, is history. And from the same lead, Air Chrysalis Music in Sweden pitched 'Come On Over Baby (All I Want Is You),' which also went to number one around the world. Over the years, leads in *SongLink* have led to top 10 records and some number ones in various countries, many by local artists you may never have heard of, but who are often huge in their own markets."

Although many of the European listings are strictly for songs, sometimes there are additional opportunities, Stark says. "There are always some new and upcoming artists whose managers or labels are looking for more than just a great song, they need someone who writes and can produce to help nurture and develop the artist's style. There are a number of highly talented writer/producers around who can fulfill these duties pretty well. In fact, just recently I had a call from the manager of a top UK girl act who had a rough idea for a song but needed the input of a writer/producer to see it through. I thought of someone who would be suitable, and I've heard they've since hit it off very well indeed."

Highly Contested

Stark is co-founder of Unisong, a worldwide songwriting contest. "UniSong has provided some incredible opportunities and prizes for songwriters all over the world, from cash, to products and services, to amazing and unique co-writing trips. Probably the most memorable week in my career was taking the 1998 UK Grand Prize winner, Ruth Merry, to attend the 'Music Speaks Louder Than Words' songwriting week in Havana, Cuba, at which we not only hung out with names like Burt Bacharach, Bonnie Raitt, Gladys Knight, Mick Fleetwood, Andy Summers, Stuart Copeland, Peter Buck, Peter Frampton, and many others, but also got to meet President Fidel Castro—quite a surreal experience! I'm not as actively involved in UniSong these days, but still provide free subscriptions to the prize winners. I also now do the same with the Indie International Song Contest, which launched in 2008 and has proved to be a highly efficient and songwriter-friendly contest run by a great team out of Washington State."

Why Not Your Song?

For aspiring and working songwriters alike, Stark offers this advice: "It's tough out there and the cuts are hard to come by, even for the most established writers. My advice is always do the best you can, make the best possible demos with the best voices you can find and production you can afford. Also make sure your songs are properly registered with one of the performing rights organizations; they can also be very helpful for practical advice."

"Before pitching, you should always do your research as to what type of songs the artist has previously recorded; check out their songs and history online and only submit up one or two of your best shots. If you've got that killer song, it will get noticed eventually. Also use the Internet and tools like *SongLink* to the max without making a nuisance of yourself. Remember, this is a people business based on relationships. Be easygoing, reliable, and, of course, talented. If you've got a knack for good songwriting or production, or co-writing with others, this is all part of the process. But at the same time, don't forget the dream—just try and imagine how your song would sound at the top of the charts, who would be singing it, and how it could possibly come to be in that position."

"Of course, luck plays a big part in it, but these days, the songwriting industry revolves around a relatively small number of seasoned writer/producers who come up with the goods, even if they don't have a smash every time. But also remember that despite all this, there are basically no rules: If you're an unknown songwriter but have got something really special, there's no reason at all why it shouldn't happen. Everyone in the industry is always looking for the next big thing, so why shouldn't it be your song?"

www.songlink.com

Yenn: Pop's New Directives

"Music represents where you are in life, who is with you, and what's around you. Holding on to that reality is incredibly important."

Shimmering charisma, compelling mystique, and unmistakable star power—meet Yenn, a Southern California–based recording artist whose formidable worldwide audience stretches from the U.S. to Germany, Poland, Holland, Switzerland, Sweden, Australia, France, and the Czech Republic. A celebrated star in the international community, Yenn is now recording new music for her home market—the U.S.—to match her intercontinental appeal.

"Audiences everywhere are different," Yenn observes. "You can take a group of people in the Czech Republic and there is a massive difference to the U.S., where you can walk down the street in a sequined dress and 'f*ck-me pumps.' Especially if you are an artist, no one cares."

Passport to the Promised Land

Born in Vietnam, a very young Yenn moved with her family to Ada, Minnesota, where they were sponsored by a minister and his wife. From the Midwest, her family traveled to New York, then Houston and San Francisco, and eventually to Orange County, California.

"In the Vietnamese culture, girls stay in the house until they're married. Boys start to make money when they are 15. Women are not encouraged to pursue education. I was never okay with that." The work ethic, Yenn says, was ingrained in her along with many other distinctive cultural traits. "I grew up with these. I think after going through my earlier years, not understanding and fighting, as I grew up and got closer to it, I really appreciated my culture. There are differences and subtleties that get lost in translation." Orange County, home to a formidable community of Vietnamese Americans, is where Yenn launched her performing career, first as a dancer, and then as a vocalist. "No one helped me," she recalls. "I went to auditions when I decided I was going to do this for a living and I was told, 'You're too young.'" But she persevered, landing a record deal with a small label and eventually a contract with industry giant Asia Entertainment.

Although Asian Americans often work behind the scenes in the music media, there has been scant visibility for them in front of the microphones or cameras. After releasing 10 best-selling Vietnamese language CDs and several DVDs for her international fans, Yenn is now intent on tapping commercial markets stateside as well. "In the new project, we're doing something fresh, something different, a blend of flavors. We haven't done anything conventional yet. With the pop thing, you can be a little more progressive in the creative department. With the difference in cultures, there are codes by which you will be judged. For this particular journey, it's going to be freeing."

In the U.S.-based Vietnamese record industry, artists have less input in their own careers. Yenn is anticipating making more creative decisions for her English-language debut. "Sometimes, on the production side, because I'm young, Asian, and a small woman, it is assumed that I must not know what the hell I'm talking about!" But her support network takes its clues from her artistry. "I'm not a businessperson. I have a visionary manager, Raymond Ho, working for me. I've never been exposed to this side of the beast. I've always done my thing and then the label works it out. I'm seeing it now as a team—everyone on the team has to play their key roles. We find the good people to do good stuff."

"There are the same challenges of making it in any industry. You start from the bottom and go through the bullsh*t. It is the same in the Vietnamese industry and the same in the UK and Europe—the same philosophy and mentality."

Mediums and Messages

For anyone expecting a demure ballad-singing lotus flower, Yen will challenge expectations as she embraces imagination and innovation. "As an artist, you always want to push the envelope—that's the point of music," she confirms. "To really break it down, the artist is just a medium. It's the music, the emotion, and the writers, and then the vocals. In the technical sense of that, the artist embodies other factions. By the time we have a performance, so many people may have worked on it. It's so many different creative processes. We can forget the sacredness of the process, not to say we don't need the image, but I'm a Libra, so I need a balance."

Moving deeper into the mainstream pop world, she maintains keen focus on streamlining each element of her artistry. "I work every day to push forward and find that better part of myself I haven't tapped into," she notes. "The day you think you've learned it all, you have nothing left."

Iconoclastic and inspiring, Yen spins within a powerful orbit of possibility and imagination. "The music represents where you are in life, who is with you, and what's around you. Holding on to that reality is incredibly important. I'm not a perfect person. I never claim to be. I want my music to take me on a journey. Hopefully, I can leave something behind so the next traveler has an entry point and a guide to go by."

www.yennmusic.com

Haikaa: Sailing on the Ocean with No Map

"If you follow in somebody else's steps, you only get as far as somebody else has gotten. That's not what I'm interested in."

Born in Brazil, emerging international singer/songwriter Haikaa grew up in Japan and also in the United States, where she attended college. "Although that was a wonderful opportunity, it was very confusing growing up in different cultures, because I felt like I had a different identity for each of them. For some time, I considered myself a bewildered animal. I had no identity and no home, but then I identified the person who I really was. Honesty, love, and respect—what matters most to me—have nothing to do with nationality, race, or gender. This perception of who I am has guided my art. The music I write is about what I consider important in a human being."

"Work of Art" is both a song and an album title. It is Haikaa's personal philosophy as well, the end result of these considerations. "When I wrote this, it sounded pretentious. Then I started singing it, and it felt really good. It is an affirmation and recognition that we are all born as works of art, but somehow we may end up forgetting that and trying to become something else when we could be looking inside and finding our treasures. It inspired me to think about millions of people around the world singing, 'Work of Art,' and how good that could feel, and how liberating it would be. It's an appreciation for yourself. When you realize you're a work of art, your life changes and it starts changing the environment around you. It can lead to good things."

All Over the Map

After living in disparate locales, Haikaa eventually settled in the U.S. for her professional career. "I had been living in Brazil, and it was an interesting place to be, very rich, culturally and musically, so I got to experiment with different rhythms. But there wasn't a place for my type of music in Brazil, and I wasn't willing to change my style to have a market there. I started to think in global rather than domestic terms. What I wanted to do was pop music and that there would be people out there in the world that would be willing to listen to that music. That's when I made the decision to take this project to an international level and to come to Los Angeles.

Prior to her move to the U.S., Haikaa lived in Japan, where she was signed to Sony Records as a member of the teen pop group, Girl's Club. "Being noticed at such an early age, it was clear to me that yes, I liked music, but I wanted to express who I really was. And when you're wearing striped suits and hats, and everything is imposed on you, the last thing you have is freedom. It was an important experience for me to figure out I had to go out and find out who I was before I could do more music."

"All of the interviews, everything we had to say, how we expressed ourselves when we were singing—everything was absolutely choreographed. That to me was a very suffocating feeling. I felt uncomfortable with who I was, and artists are supposed to feel exactly the opposite. You have to be a work of art no matter what."

"The most important aspect of this change the music industry is going through is that now artists can have their freedom. What makes an artist special is his or her own DNA. And if someone at a label tells them exactly what to wear, they are no more than a puppet. It's not the kind of art I'm interested in. I think there are great artists in the major labels, but for me it is important to make sure I have the creative freedom in the process from the music to the image to the marketing strategy. My sense of who I am needs to be presented in all of these aspects. So in regard to the classic way of doing business through major labels, it became clear I wouldn't fit. They wouldn't be happy, and I wouldn't be happy. It's better to figure out an individual path. If you follow in somebody else's steps, you only get as far as somebody else has gotten. That's not what I'm interested in."

Since she has a mastery of three languages, it is natural that Haikaa thinks across geographical lines. "At the point of creation, I don't think about the market so much. First I consider what I want to say, then I think, 'How can I place this in the market?'"

"With globalization, a lot of cultural boundaries have fallen, so you can reach a lot more listeners on a global level now. My perception, and I'm saying this as a music fan, is that the most important thing people are looking for is truth. Truth is inspiring; it can be a simple truth. When you perform your art truthfully, there are people who will connect."

Wrapping Arms Around the World

"What I would say to aspiring artists is to live your life to the fullest; every minute. When you do that, you acquire a sense of respect for yourself and you start loving yourself more and then you become even more creative. You write even more songs and you will start playing better. It really is about loving who you are, and becoming aware of what aspects and relationships you are living. Then you become creative, and people begin believing that you are an artist, not just an egocentric person who wants to be famous. If your profession is to be an artist, live your truth every minute and the rest will come as a consequence of that."

"It takes a lot of changing, but this was the path for me and it's been very rewarding. I have this stage of music as a stage for my self-discovery. And I am blessed because I get to expand my limits because I love music. It is about being truthful."

Derek Bramble: Rhymes and Bass Lines

"If you're a good producer and writer, there couldn't be a more perfect time for you than right now. For a long time, the biz has been a big fat pig that's been very wasteful. Now, companies have to be lean and mean."

British-born bassist Derek Bramble was only 14 when joined up with a top R&B band, Heatwave, who rocked the charts with hits like "Always and Forever," "Groove Line," and "Boogie Nights." Fortuitously, one of the band's members, Rod Temperton [later the writer of the Michael Jackson song "Thriller"] was impressed enough by young Bramble's songs to become his mentor.

After leaving Heatwave at age 20, Bramble went on to write and produce a string of top 20 hits of his own in England and Europe with various artists and bands. Moving to Los Angeles, he displayed his diversity by working with some of the biggest names from opposite ends of the musical spectrum, recording or writing with artists such as David Bowie, Faith Hill, Will Smith, and Whitney Houston.

International Appeal

Bramble has worked with acts that are huge sellers in the UK but might be less known in the U.S. He reflects on the differences in tastes on both sides of the Atlantic as in a reference to Anastasia, a U.S. artist with whom he worked who became a huge star on the continent. "Sometimes, for the U.S. market, the music from Europe can be a little too novelty-driven. Sometimes it could be a cultural thing that doesn't translate or a situation where there aren't enough funds to keep the artist in the public's face long enough for them to register. I think with Anastasia, she was an acquired taste, and I don't think her records translated across to this country. Maybe she had success in Miami and other spots, but it didn't catch on everywhere."

"That is what you need to do, to catch that wave. Craig David is another example. He made a European-sounding record that did very well on both sides of the ocean and on his second album he used American producers and lost his identity and never really recovered."

As a songwriter, Bramble has had cuts with marquee artists such as Tina Turner and Whitney Houston. He relates how one Faith Hill cut evolved. "I gave it to my publisher to send to Nashville. It didn't have anything to do with Nashville really; it was just a good song. I wanted other people to hear it. I was in the studio with Mandy Moore, who wanted to cut it. We sent it to her A&R man and he didn't like the song. Then I got a call from Nashville that Faith also loved the song, so I told Faith that she had it. But Mandy went back to her manager; now they both loved it. Then, I was called back about Mandy doing vocals [on it], and when I said they lost it, the people she was working with went ballistic."

Songwriting is one facet of Bramble's diverse career. "Diane Warren was one of my first co-writers when I got here. I've had more joy writing with people than writing by myself. I tend to write with people whose style fits with mine. So I am always looking for co-writers that I can elevate and can help elevate me."

The Fame Game

Bramble has also worked in the studio with an illustrious retinue of major artists. As a producer, his biggest hit was "Blue Jean" by David Bowie (Bramble is credited as a co-producer with Bowie and Hugh Padgham). He relates that when he tracked with David Bowie, the pop chameleon had just come off of a major career boost with "Let's Dance." More recently, he relates that recording with Elliot Yamin for his very successful first album was a joy. "What an amazingly wonderful human being he is and talented beyond even his belief. It's very special when someone doesn't realize how good they are. He is one of most wonderful people I've ever worked with—so grounded. It is so refreshing to work with people like that. If anyone ever deserved it, it is this kid and for the right reasons."

Ch-Ch-Changes

Bramble says that if someone is a good producer and writer, there couldn't be a more perfect time for them than this moment. "For a long time, the biz has been a big fat pig that's been very wasteful. Now companies have to be lean and mean. Those days of frivolous albums, spending millions and having the record never come out, are basically behind us, thank goodness. There are so many other areas to break yourself through, if you can do something to get yourself started. At end of the day, you do need major labels to help take you to the next level, but I definitely think there's more control for artists. This wasn't there for the longest time, when people were forced to sacrifice integrity to keep a gig. Back then, the days were few and far between when someone was willing to go to the wall for artists because they believed in them."

Although he avows that the general music loving public is increasingly sophisticated in finding what they want, Bramble still believes that outlets like Top 40 radio will remain a vital vehicle for new music. "I think quality of recording and singing is going to come back. People want to hear something timeless that transcends a moment. That is going to be focal point for a lot of producers who will stand the test of time and technology."

What impresses Bramble initially in a potential artist he might be interested in working with is a solid work ethic. "They have to be willing to stay [in the studio] and battle with me for nine hours a day; that will earn my respect. Especially if someone has a definite sense of themselves, but not if they expect the producer to tell them who they are and mold them. Michael Jackson, Tina Turner, and David Bowie—all of them knew who they were as artists. They didn't need a producer to get their voices heard, but used producers to capture their magic in the studio. It's very important for artists to know who they are. And it's hard to find these days. The artist has to be that jockey that guides that horse to the finish line."

"I tell everyone: Be committed. You might hear a thousand 'No's' before you hear one 'Yes.' Put the work in because you won't get something for nothing. And lean forward into the wind and don't be afraid of it. Don't phone it in. If you want it, show up for it. Come and find it. Success is always 90 percent hard work and 10 percent luck."

Index

0 1341 1274543 2